Redeeming the Gospel

Redeeming the Gospel

The Christian Faith Reconsidered

David A. Brondos

Fortress Press
Minneapolis

REDEEMING THE GOSPEL
The Christian Faith Reconsidered

Cover image: The Green Christ, 1890 (oil on cardboard) by Maurice Denis (1870–1943); © Artists Rights Society (ARS), New York / ADAGP, Paris
Cover design: Ivy Palmer Skrade
Book design: Carolyn Banks

Library of Congress Cataloging-in-Publication Data
Brondos, David A., 1958-
Redeeming the gospel : the christian faith reconsidered / David A. Brondos.
        p. cm. – (Studies in Lutheran history and theology)
Includes bibliographical references and index.
ISBN 978-0-8006-9745-7 (alk. Paper)
1. Salvation—Christianity. 2. Lutheran Church—Doctrines. I. Title.
BT751.3.B77 2010
234—dc22   2010019366

The paper used in this publication meets the minimum requirements of American National Standard for Information Sciences—Permanence of Paper for Printed Library Materials, ANSI Z329.48-1984.

Manufactured in the U.S.A.

15   14   13   12   11   1   2   3   4   5   6   7   8   9   10

For my bishop, Floyd M. Schoenhals

Contents

Introduction

As we approach the five-hundredth anniversary of the events surrounding the Protestant Reformation, one can hardly avoid the sensation that the gospel that Martin Luther and the other Reformers so boldly proclaimed is in a state of serious crisis. To some extent, of course, that is nothing new. From the time that Luther and those who followed him defined the essence of the gospel in terms of the justification of sinners by grace through faith alone for Christ's sake, their understanding of the gospel has been criticized and rejected by the majority of Christians in the world. The chief objection has no doubt had to do with the Lutheran rejection of the necessity of "good works" for one to be justified and saved by God in the end; once it is argued that justification is based entirely on God's grace in Christ and not on anything human beings do, so that God's decision to *declare* sinful believers righteous is in no way dependent on any actual righteousness of their own in life and deed, then such a life of righteousness appears to be superfluous and unnecessary.

Although ecumenical dialogue has led to a greater appreciation of the Lutheran understanding of the gospel on the part of other Christians and even to ecumenical agreements and documents such as the 1999 Lutheran–Roman Catholic *Joint Declaration on the Doctrine of Justification*, the general consensus still seems to be that significant and even profound differences remain. Many non-Lutherans may agree that their own understanding of the gospel can be reconciled to some extent with the Lutheran understanding but would nevertheless insist that the Lutherans still have not got it quite right. In fact, it has become increasingly evident that among Lutherans themselves there are serious disagreements over the way in which the doctrine of justification should be understood, which means that we cannot even speak properly of *the* Lutheran understanding of the gospel but only *Lutheran understandings* in the plural.

Yet even though all of this raises difficulties, the real crisis concerning the gospel today stems from two other factors that appear to be even more serious and present challenges not only to Lutherans but to Christians in general. The first of these is that our modern worldview has changed so dramatically from both biblical times and the period of the Reformation that the gospel appears to have become irrelevant and even incomprehensible, not only to people outside of the church, but to many who have chosen to remain within it as well. It has been more than four decades since the Fourth Assembly of the Lutheran World Federation affirmed that the world was no longer asking Luther's question regarding how to find a gracious God but instead questioning the very existence

1

and meaningfulness of God.[1] Even this latter question has become a matter of indifference for many today. However, the proclamation of the gospel in its biblical form and in most of the forms in which it has appeared over the centuries has been dependent on a notion of salvation that has to do primarily with a future life: the risen Christ, now "seated at God's right hand," will return some day to judge the living and the dead, receiving the "elect" into eternal life in a new world while condemning the rest of humanity to everlasting death and destruction. For many people today, such beliefs can only be regarded as myth and fantasy, along with many of the other things we find in the Bible, including not only the miraculous events narrated there but the claim that Jesus of Nazareth was God incarnate.

Up until very recently, this clash between worldviews has forced Christians to choose between holding fast to the ancient worldview so as to reject any aspect of the modern scientific worldview that conflicts with it (as biblical fundamentalists have generally done) or attempting to accommodate the gospel to the modern worldview through some approach such as Rudolf Bultmann's "demythologizing" program, which sought to strip away from the gospel all of the "mythical" elements surrounding it in the Scriptures and thereby arrive at its true essence.[2] Today, however, the modern worldview itself has entered a state of crisis. This means that rather than following Bultmann in attempting to accommodate the gospel to the modern scientific worldview, we might now speak of the need to demythologize that worldview itself—though perhaps a different term is necessary, given the post-modern recognition that, like all worldviews, the modern one is mythical in nature and thus, strictly speaking, *cannot* be demythologized. As one or more new worldviews come to establish themselves alongside the modern scientific worldview, to some extent replacing it, it will no doubt be necessary to carry out once more the task of relating the ancient worldview underlying the biblical gospel to the new one(s).

Of course, even though many Christians now find it hard to accept literally the traditional portrayals of heaven and hell, the vast majority continue to hold to a hope of a future salvation having to do with some type of transformed existence in a new world or realm. Yet while they generally attribute this coming salvation in some way to what God has done and will do in Jesus Christ, the spirit of pluralism and tolerance that has become characteristic of our age has led to a growing tendency to maintain that this salvation is open to people of all religious faiths and even to those who practice no religious faith at all. This belief is often closely tied to a similar belief that the idea of some type of eternal condemnation should no longer have any place in the Christian proclamation. Thus, while the notion of a future salvation undoubtedly persists among Christians, it is not entirely clear in what way that salvation depends on accepting the gospel of Jesus Christ; nor is it always clear what the plight from which people must be saved is.

Undoubtedly, salvation has always been defined in broader terms than eternal life, both in Scripture and the Christian tradition. To be "saved" has to do not only with a future life but also with experiencing well-being and wholeness in the present. It involves deliverance from physical and emotional ailments as well as from various types of oppression, not only on an individual level but also on the level of communities and societies. In our world today, however, there seem to be better places than the church and the gospel to look for this kind of salvation. For physical well-being we go to doctors and for emotional healing we turn to mental health specialists. Even the goal of "changing the world" to make it a better and more just place for all is no longer seen primarily as a Christian task but one to be undertaken by governments and other institutions and organizations that have no ties to the church. Thus all of these other forms of "salvation" have ceased to be a particularly Christian concern related to the gospel and there no longer seems to be any need to look to that gospel as their ground and source.

The second major factor contributing to the gospel's state of crisis is the interpretation of Scripture today. In the past few decades, New Testament scholars have increasingly come to maintain that St. Paul's teaching concerning justification by faith was in important ways distinct from that which has been attributed to him by Protestant biblical scholars since Luther's day. Those embracing this "New Perspective on Paul" have argued that what Paul fought against was not the idea that salvation could be earned by good works, since Judaism preached grace rather than works-righteousness, but that Gentiles had to become practicing Jews in order to belong to the church.[3] This involves a rejection of the "Lutheran Paul" and to some extent the "Lutheran gospel" as well: while the "good news" proclaimed by Paul and the other apostles undoubtedly had to do with both Jews and Gentiles being able to participate in the new age of salvation on the basis of faith, it was never a matter of believers' being delivered from their futile attempts to earn their salvation through their own works so as to find certainty of salvation instead through faith alone in Christ and his death. The traditional Lutheran distinction between law and gospel is also called into question by this understanding of the New Testament message: in neither Jewish nor Christian thought was the law thought to constantly accuse God's people, driving them to despair of themselves as Luther did so that they might then flee to God's grace as found in the gospel.

One point on which both the "old" perspective and the "new" have remained somewhat in agreement is the centrality of Jesus' redeeming death for the New Testament gospel. According to many of the traditional interpretations of Scripture, believers are saved either because of Jesus' substitutionary death on their behalf or because they "participate" in some way in that death. At times, these two ideas are combined: Jesus' death and resurrection are "for others" in that these events enable believers to die to the old age and rise to the new with him through participation. As has been the case throughout almost all of the church's history, there are still many different answers to the question of *how* Jesus' death saves believers from sin, yet virtually all agree that in New Testament thought it was believed to effect deliverance from both the *guilt* and the *power* of sin. Jesus' death has therefore been seen as providing the basis upon which believers are justified.

Today more than ever in the church's history, however, many of the traditional interpretations of Jesus' death (often referred to as "theories" or "models" of atonement) have been heavily criticized, primarily on theological grounds. Feminist and womanist theologians in particular have argued that virtually all of the various ways in which Jesus' death has been interpreted in the history of Christian thought are oppressive, leading to violence, abuse, and injustice, particularly toward women; this involves the rejection of the "satisfaction" and "moral influence" views as well as the *Christus Victor* idea.[4]

However, in my 2006 work *Paul on the Cross: Reconstructing the Apostle's Story of Redemption*,[5] I have argued that *all* of these traditional interpretations of Jesus' death or "models of atonement" are to be rejected not only on *theological* but on *historical* grounds as well, since they are based on ideas that are foreign to the thought of Paul and the rest of the New Testament writers. This makes it necessary to call into question as well the idea that has traditionally been at the heart of the Lutheran understanding of justification and the gospel, namely, that Jesus' death constitutes the basis upon which believers are justified and forgiven. According to the understanding of the cross I have attributed to Paul, justification and salvation are instead based on *all* that God has done and will do through Christ and the Holy Spirit. In itself, Jesus' death saved no one; the cross can only be understood properly when it is viewed in the context of the entire story of God's redeeming activity from creation to the *eschaton*.

As suggested by its title, the present book is written in the conviction that in order for the gospel to be truly redeeming in our world today, it must itself be redeemed. Above all, this involves redeeming the gospel from many of the later theological ideas that have become associated with it, ideas that I have discussed not only in *Paul on the Cross* but in my more recent book, the *Fortress Introduction to Salvation and the Cross*.[6] In both of these works, I have argued that, from at least the end of the second century to the present, the biblical message regarding salvation through Christ and the cross has undergone significant alterations that have distorted it. It is my conviction that this contributed in important ways to the historical conflicts over how the gospel should be understood as well as its current state of crisis. In order to address that crisis, we must understand the gospel once more in the context of the ancient Jewish worldview in which it originally arose and developed.

Yet while it is necessary to reconstruct properly the gospel in its original context in order to be faithful to it and redeem it from misrepresentations, for the reasons mentioned above, this is not enough. For while the gospel may have been redeeming in that context, the fact that we live in a very different world today requires that we "translate" it into our own context to address the issues and questions of our own day and age. This means that we must go beyond the descriptive task of historical reconstruction, which was my objective in the two works just mentioned above, and carry out the *theological* task of speaking of the gospel in a way that unleashes its redemptive power in the contexts in which we find ourselves today. Nevertheless, we cannot hope to carry out properly the theological task until the historical task has been properly done; if the gospel is not reconstructed faithfully, we inevitably end up with what Paul called "another gospel" (Gal 1:6-9) that by definition cannot be regarded by Christians as redeeming.

One of the primary aims of the present work, therefore, is to address the theological questions raised by the historical reconstruction of the Christian proclamation of salvation that I have laid out in my previous writings. This includes the questions raised not only by the New Testament writings but the work of Christian theologians past and present, such as those whose work I discussed in the *Fortress Introduction to Salvation and the Cross*. Yet because we cannot speak of the gospel of Christ and the cross without dealing with related questions regarding our understanding of God, salvation, God's law, sin, grace, faith, and eschatology, among others, it will be necessary to consider all of these subjects as well. In fact, for the gospel to be redeemed from the misrepresentations of which it has often been the object, all of these concepts must be redeemed together with it. This, of course, is the task not of any one individual but of Christians together through interaction and dialogue such as that which this book seeks to foment.

Because the gospel is ultimately a proclamation concerning God and human salvation, the opening chapter of this book will discuss some of the basic problems and questions related to the way God and salvation have been understood in Christian thought past and present. This will provide the foundation necessary to discuss the central doctrines of the Christian faith as the Lutheran tradition has defined them, namely, the role of God's law in justification and salvation (Chapter 2), the relation between justification and the work of Christ (Chapter 3), the gospel of justification by grace through faith (Chapter 4), and the Christian life that follows upon justification (Chapter 5). The objective of these chapters is to compare Lutheran teaching on these questions with ancient Jewish beliefs, biblical thought, and the teaching of other Christian traditions, most notably Roman Catholicism, not only to explore similarities and differences but to examine the theological problems associated with the various views. Each of these four chapters will end with a reconsideration of the New Testament teaching on the subjects discussed. On the basis of this discussion, which to a great extent should be seen as having a deconstructive purpose, the final chapter offers a constructive proposal regarding how we should understand and proclaim the biblical gospel of salvation today.

This book is markedly Lutheran both in its concern for "getting the gospel right"—historically a typically Lutheran concern—and in its attempt to be faithful to the principle of *sola Scriptura*, looking to Scripture alone as the ultimate norm and basis for our theology, while of course not ignoring the difficulties involved in any attempt to adhere to this principle. Perhaps somewhat paradoxically, this book is also markedly Lutheran in that it is not intended exclusively or even primarily for a Lutheran audience but for the church at large. The Lutheran church body of which I am a member sees itself not as the "true church" but as a movement within the one, holy, Christian, and apostolic church to which all Christians belong; for this reason, as Lutherans we seek to give witness through accompaniment, sharing, and dialogue even as we receive the witness of others. It is in that spirit that this book is written.

I would like to express my gratitude and appreciation to all those at Fortress Press who played a role in the publication of this work, including especially Neil Elliot, Susan Johnson, and Marissa Wold. Above all, I am deeply indebted to Michael West, Editor-in-Chief at Fortress Press, for his encouragement, willingness to listen, and the confidence he has shown in me over the past ten years. This work was also made possible in part by the materials loaned to me by extension by the Luther Seminary Library at Luther Seminary in St. Paul, Minnesota, and the JKM Library at the Lutheran School of Theology at Chicago. In particular, I am thankful to Karen Alexander at the Luther Seminary Library and Chad Pollock at the JKM Library for their kind assistance in this regard. In addition, I am profoundly grateful to all those at the Global Mission Unit at the Evangelical Lutheran Church in America, to my coworkers and students at the Theological Community of Mexico and Augsburg Lutheran Seminary in Mexico City, and most of all to my wife Alicia for giving me the inspiration, patience, and support necessary to make the publication of this work a reality.

CHAPTER 1

God and Salvation

"How can I find a gracious God?" It is generally acknowledged that this question constituted the starting point for Martin Luther's theology. Toward the end of his life, Luther described in the following terms the personal struggle he had experienced in his younger years before his discovery of the gospel:

> Though I lived as a monk without reproach, I felt that I was a sinner before God with an extremely disturbed conscience. I could not believe that he was placated by my satisfaction. I did not love, yes, I hated the righteous God who punishes sinners, and secretly, if not blasphemously, certainly murmuring greatly, I was angry with God, and said, "As if, indeed, it is not enough, that miserable sinners, eternally lost through original sin, are crushed by every kind of calamity by the law of the decalogue, without having God add pain to pain by the gospel and also by the gospel threatening us with his righteousness and wrath!" Thus I raged with a fierce and troubled conscience.[1]

These words of Luther reflect a certain concept of God: the God with whom Luther struggled was a personal God standing over against Luther as judge, angrily accusing and condemning him for his sins. Although Luther eventually came to see God as a merciful and forgiving Father, his belief that God related to human beings as a personal being remained the same throughout his lifetime. There can be no doubt that in conceiving of God in this way, Luther was in continuity with biblical thought. Yet, in both ancient and modern times, many have found such an understanding of God problematic.

God in Biblical Thought

While one can undoubtedly find many different concepts of God throughout the biblical writings, from beginning to end God is spoken of as a divine person who is constantly active in the world. As almighty and sovereign Lord, God not only created all things in the beginning but is constantly at work to preserve and sustain them. Psalm 104, for example, presents God as the one who moves land

and waters, sends rain and thunder, and makes grass and plants grow so that animals and people may be fed (Ps 104:5-18). Although at times this implies some type of natural order that God has established, so that the sun and the moon and the seasons follow certain set patterns (Ps 104:19-22), God is still spoken of as being involved in all that happens. God gives the "living things small and great" their "food in due season": "you open your hand, they are filled with good things. When you hide your face, they are dismayed; when you take away their breath, they die and return to their dust. When you send forth your spirit, they are created; and you renew the face of the ground" (Ps 104:27-30). Such ideas run not only throughout the Hebrew Scriptures but the New Testament as well. In Matthew's Gospel, for example, Jesus affirms that God makes the sun shine and the rain fall on good and bad, clothes all living beings from plants to people, and feeds the birds of the air, none of which falls to the ground independently of God's will (Matt 5:45; 6:26-30; 10:29-30).

In biblical thought, then, God is active in all that takes place in the world.[2] Undoubtedly, we can find in the biblical writings the idea that God has established in the created order what we would today call "natural laws." Yet these laws do not function independently of God, as if things happened entirely on their own. Instead, God is constantly upholding and maintaining the created order, yet can alter the course of things at any moment. Thus, for example, while God has established a course for the sun to follow day after day (Ps 19:4-5; 74:16-17; 104:19), God can make the sun stand still (Josh 10:12-13), command it not to rise (Job 9:7), or make it go down at noon (Amos 8:9). Thus God is behind not only the extraordinary or supernatural events that take place but the everyday, ordinary, natural events as well: *everything that happens is ultimately to be attributed to God's will*, since even what is not directly *caused* by God is still *allowed* by God, who could prevent anything from happening at any time.

Such an understanding of God can, of course, imply a determinism in which everything is decided by God alone, leaving no room for chance or human freedom. In that case, all things have been determined by God ahead of time, so that even the smallest and most insignificant of occurrences must be attributed to God's activity. This would mean that human beings are not responsible for their actions, since they can only do what God has ordained and determined beforehand. Yet in spite of the tensions or even contradictions that this involves, the Scriptures consistently avoid that conclusion, insisting instead that human beings themselves choose between good or evil and on this basis are accountable to God for what they do. For this reason, God is consistently presented as the one who *judges* human beings, rewarding them for doing what is right and punishing them for doing what is wrong. This clearly implies that when human beings behave in certain ways, it is not *God* who is ultimately responsible for their actions but those human beings themselves. Though at times God or some other power such as an angel, demon, or serpent may influence or occasionally even compel human beings to do good or evil against their will, they are still held accountable for their actions. The Scriptures repeatedly let this apparent contradiction stand, affirming human freedom and responsibility while nevertheless claiming that ultimately all things are determined by God's sovereign will.

In the Hebrew Scriptures, which for the most part reflect a worldview predating the New Testament worldview by at least several centuries, it is repeatedly affirmed that God responds to what human beings do by rewarding or punishing them in *this* world. If God's people do what God has commanded, God is content and gives them peace, health, abundance, well-being, and victory over their enemies; if they do not, God becomes angry and sends plagues, desolation, oppression, and many other ills resulting in suffering and hardship for the people (Leviticus 26; Deuteronomy 28). This is true with regard to peoples and nations as a whole, who are blessed or punished collectively by God for their actions, as well as individuals. The idea that God rewards those who do good and punishes those who do evil often forms the basis for concluding that, when things go well for certain persons or a people as a whole, it is because God is blessing them for their obedience and righteousness; but when things go poorly for them, the reason is that they have done something wrong and thus are being afflicted by God.[3]

In Old Testament thought, the sufferings sent by God are seen as having a goal or purpose rather than constituting an end in themselves.[4] Hardships may serve to test people and see how strong their faith is, as in the case of Job. At other times, by afflicting those who sin, God attempts to bring them to repent of their sinful ways and return to a life of obedience in the context of the covenant. This is an act of love on God's part, since God does not merely let them continue in their errant ways (2 Macc 6:12-16; 7:32-33). When God destroys those who do harm to others, the purpose is also a loving one, namely, to deliver the needy and oppressed from their oppressors. The destruction of evildoers may also serve to keep sin from spreading as well as demonstrate to all that God does not tolerate sin so that they may be moved to refrain from sinning out of fear of divine retribution. Thus the fact that God becomes angry and punishes human beings when they sin is seen as a sign of God's love, rather than a *lack* of love, since God's ultimate purpose is promoting human justice and well-being. These ideas are found in the New Testament as well. God can send sufferings to test and refine the faith of believers (1 Pet 1:6-7; 1 Thess 2:4; Heb 11:17), as well as to discipline them and bring them to repentance (Heb 12:5-11). God strikes down Ananias and Sapphira for their dishonesty (Acts 5:1-11) and Herod for his insolence (Acts 12:20-23), apparently to provide an example and warning for others.

By New Testament times, however, it had become common to maintain that sin would be punished and righteousness rewarded primarily in a *future* life or world.[5] God would judge all people for their deeds, ultimately rewarding the righteous with a life of eternal bliss and punishing evildoers with eternal death and destruction. This belief no doubt arose in response to the problem of why sinners so often prosper in the present life, while the righteous suffer: accounts will indeed be settled but this will take place in the coming world rather than the present one. Thus the New Testament affirms that in this life God may send suffering or hardships on the righteous: Paul, for example, endured a "thorn in the flesh" as a result of God sending a messenger of Satan to torment him to keep him from being too elated (2 Cor 12:7). Conversely, those for whom all goes well in life are not necessarily the object of God's blessing, since they may actually be unrighteous persons and evildoers (Luke 6:24-25; 16:19-31). God may even allow a man to be born blind, not as punishment for his parents' sin, but simply "so that God's works might be revealed in him" (John 9:3).

In both the Hebrew and Christian Scriptures, therefore, God is viewed as a sovereign Lord who is constantly active in the world and in human history to accomplish God's purposes. At times, of course, God may choose to withdraw from human beings, abandoning them to their own deserts, so that God becomes *inactive* and is no longer "present" among them; yet even God's inactivity is ultimately aimed at accomplishing God's gracious purposes among human beings.

Finally, it is important to stress that in biblical thought the God of Israel is regarded not merely as a *personal being* but an actual *person*. While God is no doubt far greater in many ways than any human person and is the *judge* of all people rather than their *equal*, as a divine person God consistently behaves like other persons: God has a will, acts with certain intentions, and can even experience emotions such as joy, sadness, or anger, depending on what human beings do.

Because the Reformers sought to be faithful to Scripture, this view of God is found throughout their writings as well. Philip Melanchthon, for example, affirmed that "God, even in this life, fiercely punishes external disobedience with plagues, illness, poverty, hunger, war, disastrous government, and even adversity for our children."[6] Thus God is thought to reward and punish human beings personally for their actions both in this life and the life to come.

Modern Thought concerning God

Even before New Testament times, this biblical understanding of God began to be challenged by those adhering to certain conceptions of God associated with Greek philosophical thought. Some have claimed that evidence of this Hellenistic influence can already be observed in a tendency to avoid ascribing to God some of the traits characteristic of human beings or "anthropomorphisms" in the Septuagint (the Greek translation of the Hebrew Scriptures) as well as other Jewish writings in antiquity.[7] The writings of the Christian Church Fathers demonstrate that, by the fourth century C.E., the biblical view of God had been transformed further. God was described as immutable and impassible and as such could not suffer or be affected by anything human beings do.[8] In effect, this made God more detached from human affairs; the world came to be seen as being governed by natural laws which, though established by God, functioned to some extent on their own independently of God. Of course, because the Fathers still strove to be faithful to Scripture, the biblical view of God never disappeared entirely, instead co-existing with the conceptions of God found in Hellenistic philosophical thought. Nevertheless, this led to constant tensions and problems. Thus, for example, the claim that Jesus was divine raised the problem of how it was possible for him to have suffered and died, since neither of these things are possible for God according to a Hellenistic understanding of divinity.

This tension between two different conceptions of God has persisted in Christian thought throughout most of the church's history. Since the Enlightenment, however, it has become particularly acute. Whereas in ancient times people such as the Hebrews attributed things like the weather, illnesses, and misfortunes to the hand of God, ever since the establishment of the scientific worldview in the West we now regard such things as natural occurrences that can be explained on the basis of natural laws that are inherent to the universe. According to our modern worldview, almost everything has a natural explanation; even when we are not able to explain and understand fully the laws that govern our world, we nevertheless believe that such laws exist and also generally view them as inviolable.

The adoption of the modern scientific worldview by Christians has had significant consequences for Christian theological thought. According to the biblical and ancient Jewish worldview, there is often an *extrinsic* relationship between an action and its result: God acts to punish human sin and to reward acts of righteousness. When Ananias and Sapphira are dishonest and consequently fall to the ground and die, it is believed that God has intervened from above to punish them for their wrongdoing; *God* causes them to die. Today, however, "modern" human beings tend to posit an *intrinsic* relationship between actions and their consequences, seeking natural explanations based on the idea of cause-and-effect. Thus, according to this worldview, Ananias and Sapphira probably fell dead to the ground because Peter's accusation caused such stress and anxiety in Ananias that he suffered a fatal heart attack; this in turn led to another fatal heart attack in Sapphira when she was overcome by emotion after learning what had happened to her husband. In this case, there is no *extrinsic* relationship between what Ananias and Sapphira had done and the fate they suffered, since God did not intervene from the outside in any way or cause something supernatural to take place; the relationship is solely *intrinsic* and can be explained on the basis of natural laws.

These modern ideas of God have become quite prominent in the work of contemporary Christian theologians. In his *Systematic Theology*, for example, Paul Tillich argued against the idea that "God is *a* person," instead asserting that "God is the ground of everything personal and that he carries within himself the ontological power of personality. He is not a person, but he is not less than personal.... Ordinary theism has made God a heavenly, completely perfect person who resides above the world and mankind. The protest of atheism against such a highest person is correct.... 'Personal God' is a confusing symbol."[9]

Similarly, although at times she speaks of God in personal terms, Rosemary Radford Ruether conceives of God as a "Great Matrix of Being" that is the "ground of life-giving relations and their ongoing renewal."[10] Like many modern theologians, Ruether often refers to God as "the Divine," which can involve viewing God more in terms of some type of power, force, or nature than a person.[11] When personal pronouns, whether masculine or feminine, are avoided when speaking of God so that God is neither a "he" nor a "she," the result can be the same: God seems to be viewed more as some*thing* rather than some*one*. Such a God, of course, is no longer conceived of as a judge standing over against human beings to reward or punish them for their deeds. According to Ruether, human beings merely disintegrate after death and are dissolved "back into the cosmic matrix of matter/energy, from which new centers of the individuation arise."[12] Thus, for Ruether, the "God of omnipotent control over history" does not exist; ultimately, it is human beings who control history, though nature and its laws are of course also involved.[13]

Gordon Kaufman has also argued against such a personal idea of God. According to Kaufman, we can no longer "think of God as a person-like creator-God" or as "an all-powerful *personal* reality existing somehow before and independently of what we today call 'the universe'...." Today, therefore, we must reject the anthropomorphic view of God that is characteristic of theism so as to refrain from attributing to God the features commonly associated with personality, such as "conscious intention, purposive action, deliberate creation of artifacts, loving attitudes and behaviors, and the like. . . ."[14] Needless to say, these views of God are fundamentally at odds with the biblical view of God as one who loves human beings, becomes sad or angry when they sin, rejoices when they repent, and is constantly active in human affairs.

Concepts of God and the Doctrine of Justification

All of this has important implications for the Christian doctrine of justification. According to Paul's teaching, justification involves a divine judgment of individual human beings on the basis of their actions: God "will repay according to each one's deeds: to those who by patiently doing good seek for glory and honor and immortality, he will give eternal life; while for those who are self-seeking and who obey not the truth but wickedness, there will be wrath and fury" (Rom 2:6-8). Obviously, this involves an *extrinsic* relationship between the actions of human beings and their salvation or punishment, not only because the consequences of those actions depend entirely on God's sovereign decision rather than following naturally and inevitably from them, but also because salvation and condemnation ultimately take place in another life or world distinct from this one. Furthermore, the God who justifies or condemns reacts to the actions of human beings like a human person, either being content and rewarding them for doing good or becoming wrathful and punishing them for doing evil.

In Western Christian thought, which has always displayed a special affinity for legal and juristic categories, salvation and justification have commonly been regarded as virtually synonymous: being saved has to do with God declaring a person righteous and forgiving that person's sins at the final judgment, as Paul teaches. In Eastern Christianity, however, the situation has been different. When asked to comment on the discussions in the West concerning the doctrine of justification, Eastern theologians almost invariably make the observation that "Eastern Christianity from its origins shows a singular lack of interest in discussing its soteriology in terms of justification."[15] The reason for this is precisely the distinct view of God and God's relation to believers found in Eastern thought, which was heavily influenced by ancient Hellenistic philosophy and anthropology. There the plight of human beings is not understood primarily in terms of sinners standing under the judgment of a wrathful God. Divine forgiveness of human sin and guilt is "not a problem for God"; rather, the problem is that human beings have a "mortal and corrupt nature" that must be healed.[16] Sin stands in the way of salvation, not because God threatens to punish it, but because it has "cosmic consequences," namely, "ontological separation from the divine source of life, the moral instability of the human heart as well as physical instability, and death as ultimate destruction."[17] According to this way of thinking, there is an *intrinsic* relationship between human sin and its consequences, such as separation from God and death; these *follow naturally* from sin rather than being some type of punishment imposed by God from above.

The solution to the problem of sin and death is therefore to introduce into humanity a divine power or energy capable of reversing, overcoming, or neutralizing the effects of sin in human nature. This takes place in the incarnation of God's Son, when the divine was joined to the human so that the human might become divine or "deified." Salvation is a matter of "participation in divine life" and "sanctification through the energy of God, which penetrates humanity and restores it to its 'natural' state."[18] The penetration of this divine energy into the human nature assumed by Christ, which is the same nature shared by all people, effects a transformation of human beings as well as the cosmos as a whole.

Just as there is an intrinsic relationship between sin and its consequences, then, there is an intrinsic relationship between the incarnation of God's Son and the restoration of human beings to divine life and union with God. While Orthodox theologians insist that human beings must "cooperate" with this divine grace or energy in order for it to be effective, it is still something that "works" through some type of salvific "effect" it has on the human nature in which all share.[19] Of course, because Eastern Orthodoxy seeks to remain faithful to the Scriptures, it does not abandon entirely the ideas of divine judgment and the forgiveness of sins.[20] Yet the judgment that ultimately seems to save human beings is the judgment *they* make about whether to cooperate with God's grace in Christ rather than the judgment *God* makes regarding what they have done. In effect, God has set up a system by which they can obtain salvation for themselves by receiving divine grace or energy through the church and the sacraments and cooperating with it. Salvation is thus an "organic process" that begins in this life and is perfected in the next as believers grow into the divine likeness so as ultimately to attain a perfect union with God.[21] This understanding of salvation leads Orthodox theologians to reject the Western interpretation of Christ's death as a satisfaction offered to God to avert God's wrath or enable God to forgive. This is not only because "God did not need the cross to forgive sins" but because "simple forgiveness was not enough to solve the problem of sin."[22] A real, ontological transformation of human beings is necessary, because their problem is not that of being guilty before God but of suffering the intrinsic consequences of the sin that resides in their fallen nature.

Since at least the nineteenth century, the idea of God as a righteous judge who will ultimately justify some but punish others in wrath for their sins has found increasing opposition in the West as well. Liberal theologians like Albrecht Ritschl (1822–1889) rejected the notion that God punishes sin and instead claimed that "punishment of sin" involved a "permanent consequence of sin," namely, "*the separation of sinners from God*, the suspension of man's proper fellowship with him."[23] This "punishment" is thus an *intrinsic* consequence of sin rather than an *extrinsic* one. Ritschl also rejected the conception of God as judge: "the attitude of God in the act of justification cannot be conceived as that of Judge."[24] While not ruling out entirely the concept of divine wrath, Ritschl nevertheless insisted that when evil things happen, they should not be understood as divine punishment; instead, "evil is always a natural event."[25] For human beings to be justified and saved from guilt, it was not necessary for God's wrath to be taken away by Christ's death, since God is always loving and willing to forgive; the problem of sinners is not that God holds them guilty but that they allow their feelings of guilt to alienate them from God.[26] Because the alienation lies on their side rather than God's, it is they who must come to accept God's love and forgiveness rather than an angry God who must come to accept them.

Today, even among more "orthodox" Protestant theologians, ideas similar to these have become common. Wolfhart Pannenberg, for example, questions the notion of divine punishment for sins, noting that "the word 'punishment' is not entirely appropriate, since this word suggests an arbitrary sanction."[27] Instead, Pannenberg affirms that in biblical thought there is a "natural relation between deed and consequence"; thus "death is built into the essence of sin as the most extreme consequence of sin's desire for separation from God, the origin of life. Death is not added externally to sin, as an arbitrary 'punishment' imposed upon it."[28]

In his treatment of the doctrine of justification, Eberhard Jüngel looks to a similar understanding of sin and divine wrath. He notes: "It has become customary for theologians to avoid the concept of divine punishment as too painful. However, when it is understood correctly it is indispensable. Of course, it is not a punishment which is especially linked to sin. It is simply the logical consequence of our sin which we would only too gladly escape, but God has handed us over to it."[29] The idea of God's wrath should therefore be understood simply as God allowing nature to run its course: "sin as it exists must be taken seriously in its consequences; all sinners must suffer the punishment of being handed over to the curse of the evil of their sin. This is God's wrath, rightly understood: that sinners be delivered up to the consequences of their sin."[30] Here God's wrath is no longer an active response to human sin, as it is in biblical thought, but a passive non-intervention on God's part in which God merely stands back and lets human beings suffer the natural consequences of their actions.

Such an understanding of sin and divine wrath can lead to the conclusion that salvation and justification ultimately depend not on an act of God but on a human decision. Just as God merely lets human beings suffer the consequences of their sin in this life, so also does God let them make their own judgment as to whether they will be saved. Douglas John Hall, for example, writes that although "God *wills* life, abundant life (*salus*) for all," nevertheless "no one under the loving dominion of this God will simply have salvation imposed upon him or her."[31] Similarly, David Scaer affirms that God's final verdict on unbelievers "only confirms the path they have chosen for themselves."[32] This implies that God merely respects the decision of human beings as to whether they wish to be saved or not, neither forcing them to accept salvation nor preventing them from attaining it; everything is up to human beings themselves.

Concepts of God and Human Salvation

These conflicting conceptions of God as one who intervenes actively in human history and ultimately will justify or condemn human beings for their behavior and as one who simply lets human beings receive the natural consequences of the decisions they make for themselves without intervening have important ramifications for the Christian teaching regarding salvation. The former view of God's saving and judging activity is problematic on several accounts. With regard to life in the present world, if we claim that God is constantly active to bless with happiness and well-being those who do good but to punish with suffering and afflictions those who do not, then we must interpret prosperity in life as a reward from God for righteous behavior but misfortune and hardships in life as divine punishment for sin. While this view is found in many passages of Scripture, even in biblical times many considered it problematic in light of the fact that many who consistently practice sin and injustice seem to prosper while those who strive to do God's will suffer. Precisely because of this problem, many came to interpret suffering in this life as having some purpose other than to punish sinners, as noted above: it might serve to discipline or test them or strengthen their faith and dependence on God. Once it is affirmed that righteousness is not always rewarded and sin is not always punished in *this* world, however, in order to maintain the idea of a just and loving God, some type of *future* reward and punishment must be posited: those judged righteous by God will receive blessing and prosperity in the next life, while those who are not judged righteous will be excluded from that blessing and prosperity in some way. Generally, this is said to involve some type of eternal suffering such as hell, though some have argued instead in favor of the destruction or annihilation of those condemned by God, which would appear to be somewhat less drastic on God's part.

What many people have found objectionable in this traditional view is not so much that God graciously *saves* and *rewards* some (even those who are not deserving of such salvation) but that God *condemns* and *punishes* some by subjecting them to pain and suffering both in this life and the next. It is not God's *grace* but God's *wrath* that creates difficulties. Even if some type of divine loving purpose is said to be at work, for many the idea that God afflicts people in *this* life for their sins remains problematic: a God who willfully and intentionally makes people suffer for whatever reason seems heartless and even cruel, rather than loving and merciful. Perhaps the most common response to such an objection is to maintain that God *must* punish sin if there is to be justice and well-being for all in this world; to fail to act against evil would constitute a *lack* of love on God's part. Yet this argument seems to be undermined once more by the fact that evildoers often prosper while the righteous suffer; in meting out blessings and afflictions in this life, God appears to be capricious and arbitrary rather than just.

These difficulties are not resolved merely by positing some type of eternal punishment for sinners that will provide a settling of accounts. It would seem that the only loving purpose behind such a future punishment might be to serve as a deterrent in the present life: supposedly, when people know that what they do in the present will have eternal consequences, they will be moved to avoid evil and do good. Eternal condemnation might also be seen as a loving act on God's part if its purpose is said to be that of saving the oppressed from the oppressors, making it impossible for those who bring pain into the lives of others to continue to do so in the world to come. Yet one cannot help but ask if people can so easily and neatly be divided into two groups, such as oppressors and oppressed, righteous and wicked, good and bad; do not all people belong to both groups? In any case, once the final judgment has been made, it appears that there can no longer be any loving purpose on God's part in relation to those who are condemned to some type of eternal suffering or simply destroyed and annihilated permanently.

One solution to these problems has been to posit the existence of something such as purgatory in which people are sentenced by God to some type of *temporary* suffering after they die.[33] Here the loving purpose may be either that of deterring people from committing sin in the present world, since they know that the more they sin the more they will have to suffer, or else that of purging people from their sinfulness like precious metals are refined and purified; the former idea has been more characteristic of Roman Catholicism, while the latter has been found in Eastern Christian thought, most notably that of Gregory of Nyssa.[34] The idea of a future purification from sin has at times been combined with that of *apocatastasis*, according to which all persons and beings (including even the devil in some views) will be saved after they have been purified through suffering.[35] The advantage of views such as these is that they uphold both God's justice and God's love and mercy: all people are repaid for what they do in life, yet ultimately salvation is open to all. For Protestants, however, the main problem with this type of view is that there is no clear basis for it in the Christian Scriptures. The idea of God intentionally subjecting people to pain and suffering after death also remains troublesome for many.

Yet the notion that there is some future realm of existence in which God will not only reward people for doing good but punish them for doing evil is problematic in other regards as well. Why should God wait until then rather than putting an end to suffering and evil in the present or at least punishing those who do evil now, instead of letting many of them prosper in this life? By positing a future existence in some other realm in which what we do in this life will be rewarded or punished, do we not make the present world secondary in importance to the coming world? Is this life merely a testing ground for a future life, so that our only concern here should be doing what is necessary to be rewarded in eternity rather than being punished there? In addition, if persons will be judged and either saved or condemned as *individuals*, why should we be concerned about social justice and making this world a better place? All of our actions would seem to have as their ultimate goal merely attaining an eternal reward or avoiding eternal punishment on an individual level, so that they are motivated by a concern for our own future personal salvation rather than a real concern for others. In that case, as Douglas John Hall has observed, the purpose of the world seems to lie *above* and *beyond* it rather than *in* it, so that the present world is abandoned to vanity and there is no need for us to work to change it.[36]

For these and other reasons, many prefer the alternative of viewing God as a being who simply lets human beings suffer the natural consequences of their actions. In that case, God does not act either to reward righteousness or punish sins in this world but only instructs and illumines human beings through different means (such as the Scriptures) so that they may know what is best for them. Of course, the problem with this view is that it still cannot address satisfactorily why there is such widespread suffering and injustice in this world and why those who do good so often suffer most in this world, while those who practice sin and oppression at times prosper. Furthermore, if God does not act to overcome evil and injustice in our world but leaves it up to us to resolve our problems, we can no longer speak of a God that "saves" us in this world; at most, God reveals to us what we ought to do, yet in the end we must save ourselves. The same problem arises when it is said that both in *this* life and in the life to come God merely lets us receive the consequences of our actions, which either unite us to God or separate us from God, whether temporarily (as a doctrine of purgatory maintains) or permanently. Once again, if in a future world we merely "reap what we sow" in this world, then our salvation is left up to *us*; it is *we* who judge union with God as desirable or not rather than God judging us.

Although it is problematic to affirm the existence of a future world in which all will receive either blessings or sufferings depending on the choices they have made in life, it seems just as problematic to deny such a belief. If at death we merely disintegrate into the earth so as to be absorbed once more into the "cosmic matrix of matter/energy," as Rosemary Radford Ruether affirms, then for each of us as individuals there are no consequences for the choices we make in life beyond those we experience in this world. At most, we might speak of some type of collective salvation in that our actions affect others both now and in the future, making our world either better or worse; yet it is not clear how Ruether can affirm that we "are ultimately accountable for its welfare to the true source of life, God."[37] In what way can we be accountable to God if we will not be judged, either as individual persons or collectively, and if God neither rewards nor condemns people for their actions? The same difficulties arise with regard to universalistic views of salvation according to which all will be saved and no one condemned in the world to come:[38] in that case, in the end it makes no difference whether we do good or evil outside of the natural consequences that our actions have for us and others in this life.

Perhaps the greatest problem that most people would have in accepting the idea of an impersonal God is that such a belief seems to undermine the hope of believers, which is based on the conviction that their salvation in both this life and the next is based on God's intervention. An impersonal God does not act in human history to save people from their problems and difficulties, bless them, or even teach and guide them; such saving activity can only be attributed to a God who relates to us as a person. What sense is there in asking God to intervene against evil in our world if God merely stands by passively, letting us suffer the consequences of what we do? In that case, prayer to God must be regarded as senseless and futile (unless we affirm that we are to pray for our own benefit but not because it will affect in any way what God does). To say that God *can* and at times *does* intervene when people pray involves a return to the biblical worldview, according to which God's hand is actively involved in the affairs of this world. Similarly, only if one confesses belief in a personal God can one hope and pray that God will some day save the world from evil and bring the faithful into an existence of eternal bliss. Thus to reject the idea that God relates to us as a person necessarily involves rejecting a view of God that provides hope and consolation not only for Christians but people of other faiths as well.

CHAPTER 2

Justice, Righteousness, and the Law

According to traditional Lutheran teaching, the gospel cannot be proclaimed apart from the law. This is because, as a proclamation of the forgiveness of sins and salvation from divine condemnation, the gospel presupposes a condition in which people have not observed God's law and thus stand under the judgment that the law pronounces on those who disobey God's commandments.

In recent years, however, the Lutheran understanding of the law has been seriously called into question, particularly by scholars associated with what is now known as the "New Perspective on Paul."[1] In addition to the problems raised by the New Perspective, however, there are a number of others that make it necessary to reconsider the role ascribed to God's law in human salvation and justification.

The Law in Lutheran Thought

Although the writings of Luther have provided the basis for Lutheran teaching regarding the law, Luther himself sought merely to expound the New Testament teaching on the subject, particularly that of Paul's Letters to the Romans and the Galatians. Drawing on passages such as Rom 13:8-10, Gal 6:14, and the teaching attributed to Jesus in the Gospels (Matt 19:16-19; 22:35-40, and parallels), Luther understood the law primarily in terms of the Decalogue or Ten Commandments, which in turn are summarized in the commandments to love God and neighbor.[2] These commandments can be fulfilled only by trusting in and clinging to God with all of one's heart.[3]

Following Paul, Luther maintained that, while in principle the law is good, because human beings exist in a fallen state it is no longer possible for them to obey the law; even when they try to do good, they cannot (Rom 5:12; 7:8-23; Gal 3:10-11). Although at times they can keep many of the law's commandments outwardly, they cannot fulfill the law in the way God desires by loving God above all else and doing what God commands willingly and with joy.[4] For this reason, in their fallen condition, it is impossible for human beings to attain the salvation that the law promises to those who are perfect in obedience and righteousness. Instead, they are under God's wrath and condemnation (Rom 2:5-8; 5:16-18).

All of this results in a situation in which the law is constantly accusing human beings of their sin and making it manifest to them. This idea is based on Paul's affirmation in Rom 3:20 that "through the law comes knowledge of sin" as well as his teaching in Rom 7:7-24 that the law reveals to human beings that they are in "slavery under sin" and need to be rescued by Christ. According to Lutheran theology, "the law always accuses" (*lex semper accusat*). It stands over sinners with the demand that they obey it and live righteously but it cannot give them the power to do so (Gal 3:21). Thus the law is not a manifestation of God's grace but of God's righteousness to which human beings must conform.[5] Faced with the incessant accusation of the law and their inability to fulfill it and thereby attain salvation, sinful human beings can only despair of themselves. They realize they are under God's wrath and judgment: "The law works the wrath of God, kills, curses, accuses, judges, and damns everything that is not in Christ."[6] Luther calls this the "primary purpose" of the law: "the true function and the chief and proper use of the Law is to reveal to man his sin, blindness, misery, wickedness, ignorance, hate and contempt of God, death, hell, judgment, and the well-deserved wrath of God."[7] By driving sinners to despair of themselves, at the same time the law drives them to look to God and the gospel of God's grace in Christ for salvation. In Lutheran thought, this is referred to as the second or "theological" use of the law (*usus theologicus*): it serves both as a mirror to show sinners their sin and moral impotence as well as a hammer to crush any self-righteousness on their part.[8]

The law does, of course, have a first use as well, which Luther called the "political" or "civil" use (*usus politicus/civilis*): "God has ordained civic laws, indeed all laws, to restrain transgressions. Therefore every law was given to hinder sins. . . . Thus the first understanding and use of the Law is to restrain the wicked."[9] Luther found this idea in Rom 13:1-7, where Paul teaches that God has established authorities to suppress evil conduct in the world, and in 1 Tim 1:9, which affirms that "the law is laid down not for the innocent but for the lawless and disobedient." To some degree, human beings can fulfill the law in the sense of refraining from evil and doing good in the civil realm, thereby attaining a "civil righteousness" that avails before other human beings (*coram hominibus*). Yet such fulfillment does not contribute in any way to salvation, since it merely affects life in this world and not one's standing before God (*coram Deo*).[10]

Paul's words in Gal 3:24 have been understood against the background of both of these ideas: the law can be seen as "our disciplinarian (*paidagōgos*) until Christ came" in the sense that it constrained God's people from falling into utter lawlessness (first use) and in that it pointed them to Christ for salvation (second use).[11] The same is true of Paul's affirmation that the law was "added because of transgressions" (Gal 3:19): this can be interpreted to mean that God gave the law so that human beings might become aware of their transgressions and thus come to see their need for a savior (second use) or in the sense that God's purpose was to curb transgressions so that the world might not become a place of unrestrained evil and wickedness (first use).[12]

Both Lutheran and Reformed theologians have also spoken of a third use of the law in addition to the first two: according to this idea, the law serves to guide and instruct believers in their Christian life. Although this idea is found in the writings of Philip Melanchthon and the Formula of Concord, Luther never spoke explicitly of a third use of the law and Luther scholars are in disagreement regarding whether such an idea is actually in continuity with his thought, as we shall see in chapter 5.[13]

The Law in Ancient Judaism

Certain aspects of this Lutheran understanding of the law have come under growing criticism since the 1977 publication of E. P. Sanders' *Paul and Palestinian Judaism* and the subsequent development of the New Perspective on Paul. Although many of the things Sanders questioned had to do with the Lutheran characterization of Judaism as a religion based on "works-righteousness" rather than the Lutheran understanding of the law per se, several of the points he raises are relevant here.

First, Sanders stressed that, in Jewish thought, the Mosaic law was seen as a gracious gift to Israel rather than a heavy and oppressive burden, constantly making impossible demands on them and accusing them of their sin. "Judaism does not regard the obligations which God imposed upon his people as onerous. They are instead regarded as a blessing, and one should fulfil them with joy. They are accompanied by strength and peace, and they are a sign of God's mercy. . . ."[14] This idea is found in the Hebrew Scriptures themselves, most explicitly in Psalm 119, where the Psalmist repeatedly speaks of delighting in God's statutes since they give understanding and guidance, like a lamp in the darkness (Ps 119:14, 16, 24, 47-48, 77, 97, 103-5, 111, 129-30). This means that the law is a manifestation of God's grace, just like Israel's election as God's people.

Second, although salvation was linked to the fulfillment of the commandments, Sanders pointed out that in Jewish thought perfect obedience was not required or expected. In fact, the law itself anticipated that people would transgress and therefore established means of atonement for sin. All that was expected of those in the covenant was that they be committed to obeying the commandments to the best of their abilities and repent and make atonement when they sinned. Fulfillment of the law was therefore not an impossibility, nor was it beyond the power of human beings to love God and obey God's commandments with a joyful heart (see Deut 28:47; 30:11-14). God was always willing to show mercy to those who sincerely repented of their sin. Forgiveness, then, was not a problem.[15]

Third, Sanders notes that salvation was not understood exclusively in terms of the life of the age to come: "Judaism in general and Rabbinic Judaism in particular is not a religion which is primarily other-worldly."[16] While many Jews in Jesus' day awaited the arrival of a new age and stressed that the rewards and punishments for sins committed in the present would be received when that age arrived, they also believed that God rewarded obedience and punished sin to some extent in the present life. Thus, although salvation undoubtedly involved a future hope, it was also something that could be experienced at least partially in the present.

The main point Sanders makes, however, is that in ancient Judaism it was not believed that one could *earn* salvation by obeying the commandments. Salvation was a divine gift, based on election; obedience was merely the condition for continuing to belong to the elect people to be saved by God, that is, "staying in" that group rather than "getting in." On this point Sanders' argument has been heavily criticized since, when obedience to the commandments is made the condition for salvation, then it does appear that ultimately salvation must be earned or at least merited by striving to obey those commandments.[17] In other words, even if obedience is not what enables one to "get in" to the community of the elect to whom God has promised redemption, the fact that one must "stay in" through obedience to the commandments if one is to be saved means that one must merit one's continued inclusion in that group through one's deeds.[18]

Obviously, Sanders' presentation of Jewish thought represents a challenge for Lutheran teaching on the law; it is clear that there are fundamental differences in the way that the law is viewed in Judaism and in Lutheranism. Of course, the fact that Luther and Lutheran theologians looked to Paul's writings to define their understanding of the law raises the question of the extent to which the differences between the Jewish and Lutheran views are actually differences between Judaism and Paul. And the fact that Paul was a follower of Jesus raises the further question of the extent to which Paul was drawing on Jesus' teaching on the law in developing his own.

Defining the Law

Before discussing the role of the law in human salvation, it is necessary to define what is meant by the term *law*. As noted above, in Lutheran thought the law has been understood primarily in terms of the Decalogue. In contrast, in Jewish thought, the law includes all of the commandments given through Moses in the Pentateuch or Torah. According to Jewish tradition, these commandments number 613, of which 365 are negative commandments or prohibitions and 248 are positive commandments.[19]

The majority of both Jews and Christians have agreed that the commandments of the law given to Israel through Moses are not binding on non-Jews, or Gentiles. Jewish tradition has often spoken of seven commandments that apply to non-Jews; these are generally referred to as the "Noahic" commandments (Genesis 7–9) and include refraining from stealing, murdering, blaspheming God, idolatry, sexual immorality, and cruelty to animals in addition to establishing courts of justice.[20] In the book of Acts, there seems to be evidence that the first Christians took up a similar view, since the apostles are presented there as ordering Gentile believers to abstain from eating food offered to idols, blood, and that which has been strangled, as well as to avoid fornication (Acts 15:10-20, 29).

The question of whether the Mosaic law was to be binding on Gentile believers was the subject of much debate and controversy among believers in Jesus in the years immediately following his death. Seemingly conflicting views can be found even in the New Testament.[21] Thus, for example, in Matthew's Gospel Jesus is presented as teaching that "not one letter, not one stroke of a letter, will pass from the law until all is accomplished" (Matt 5:18), whereas in Mark's Gospel it is said that Jesus "declared all foods clean" (Mark 7:19). Eventually, the majority of Christians came to agree that Gentiles did not need to be circumcised or submit to the commandments of the Mosaic law in order to belong to the church, although there were clearly dissenting voices among many believers, as Paul's letters amply demonstrate.

In reality, the problem regarding which of the commandments of the Mosaic law remain binding has never been entirely resolved by Christians. Virtually all Christians continue to maintain that the Decalogue must still be observed, though many have claimed that the prohibition against making images (Deut 5:8-10) is no longer applicable. Most have also interpreted the commandment regarding observance of the sabbath in ways that are foreign to Judaism, either understanding it in a spiritual sense or considering Sunday rather than Saturday the day of rest. The other commandments have also been subjected to a wide variety of interpretations by Christians, including especially those that prohibit taking the Lord's name in vain, killing, and stealing.

Yet the fact that the Decalogue forms only part of the Mosaic law means that some justification must be given for continuing to regard the Ten Commandments as universally valid while setting aside most of the other commandments of that law. This has been done primarily in two ways. One way has been to make a distinction between the civil, ceremonial, and moral law of the Old Testament and then to claim that the civil and ceremonial laws are abolished but the moral law remains binding.[22] This view is problematic, not only because such a distinction is nowhere to be found in either the Old Testament or the New (not to mention ancient Judaism and Christianity in general), but also because it is not always clear which commandments fall under the category of moral law. For example, is the commandment to present one-tenth of the produce of one's fields as an offering before God so that it might be given to the Levites and to the needy (Deut 14:28-30) to be considered part of the ceremonial, civil, or moral law? Furthermore, certain of the commandments that legislate moral behavior also legislate punishments such as putting people to death, often by stoning (Lev 20:27; 24:16-21; Deut 21:18-21; 22:20-24). Clearly, it is problematic to claim that only the part of the commandment dealing with moral behavior remains valid but not the punishment prescribed.

While this threefold distinction appears in both Lutheran and Reformed writings, Luther himself preferred to follow a different approach by regarding the Decalogue as the clearest expression of a *natural law* given to humanity as a whole.[23] This is the law of which Paul speaks in Rom 1:18-32 and 2:14-16, where he claims that God has made plain to all people what is right, writing on their hearts what the law requires so that their conscience bears witness to it. Undoubtedly, this natural law can be said to be reflected as well in the commandments generally associated with the moral law of the Old Testament, yet the two must nevertheless be distinguished from one another: the moral questions legislated by the Mosaic law are an expression of an underlying natural law.

This approach is equally problematic, however. Neither Judaism nor early Christianity understood the Decalogue as a whole constituting a natural law binding on all people; while Paul speaks of a law written on human hearts, he never defines exactly the content of this law or identifies it explicitly with the Decalogue. It might be argued that the two great commandments to love God and love one's neighbor constitute the content of this natural law. Yet this is so vague that virtually anything can be justified in the name of love for God and others, including practicing violence or hurting people. The same problem arises even if the natural law is identified with the commandments of the Decalogue:

these too must be interpreted and fleshed out in some way and can certainly not be said to address all moral questions and dilemmas.

A further problem with positing a natural law arises when it is claimed that human understanding and judgment have been clouded by the fall of humanity into sin. In this case, any attempt to define the content of the natural law must be seen as imperfect, since human sinfulness does not permit human beings to grasp God's will fully and properly.

In spite of the problems it entails, however, Protestant theologians have generally continued to follow Paul, Luther, and the other Reformers in speaking of a natural law written on human hearts and embedded in the conscience of all human beings. They have also continued to regard the Decalogue as the clearest expression of this natural law, which is said to be binding on all people, both Christians and non-Christians.[24] This means that human beings innately possess a sense of right and wrong together with the knowledge that they are to love other human beings and perhaps God as well; this natural law can therefore also be spoken of as a universally valid moral law. The claim that people must love and respect one another, in fact, is found not only in the Hebrew and Christian Scriptures but in the belief system of almost all human beings, including adherents of other religions as well as those who do not identify with any religion. In modern times, the idea of a natural law provides the basis for most of the legal systems found throughout much of the world (particularly in the West), which are no longer regarded as resting on a theological foundation but instead on something such as natural human rights. Just as this natural law is used as a basis for making decisions concerning what is right and wrong in this world, so also in Christian thought is it regarded as the basis upon which all people will be judged by God, as Paul affirms.

Salvation and the Purpose of the Law

How does the law relate to human salvation? The answer to this question depends not only on how *law* is defined but the manner in which the concept of salvation is understood. As was noted in chapter 1, salvation can be understood as having to do with both the present world and a world to come.

In the Hebrew Scriptures, the Mosaic law establishes a clear and straightforward relationship between observance of the law and the salvation of God's people. This salvation, however, is understood in terms of blessings to be given in the *present* world: in passages such as Lev 26:3-13 and Deut 28:3-14, God promises to give the people abundance of food, health, security, protection, and well-being in their land if they obey the commandments. The Hebrew word *shalom* reflects and summarizes well these different aspects of salvation.

While this word is generally translated as "peace," it involves a great deal more than that: "The verbal root from which it derives conveys the conception of being whole or being complete or sound; consequently the transitive form of the verb [*shalam*] means to make whole, to restore, to complete." Therefore, *shalom* has to do not only with a lack of conflict and oppression but with "fulness of life, harmony, satisfaction, completion, integrity," and well-being in every aspect of life, both on an individual and community level.[25] At the same time, both Leviticus 26 and Deuteronomy 28 affirm that if the people disobey God's commandments, they will face untold hardships, destruction, and death. All of this is spoken of in terms of an *extrinsic* relation between what the people do and God's reaction to it; the blessings or hardships that they will face will not simply be the intrinsic and natural consequences of their actions but rather a divine reward or divine punishment, depending on whether their behavior conforms to the law. Salvation is thus *conditional* on obedience to the law.

Yet *why* does God demand obedience to the law, rewarding obedience and punishing disobedience? While this question is not addressed explicitly in the Hebrew Scriptures, it is possible to discern an *intrinsic* relation between obedience to many of the commandments and the people's well-being. The observance of commandments having to do with sanitary and alimentary questions, for example, can be seen as contributing to the people's physical health, while the commandments that regulate social and economic relations, such as the Jubilee laws, are intended to promote justice and equity for everyone, especially the poor and those who suffer most.[26] When the people disobey the law, they do harm not to God but to themselves and other people for whom God also cares. Obedience to God's commandments, therefore, can in many cases be seen to bring well-being and wholeness as a *natural consequence*.

In Old Testament thought, then, God gives the law out of a desire for the well-being of God's people, especially the oppressed and needy (Deut 10:18; Ps 9:8-9; 113:5-9; 146:5-9; Isa 3:14-15; Zech 7:9-10). God wants the people to observe the law, not for *God's* sake, but for the sake of the people as a whole. Because social justice depends on obedience to God and God's law, God prohibits the people from serving other gods or replacing God's law with their own laws, since submission to these other gods and laws leads to injustice and oppression (Isa 10:1-2; Jer 9:13-14; 44:7-10; Ez 5:5-7; 22:23-29; Amos 2:4-8). Israel's God YHWH is thus a "jealous God" not out of any concern for himself but solely out of a concern for his people (Ex 20:5; 34:14; Deut 4:24; 5:9; 6:15). This concern also extends to the other nations: God wants Israel to be obedient so that they may be a "light to the nations" (Isa 42:6, cf. 49:6; 60:3; Mic 4:1-2), drawing them to worship and serve Israel's God together with Israel so that they too may be blessed by living in the way God desires. When God's people disobey the law and practice evil and injustice, they give a negative witness and profane God's name among the other nations, thus preventing them from being attracted to Israel's God (Ez 36:16-23).

While there is both an *intrinsic* relationship between obedience to the commandments and the people's well-being and an *extrinsic* one, then, it is the former that provides the basis for the latter. In other words, God gives the commandments and demands that the people keep them, rewarding obedience and punishing disobedience, *for their own sake* rather than for God's sake, because of the positive consequences that obedience brings in and of itself and the negative consequences disobedience brings. Although this idea does not appear explicitly very often in the Hebrew Scriptures, several passages do suggest it. The prophet Jeremiah, for example, tells the people that when they sin and abandon Israel's God for other gods they do themselves harm, digging out for themselves "cracked cisterns that can hold no water" and choosing "something that does not profit"; their wickedness thus brings its own punishment (Jer 2:11, 13, 17-19). Similarly, the book of Proverbs teaches that the wicked and treacherous "fall by their own wickedness" and are "taken captive by their own schemes," so that their wickedness itself "destroys them," as well as that "the cruel do themselves harm" (Prov 11:3, 5-6, 17). And in Deut 10:13, Moses tells the people that they should keep the commandments "for your own well-being."

The idea of an intrinsic relation between obedience to the law and salvation, however, becomes problematic when salvation is defined in other-worldly terms, as was the case in much of Judaism by the time of Jesus. Once salvation is understood as a future reality based on a divine judgment, one's actions cannot be said to result in salvation in and of themselves; there can be only an *extrinsic* relation between one's behavior and one's salvation. Undoubtedly, God can still be said to demand that human beings obey the law for their own good due to the intrinsic relation between one's actions and their consequences in *this* life. Yet salvation is no longer the *natural consequence* of one's actions but solely an act of God, who rewards obedience and punishes disobedience in the life to come.

When salvation is understood in this way, however, then the salvation that ultimately matters is not the limited, temporary salvation that can be experienced in the present life but the full, perfect salvation that will last indefinitely in a future, other-worldly realm. The doctrines of an afterlife and a future judgment originally provided a basis for insisting on the need to practice love, justice, and righteousness in the *present* age: because a life of righteousness does not always lead to blessings and well-being in *this* world and the practice of injustice and unrighteousness often seems to result in prosperity rather than suffering, it came to be maintained that accounts would be settled at a future judgment in which some would be rewarded for what they had done in this life while others would be punished. According to this idea, *the world to come existed for the sake of the present world*: by maintaining that what one did in the present would have eternal, irreversible consequences, it was possible to demand that people do good and avoid sin and evil here and now. Ironically, however, this eventually had the opposite effect of shifting the focus from life in the present to life in the future: rather than the future world existing for the sake of the present, *the present world inevitably came to be seen as existing for the sake of the future one*, since the future life was definitive and permanent rather than transitory like the present life.

Once this shift has taken place, then the question of the law's purpose arises once more. If the law promises salvation to those who observe it and condemnation to those who do not and this salvation and condemnation are now primarily something to be experienced in a future realm, then observance of the law comes to have as its primary objective attaining eternal life in that future realm, rather than merely obtaining blessings in this life or bringing about justice and well-being in the here and now. Furthermore, when the intrinsic relation between observance of the law and salvation is lost, then it can no longer be maintained that God insists that God's people keep the law *for their own good*, since the "good" that they obtain through obedience is not the natural consequence of their own obedience but an other-worldly reward granted by God. One's motivation for keeping the law then ceases to be that of bringing about a situation of salvation and wholeness for oneself and others in the present world and instead becomes that of obtaining a favorable divine verdict at the final judgment so as to attain the eternal reward in the life to come, which is ultimately what really matters.

Both the New Testament and the literature of early Judaism give ample evidence that the belief in an afterlife and a final judgment led to this change in the understanding of the purpose of observing the law and doing God's will. The faithful are consistently exhorted to do what God commands on the basis of a reward to be received in a future life, rather than on the basis of the natural consequences to which obedience to God's commandments leads in the present, both for oneself and for others.[27] Undoubtedly, this latter idea is not entirely lost; the faithful are encouraged to do good, help those in need, and practice justice, mercy, and righteousness in a disinterested manner, rather than merely seeking to gain merits on their own behalf in order to ensure their own personal salvation in the world to come. However, these two types of motivation remain in constant tension and, ultimately, the motivation of attaining salvation in a future life tends to predominate, especially when it is stressed that what really matters is not what one experiences in the present world but one's eternal fate following the final judgment.

Once the present world is seen as existing for the sake of the future, eternal world and the purpose and meaning of life in the present revolve around obtaining salvation in the world to come, this world basically becomes a "testing-ground" aimed at determining who is fit to participate in the salvation of the future world. The purpose and meaning of the law must then also be understood in the same way: God gave the law as a basis for determining which human beings would be righteous and obedient and which would not. In this case, the ultimate purpose of the law is no longer that of contributing to human well-being and wholeness on this earth through the natural consequences that obedience to the law brings but that of separating the righteous from the unrighteous so that the former may be saved and the latter condemned. Thus the law must be said to exist for some reason other than the well-being of human beings themselves.

Justice and Righteousness

Intimately related to the question of the relation between the law and salvation is that of the relation between obedience to the law and justice or righteousness. In English, the words *justice* and *righteousness* are generally taken to mean two different things, though obviously they are closely related to each other. In biblical Hebrew and Greek, however, the same word can be translated alternatively as "justice" or "righteousness" (*tsedeq/tsedaqah; dikaiosunê*). The same is true in Latin (*iustitia*) and the Romance languages derived from it, German (*Gerechtigkeit*), and most of the Slavic languages (which use various forms of the basic root *prav*).

While the word *justice* admits of a wide variety of meanings, it is generally associated with ideas such as fairness, equity, and what is right, especially in human relationships. In Western thought, justice has generally been defined in terms of giving to each person what is due to him or her, that is, "*distributive* justice." Justice thus involves a balance that must be maintained. When this balance is upset, the situation must be righted. For this to happen, what has been taken away unjustly must be restored and those who acted unjustly must be punished. This involves *retributive* justice, which is aimed not only at restoring the situation to a condition of proper balance but serving both the corrective purpose of moving wrongdoers to mend their ways and the dissuasive purpose of influencing others to refrain from such behavior by letting them observe how it is punished. However, when it is claimed that those who do wrong are punished eternally in a place such as hell, the corrective purpose can only pertain to this life, since in hell there is no more opportunity for one to mend one's ways. Thus eternal punishment can have only a dissuasive purpose. According to these ideas, to say that God does justice is to say that God punishes sin and rewards righteousness. In both Jewish and Christian thought, it is maintained that this takes place to some extent in the present world but will take place definitively only at the end of this age after all people are judged.

In biblical Hebrew, however, the idea of justice is somewhat different. Both *tsedeq/tsedaqah* and *mishpat* often have to do with the absence of oppression: God "does justice" when God saves those in need from those who oppress them. Although in a sense justice can be defined as giving all people what is due to them (distributive justice), in biblical thought this goes beyond repaying people for their deeds or behavior; rather, because all things ultimately belong to God and God desires the well-being of all of God's people equally, justice can only exist when there is equity and all have what they need in life. This well-being is what is "due" to each person. The starting point is not the status quo (which may actually be a situation of inequity) but the ideal of *shalom* for all. In this case, justice can be seen as *synonymous* with mercy and compassion rather than their opposite: to do justice is to show mercy and compassion toward those who have been wronged or are in need so that they may experience wholeness.[28]

In contrast, *righteousness* has to do with behavior that conforms to a moral norm and is most commonly understood in terms of the individual. Usually righteousness is a quality or characteristic that a person is judged to *possess*, whereas justice is something that one *does* by righting a wrong in some way. The difference between the two concepts becomes evident when we consider the extrinsic/instrinsic distinction discussed previously. Righteousness involves an *extrinsic* relation between actions and their results: one is *judged* or *accounted* to be righteous by a judge when one does what the judge deems to be right. In contrast, justice implies an *intrinsic* relation between actions and their consequences: in and of itself, proper behavior or the execution of fair judgments leads to a situation in which there is equity. When understood in this way, justice can be *equated* with salvation: salvation exists when there is well-being for all people without exception. Righteousness, however, can only be regarded as a *pre-condition* for salvation, since it must be rewarded before there can be salvation. In the former case, because of the intrinsic relation between obedience to the law and justice, human activity in and of itself can bring salvation. In the latter, human activity in accordance with God's will moves *God* to save human beings; the relation between obedience and salvation is an *extrinsic* one.

The difference between these two ideas can be seen by considering Jesus' affirmation that those who hunger and thirst after *dikaiosunē* are blessed (Matt 5:6). This can be interpreted in two different ways, depending on how *dikaiosunē* is understood. If it is translated as "righteousness," Jesus is pronouncing a blessing on those who seek to behave in a way that will lead to their being judged as righteous in God's eyes; but if *dikaiosunē* is translated "justice," the blessing is for those who defend what is right and struggle against injustice. Undoubtedly, the two ideas are related in that, when one seeks justice, one is accepted as righteous before God. However, in one instance one is seeking divine approval through one's behavior, while in the other one is not seeking any response from God but merely to establish equity and well-being for all, especially those in need.

A similar observation can be made concerning the words attributed to Moses in Deut 6:25: "And there will be righteousness/justice for us (*utsedaqah tihyeh lanu*), if we are careful to do all this commandment before the LORD our God, as he has commanded us." If *tsedaqah* is translated "righteousness," the idea is that God will judge them to be righteous if they keep the commandments; they will have a right standing before God (thus, for example, the NRSV: "we will be in the right"). Here there is an *extrinsic* relation between their obedience and its result, namely, their being accounted righteous before God. However, if *tsedaqah* is instead translated "justice," the meaning changes: justice—that is, *shalom* for all—will exist among the people if they keep the commandments. In this case, there is an *intrinsic* relation between their observance of the commandments and the social justice that will follow as a natural consequence, although there may also be an extrinsic relation in the sense that God will respond to their obedience by acting to ensure that there is well-being for all in the land.

The distinction between righteousness and justice is also important for considering the concept of judgment in Scripture. The idea that God judges people as righteous or unrighteous, depending on their behavior, runs throughout both Testaments; on the basis of this judgment, they receive either a reward or punishment. Alternatively, however, to "judge" people can mean to deliver them from oppression and evil, thereby saving them and establishing social justice. This is the meaning in the Hebrew Scriptures when it is said that God or Israel's kings are to judge the poor, the oppressed, and the widows (Ps 10:18; 72:1-4; 135:14; 146:7; Isa 11:4; Jer 5:28; 22:16) and in a New Testament passage such as Matt 19:28, where Jesus promises his disciples that they will "sit on twelve thrones, judging the twelve tribes of Israel." Though in both cases justice can be said to be the objective and result of the act of judging, this justice is nevertheless understood in two different ways: as rewarding and punishing people according to their deeds (retributive justice) or as saving the oppressed from their oppressors so as to establish social justice, equity, and *shalom* for all (distributive justice). In the latter case, God's act of judgment is an *act of grace and mercy* toward the oppressed and flows from God's love, which desires human well-being. In contrast, when God's purpose is to determine whether those being judged are sufficiently righteous to be saved, then God's act of judgment is *not* an act of grace and mercy but of strict justice, which is understood as the *opposite* of grace and mercy.

On the basis of this distinction between justice and righteousness, then, the attempt to obey God's law can be seen as having *two possible objectives*. One objective would be that of *establishing justice*, that is, human well-being and wholeness *in the present world*; this would be the instrinsic, natural consequence of obedience to the law. Yet an alternative objective would be *to attain righteousness*, that is, to be accounted righteous by God and thereby be saved by God, especially *in the world to come*. In this case, salvation does not not follow intrinsically from obedience but only extrinsically.

Salvation and Obedience to the Law

This brings us back to the question of the relation between the law and salvation. Can the law save? In one sense, of course, the obvious answer is no: whether by *law* one means the Mosaic law or a universal moral law given by God, the law itself cannot act to save people; only a personal divine being can do this. However, if salvation is understood in terms of a situation of justice and well-being for people in the present world, clearly God's law may be regarded as an *instrument of salvation* and in that sense can be said to "save" those who obey it. In this case, God's purpose in giving the law was to guide human beings and teach them how to behave so that there might be well-being for all in this life. Understood in this way, the law is also an expression of God's *grace* since it is something given to human beings, not to condemn them or burden them, but to *benefit* them. God graciously indicates to them the way in which they should walk for their own good. Of course, because human beings are imperfect and can therefore never obey the law perfectly, salvation in this world will always be incomplete. Justice and salvation will also exist in varying *degrees*: there will never be full and perfect justice in this world but it is possible to come closer to that ideal, just as it is possible for injustice to increase or decrease.

If salvation is understood in terms of an other-worldly life bestowed by God on those who are accounted righteous, however, the question of whether God's law can save becomes more complex. In this case, as noted previously, if the idea of a future, eternal salvation is maintained, this must be seen as constituting God's ultimate concern for human beings, whose ultimate objective in turn must be that of attaining that future salvation rather than merely experiencing some partial salvation in the present. Here, at least in New Testament thought, there are no degrees of salvation but only two possibilities:

eternal salvation or eternal condemnation. Furthermore, when this other-worldly salvation is understood in terms of a life that is very different from the present one, in that human beings will be transformed into some condition in which they will no longer sin or die but will exist eternally "like angels" (Mark 12:25), there would seem to be no further purpose for God's law in that new life. Therefore, the law must be seen as something that pertains only to the present world.

If God's ultimate purpose in giving the law in this world was that it serve as a means for human beings to attain salvation in the world to come, rather than as an instrument for human well-being and justice in the present world, then there would seem to be no real need for the law, since God can save whichever human beings God desires to save simply by receiving them into the world to come, no matter how faithful or unfaithful they have been in observing the law. Similarly, God cannot have given the law primarily out of a concern for human well-being, since the ultimate well-being of those to be saved will be brought about, not as a natural consequence of their obedience to God's law, but unilaterally by a divine act of omnipotence when God introduces them into the the world to come. Therefore, if God did not give the law for the sake of human beings and can in fact save them without the law if God desires to do so, God must have had some other purpose for giving the law and commanding that human beings observe it: *God must have given the law for God's own sake.*

This, in fact, is what has generally been affirmed in Protestant teaching regarding the law. God gives the law to respond to an *inner need*, namely, the need for God to uphold and safeguard God's own perfect righteousness. God's righteousness will not allow God to have communion or fellowship with those who are *not* perfectly righteous, as God is, since by nature what is holy and perfect cannot co-exist harmoniously with what is *not* holy and perfect. The problem is posed in the following terms: "How does God maintain his righteousness?";[29] for God to allow unrighteousness into God's presence would involve compromising God's righteousness. This is thought not only to be improper but in some sense impossible as well: God must be "*utterly consistent with himself* and therefore *righteous.* . . ."[30] This, then, is the law's purpose: "The law declares that the unclean cannot stand before God, only the clean."[31]

This type of argument regarding God and the law is based on a certain understanding of God's *nature. By nature*, God is righteous and therefore, *by nature*, only the righteous can be accepted by God. The role of the law, therefore, is to serve as a norm that defines the righteousness necessary for human beings to be received into eternal fellowship with God in heaven. The affirmation that God's commandments are "righteous" or "just" (Deut 4:8; Ps 119:164-65) is then understood in the sense that they are a reflection and expression of God's holy and righteous nature and no longer in the sense that they intrinsically lead to justice and *shalom* among God's people when they are obeyed. In that case, it is no longer clear why human beings should "rejoice" over those commandments, whereas in contrast there is good reason for rejoicing if the commandments in and of themselves lead to justice and human well-being.

This also means that it was not God's *love* or *grace* that moved God to give the law but God's holy and righteous nature. According to this view, God's wrath is no longer a response to the injustice and oppression inflicted by some upon others, as it is in the Hebrew Scriptures. Instead of becoming angry for the sake of *human beings* who are suffering at the hands of those who do evil, God becomes angry at sin and injustice *for God's own sake*, due to an inner need for God to be in harmony with God's own nature; God's righteousness will not let God tolerate unrighteousness. And because the law is an expression of God's perfect nature, imperfect and sinful human beings must be saved *from* God and God's law, so that God, God's righteousness, and God's law represent the *problem* rather than the *solution*. In this case, the law is something to be feared and hated by human beings rather than loved because it stands opposed to God's grace rather than being an expression of that grace.

This understanding of God's righteousness seems to place God under some type of law, in particular, the law of God's own nature. It is the law that defines God rather than being defined by God, just as it is God's righteous nature that defines God, rather than God who defines righteousness. To take God's righteous nature as a starting point for defining human righteousness also raises the problem of the degree of righteousness that human beings must attain in order to be saved by God. If God is perfect by nature, so that God's righteousness is also perfect, then must not human beings also be perfectly righteous in order to be received into God's presence? This idea has also been affirmed repeatedly in Protestant thought. Martin Chemnitz, for example, claimed that the law "requires that the entire man, according to all his parts and according to all actions of each single part correspond to the norm of the righteousness in God that is revealed in the Law and, indeed, that it correspond exactly with that purity, perfection, and completeness which the Law prescribes and demands. And if anyone keeps the whole law but fails in one point, he is pronounced guilty of all."[32]

Once it is maintained that the law was given for the sake of God's righteousness, that is, for the reason that by nature God cannot accept sin and evil and therefore must demand perfect righteousness on the part of human beings by means of the law, then the original purpose of the law as an instrument for promoting justice and human well-being in the present world recedes into the background and even tends to be lost altogether. Similarly, God's purpose in judging human beings is no longer that of delivering those who suffer injustice from those who oppress them but determining who can be accepted into God's holy presence; and once it is maintained that perfection is required, the logical conclusion is that God can rightly judge no one to be truly righteous on the basis of their own actions. Thus all stand condemned.

As noted previously, however, the idea that human beings must be absolutely perfect in order to be declared righteous by God is characteristic of neither ancient Jewish nor biblical thought in general. In both the Old and New Testaments, the idea that human beings can be righteous, blameless, or even "perfect" before God is quite common (see Gen 6:9; Job 1:1; Ps 37:37; 101:6; Isa 38:3; Phil 3:6; 1 Thess 2:10; 1 Tim 3:10; Tit 1:5-7). Of course, this does not mean that they have never committed any sins in their life; such perfection is not expected of any person. Rather, when they sin, they repent of it and strive to do God's will once more. Thus, for example, when Jesus tells his followers that they are to be perfect as God their Father is perfect (Matt 5:48), he clearly appears to regard this as a possibility for them; they are to treat others as God has treated them. The argument that no human being can attain the divine standard of righteous through obedience to the law because only God is perfectly righteous is therefore based not on Scripture but on a particular theological or philosophical understanding of God's *nature*. God's nature is defined in terms of a certain idea of perfection in order then to claim that no one can attain that perfection. In reality, this argument is designed to support the claim that human salvation was impossible without Christ and his death, as we shall see in the next chapter.

If it is said that perfection is *not* required of human beings, however, it then becomes problematic to define precisely who is righteous and who is not on the basis of the law. Just as all people sin, so also at some point all people seem to do good things. How much good must one do and to what extent must one avoid sin in order to be accounted righteous? Christians of the Reformation tradition have often attributed to ancient Judaism the idea that one's good deeds must outnumber one's sins in order to be saved; yet, as Sanders argued, the evidence in support of such an idea in ancient Judaim is scanty at best.[33] Whether or not such a view was maintained by Jews (or anyone else), it is clearly problematic in that it requires that righteousness be quantified in some way so that it can be measured or weighed; the same is true of sins. It is extremely difficult to attempt to define precisely what an acceptable level of righteousness is in God's eyes and then attempt to determine when a person actually achieves that level. One must define not only what actions can be considered righteous or sinful but also attempt to quantify exactly *how* righteous or sinful each of those actions is; certain sins, for example, such as murder are generally regarded as being more serious than other "lesser" sins, such as telling a small lie. Most people would also agree that, even when one has committed grave sins, if one sincerely repents and mends one's ways one may be accepted as righteous, even though one's past sins will continue to outweigh the acts of righteousness one does at present.

At the same time, in both biblical and ancient Jewish thought, righteousness cannot be defined on the basis of actions alone. One's intentions and one's "heart" must also be taken into account. On this point both Judaism and Lutheran teaching concur, although Lutheran thought once again differs from Jewish thought in claiming that perfection is required in this regard.[34] Once a person's heart or intent is taken into account, however, it is no longer possible to claim that the law alone can determine who is righteous, since it is impossible for the law to measure intent; only God can do this. The law cannot function independently of God, judging human beings so as to save some and condemn others. Yet this means that righteousness once more involves a value judgment on God's part: ultimately, God determines who is righteous by looking into human hearts. In other words, God is the law as well as the judge. This seems to make the law unnecessary, except as a guide to indicate to human beings what type of righteousness is necessary in order for God to save them; and since they cannot attain that perfect righteousness, all that is left for the law to do is to show them their sin and thus their condition of being under God's judgment.

As noted previously, the solution of Judaism to the problem of determining who is righteous was often to affirm that what God requires is simply a commitment to obeying God's law. This was referred to in rabbinic thought as "confessing the commandments."[35] Naturally, this commitment will be manifested in concrete acts of obedience, even though one will also inevitably sin. However, as long as God sees that a person is sincerely committed to living in accordance with God's commandments, God accepts that person as righteous.

Sin and the Law

When it is claimed that through God's law God demands absolute perfection of human beings in order to justify them, their inability to attain such a standard can be attributed to two different causes. The first is simply that they are human and, by nature, human beings are incapable of perfection; only God is perfect. In this case, perfection was never a possibility for human beings, even in the condition in which they were originally created. The second possible cause of their inability to achieve God's standard of righteousness is that they have become subject to some pernicious power that prevents or hinders them from living in obedience to God. This power may be identified with one or more personal beings, such as the devil or evil spirits, or with some sinful tendency located in human nature or flesh.

In Protestant thought, human disobedience has traditionally been attributed to this latter cause. The problem is not only that God's standard is too high but that, as a result of the fall of Adam, human beings have become subject to evil desires that incite them to sin. To some extent, of course, in their fallen condition they can keep many of the commandments outwardly, doing what the law commands. In this way, they can attain a degree of "civil righteousness," yet this righteousness is still far from what God demands and thus cannot avail before God.

Because Protestant thought traditionally has defined salvation more in terms of a communion with God in eternity rather than a situation of human well-being in *this* world, it has also defined sin somewhat differently than in Jewish thought and even much Roman Catholic thought. If the objective is to achieve human well-being for all in *this* world, what matters most is what human beings *do*, since their actions have immediate *consequences* in the world. In this case, sin will be defined in terms of not doing the concrete actions that God commands and instead oppressing others and doing them harm. Undoubtedly, in order to perform the actions commanded by God, it is important that they be righteous on the inside and that in their heart they love both God and others, since if they lack the desire and motivation to do good, they will not do so. However, a righteous heart and good intentions are not sufficient to bring about a situation of justice and well-being in the world; in fact, at times one can have good intentions and still do harm to others. What ultimately matters is *practicing* righteousness or justice in one's relations to others through concrete *deeds*.

In contrast, when salvation is understood in terms of communion with God in a life to come, what ultimately matters is attaining the level of *inward* righteousness and purity that is necessary to be acceptable before God. Because salvation does not depend on what one does, since salvation is something accomplished solely by God by introducing people into a new world that is not in any way the natural consequence of human actions done in this world, those actions cannot contribute to salvation in and of themselves. The only way that they can contribute to salvation is by gaining favor with God and thereby moving God to grant the desired salvation. In that case, the law must be understood as having originally been given by God as a way for human beings to merit their salvation by doing what it prescribes; it therefore had no salvific purpose in *this* world, nor was there any reason *why* God wanted human beings to obey the law, except that their temporary situation in this world might be somewhat better as a result of their practicing greater justice and avoiding evil and oppression. However, if what ultimately mattered to God was their "purity of heart," then the only saving value their actions could have originally had would have been that of serving as an outward expression of the righteousness that was theirs on the inside.

According to this second view, sin must be understood, not so much in terms of *actions*—what people *do*—but of what is *in their heart*, that is, the type of persons they are on the inside. In this case, God's concern from the outset was not so much that they perform the *actions* God prescribed but that they do them out of the proper *motivation* with a pure heart so that they might be in harmony and communion with God's own nature. The real sin of human beings, therefore, consists in their *attitude* before God: rather than sincerely loving God and others, they love only themselves and seek to manipulate God and use God for their own ends. Even when they perform the actions prescribed by God outwardly, their inward motivation is not pure, since they are acting out of self-interest, attempting to gain merits before God so that God will be favorable to them. This is how sin has traditionally been understood in Protestantism.

For Luther, while sin consisted of a failure to love God with a pure heart, this sin was ultimately rooted in a more serious sin: the sin of unbelief, that is, not trusting in God.[36] When one does not trust in God or believe God's promises, one will not do what God desires and commands but will instead disobey God. Here again, the problem is defined in terms of what one *is* more than what one *does*: one sins because one is a sinner rather than being a sinner because one sins.

Whether sin is understood primarily in terms of *actions* or the condition of one's *heart*, in either case the human plight will be defined in terms of the inability to conform to God's will both inwardly and outwardly. This inability can be attributed either to a lack of *understanding* on the part of human beings or to a weakness of the human *will*. In the former case, the solution is to provide sinful human beings with the *knowledge* and *guidance* they need in order to change their ways and do what God commands. In the latter case, however, what is needed is a *new heart*, that is, a transformation of one's interior and will.

Although both of these ideas are present in both Jewish and Christian thought, in Judaism the emphasis has tended to be on the former. What human beings need is *knowledge* and *guidance*; this is given them through the Torah, which literally means "guidance" or "instruction." As they study the law, they come to realize that it is God's instrument for allowing human beings to experience greater happiness and well-being; in this way, they are motivated to strive to obey it. The law is thus a *remedy for sin*. According to Bruce Chilton and Jacob Neusner, in rabbinic thought, the Torah was a "regenerative force." It held the power to transform the heart of man and so turn man from rebellion to loving submission. . . . The Torah alone can deal with humanity's brokenness. . . . Through Torah God educates the heart of humanity to love, which cannot be coerced. The Torah purifies the heart of humanity, the commandments are media of regeneration and sanctification. . . . The rabbinic sages leave no doubt that Torah study changes disciples, producing humble persons prepared to love the Lord our God with all our heart, soul, and might.[37]

The idea that the Torah can serve as a remedy for sin is tied to a Jewish anthropology in which human beings are not totally depraved, as in much Protestant thought, but have a capacity to do good which stands alongside an opposing inclination to sin. According to rabbinic teaching, there are two tendencies in human beings, one for good and the other for evil.[38] The law therefore is God's instrument to educate human beings so that they can do good and resist evil. Of course, in this world they will never be able to do that perfectly but, as noted above, in Judaism perfection is not required in order to attain righteousness before God.

In Protestant thought, the problem tends to be seen more in terms of the will and sin is viewed as a power that prevents human beings from obeying God's law. Paul's words in Rom 7:15-25 have been highly influential in this regard: "I can will what is right, but I cannot do it. For I do not do the good I want, but the evil I do not want is what I do" (vv. 18-19). This inability to do God's will satisfactorily is due not to a lack of knowledge on the part of human beings but to an inclination toward sin and evil in their hearts from which they cannot free themselves. In much of Western Christianity, this inclination has been referred to as "concupiscence" and has been attributed to the fall of Adam and Eve into sin in the Garden of Eden, after which the human nature in which all people share came to be subject to sin and death. Of course, those who adhere to the modern scientific worldview would regard the Genesis story of the fall as a myth and thus would tend to reject the idea that human beings were created in some primeval state of perfect innocence or righteousness, only subsequently to fall into sin and mortality. In spite of this, however, it is still possible to see this inclination to sin or concupiscence as some type of imperfection, weakness, or disease in human nature, even if it is not regarded as the result of a fall; and in that sense, it is still possible to speak of a "fallen humanity."

When the plight of human beings is understood in terms of the inability to do God's will because of their fallen condition, it becomes evident that the law cannot be understood as a remedy for sin. While the law may have been able to serve as a guide to human beings before their fall into sin, it can no longer fulfill this function. It can tell them what to do but it cannot give them the power to do it, as Lutheran theology has affirmed.

The Christian doctrine of human fallenness raises a further problem by maintaining that human beings are *guilty* before God for their sin. If human beings in their present fallen state are totally incapable of avoiding sin and this is not the result of anything they have done personally but what their ancestors did, how can they be held responsible for their sin? If they have lost their free will and thus the ability to choose what is good because of what happened at the outset of human history and are powerless to change this situation, it would seem that God cannot justly blame or condemn them for the wrong they do out of no choice of their own. In order to address this problem, both Protestant and Roman Catholic theologians have often maintained that *all* human beings are somehow responsible for the sin of Adam and consequently their fallen condition;[39] yet this idea has always constituted a serious problem for Christian theology. It would seem that human beings can only be held responsible for their sins if they have free will and thus can choose between good and evil.

The idea of an original free will on the part of human beings is also difficult to reconcile with the idea of divine foreknowledge. If God knew from the start that human beings would fall into sin, then apparently this fall was foreordained by God, since what God foreknew had to happen. Thus it appears that God is responsible for creating a humanity that would inevitably fall into sin; apparently human beings were created with an inherent flaw that would lead to the fall. The belief that God foreknew and foreordained the fall seems to compromise God's love: If God is love, why did not God instead create a world free from sin and the suffering and evil that result from it? Theologians have often attempted to answer this difficulty by arguing that if God wanted human beings to love God and one another freely, it was necessary to create them with free will; and, by definition, one's will is not free if one has no choice but to do what God commands. Therefore, human beings had to be capable of disobeying God and falling into sin. Yet this response ends up subjecting God to nature: the nature of reality made it necessary for God to create human beings in a certain way if God's objectives were to be attained. Ultimately, all of this boils down to the problem of theodicy, that is, why a good, loving, and all-powerful God allows sin, evil, and suffering to exist.

The Uses of the Law

One of the most significant differences between the Lutheran and Jewish understandings of the law has to do with the Lutheran understanding of the "uses" of the law. In Jewish thought, the primary purpose of the law is to provide guidance and instruction for God's people; this corresponds to the third use of the law in Lutheran teaching. However, because in Christian thought it is maintained that human beings are justified not by observing the law but by faith in Christ, this use is not considered primary by Lutherans and in fact is even rejected by many Lutheran theologians, as we shall see in chapter 5. Instead, the primary use of the law is the second or theological use: the law drives one to despair by constantly pointing out one's sins and one's fallen and condemned condition. In this way, it leads one to look to Christ for salvation and justification rather than to one's own deeds or efforts.

Needless to say, it is a far cry from the Jewish concept of the Mosaic law to see the law as a "cruel and powerful tyrant over the whole human race" that accuses, intimidates, condemns, and kills all people, as Luther did.[40] Undoubtedly, the idea that the law pronounces a curse on those who do not keep it is present in both Old Testament and Jewish thought; yet because Judaism does not teach that human beings have become "slaves to sin" who are incapable of obedience and because it does not affirm that absolute perfection is required, it considers human obedience to the law as a possibility. Thus the law is not constantly accusing God's people. In fact, the law can also reward them for their obedience or lead God to bless them. While undoubtedly the law also points out the sin of those who disobey it and thus can be said to "accuse" them, the purpose of this is not to drive them to despair of themselves but to lead them to mend their ways and return to obedience.

In Lutheran and Protestant thought, to admit that one can obey the law to some extent and thereby attain some type of blessing or divine favor would lead persons to seek to earn their own salvation before God and would also lay the burden for that salvation on the shoulders of human beings themselves. The rejection of these ideas leads to the conclusion that the law can only accuse, since if the law could also save, reward, or bless, human beings would be led to seek salvation in it. In that case, they would have a ground for boasting before God and others, an idea explicitly rejected by Paul (Rom 2:23; 3:27). The doctrine that human beings in their fallen state are unable to produce any righteousness of their own that might avail before God similarly serves to lead human beings to look to God alone rather than to themselves or to the law for salvation. At the same time, because salvation is understood as something to be accomplished in the world to come and the intrinsic relationship between one's actions in the present life and one's salvation is therefore lost, the law cannot be thought to have the primary purpose of leading one to mend one's ways for one's own good or of serving as a means for human beings to attain blessings in the present world.

This same emphasis on the world to come as the realm in which salvation is to take place makes the first use of the law less important than the second and subservient to it. In Lutheran thought, what ultimately matters in this world is that people be driven to faith in Christ through the law so as to be saved in the world to come. Thus the law according to its first use only helps to hold human sin and evil in check to some extent in order that Christians may be free to proclaim the gospel and practice their faith in peace so as to attain salvation in the world to come.

Yet because in Lutheran thought the natural law is distinguished from the Mosaic law, in reality the Lutheran uses of the law must be seen as having to do with the *natural law*, not the Mosaic law. Because the vast majority of people throughout the world make no effort to live according to the Mosaic law, it must be the *natural law* written on their consciences that helps to hold sin in check in the world. Similarly, it must be the *natural law* that is constantly accusing human beings as a "tyrant," revealing their sin to them and driving them to despair. In fact, some Lutheran theologians have defined "law" in terms much broader than even the natural law. In particular, Gerhard Forde, following the Finnish Lutheran theologian Laurel Haikola, has argued that the law is to be defined in terms of the "immediate impact" it has on sinful human beings:

> This means that law, for Luther, cannot be *identified* with any set of propositions or prescriptions, be it the decalogue or any other code. Law is *anything* which frightens and accuses "the conscience." The bolt of lightning, the rustling of a dry leaf on a dark night, the decalogue, the "natural law" of the philosopher, or even (or perhaps most particularly) the preaching of the cross itself—all or any of these can and do become the voice of the law.[41]

In reality, this view affirms not simply that the law always accuses but that whatever accuses is always the law. Thus it is the "accusing" that defines the nature of the law rather than the nature of the law defining what is accused.

Whether the law in Lutheran thought is identified with the natural law or defined as anything that frightens and accuses the human conscience, it is clear that what Lutheranism is talking about when it refers to the law is something different than what is meant by the law in Judaism, where it refers to the Torah. This makes it difficult to compare the Lutheran understanding of the law with the Jewish understanding, since in reality the two traditions mean two different things when they speak of "the law."

Law in the New Testament

As the New Perspective on Paul has demonstrated, much of the discussion regarding the law in the New Testament must be seen in the context of the problems raised by the acceptance of Gentiles into the community of believers in Jesus. Did Gentile believers need to submit to the law of Moses, including the commandment to be circumcised? In Jewish thought, all of the promises of salvation were tied to the Mosaic law or Torah; thus to claim that people could participate fully in the coming age of salvation without submitting literally to all the commandments found in the Torah raised serious problems. If people were now saved simply by believing in and following Christ, what became of the Mosaic law? Was it now abolished? How could this be possible if the Torah was God's greatest gift to the world and if God had even created the world for the sake of the Torah, as the rabbis later came to affirm?[42] The beliefs of the first Christians represented a major challenge to the Jewish understanding of the Mosaic law and the covenant around which Jewish faith and life revolved.

In Paul's letters and other New Testament writings, we find a number of responses to questions such as these. One response was to claim that, while God had indeed given the Mosaic law and had made promises of salvation that depended on obedience to it, the people of Israel had not kept the law; for this reason those promises had not been fulfilled. In reality, this claim was nothing new; it is found throughout the Hebrew Scriptures and many Jewish groups in Jesus' day were making the same claim. What was new and unique about the Christian view was the claim that the most serious act of disobedience on the part of Israel consisted of the rejection of Jesus as the Messiah and God's Son. While the Jewish authorities and the inhabitants of Jerusalem are particularly criticized for this rejection (Matt 21:33-44; Acts 2:22-23; 3:13-15; 4:27-28; 5:30; 7:51-52; 10:39; 13:27-28; 1 Thess 2:14-16), eventually all Jewish people who did not become followers of Jesus were subjected to the same criticism by the Christians. The Christian argument was also unique in the sense that, at least as Paul presents it, the problem was not only that Israel *had* not kept the law but *could* not. This was because, like all human beings, the Jewish people were subject to the powers of sin and the flesh.

A second response to the Jewish understanding of the role of the law in salvation was to argue that the Mosaic law had been only a temporary dispensation given to Israel. This idea was related to the previous one in that it was claimed that, since Israel had always been a rebellious and hard-hearted people,

God had given them the law through Moses to keep sin in check until the promised Messiah might appear. Rather than being eternal and the most perfect expression of God's will, the law had been given indirectly by means of angels and was only provisional (Acts 7:53; Gal 3:19—4:5).

A third response was to claim that from the beginning the law or Torah had pointed to Christ, who constituted its fulfillment. The giving of the law had formed part of an ancient divine plan that was evident throughout the Torah, particularly in the narrative sections. Jesus was thought to have been prefigured in passages such as Genesis 22:18, 26:4, and 28:14, where God promised that all of the nations of the earth would be blessed through Abraham's seed (cf. Acts 3:25; Gal 3:16); Numbers 21:1-9, where the people of Israel were delivered by the serpent raised on a pole (cf. John 3:14); and Deuteronomy 18:15-19, which speaks of a figure greater than Moses who would come (Acts 3:22; 7:37). The Letter to the Hebrews sees Christ prefigured in Melchizedek and in the Day of Atonement rites (Heb 7:1-10; 9:1-14; 10:1-10), while Paul sees Christ prefigured in the rock from which water sprang in the desert during Israel's time there and the Passover lamb (1 Cor 5:7; 10:4). The law thus contained figures or antitypes that were fulfilled in Christ.

To say that in Christ the law was in some sense fulfilled or had reached its "end" (Rom 10:4) did not necessarily mean that it was believed to be abolished now that Christ had come. If the rites prescribed by the Torah pointed to Christ and found fulfillment in him, for example, rather than seeing them as something now to be abolished or discontinued, it might be argued that believers should continue to celebrate and practice those rites in a way that would constantly remind them that Christ was their fulfillment and gave them new meaning. The book of Acts, in fact, presents believers continuing to congregate in the Jerusalem temple and to observe Jewish ceremonies, including Paul himself (Acts 2:46; 3:1-3; 5:21, 42; 21:26; 22:17).[43] There is evidence that the Christian community in Jerusalem under James the brother of Jesus was very faithful in continuing to observe the Mosaic law. However, it seems that for the most part Gentile believers were not expected or encouraged to submit to the Mosaic law. Naturally, this created problems and even tensions when one part of the community of believers was committed to observing the Mosaic law and another part was not.

Yet while it was generally maintained that believers, at least those of Gentile origin, were not under the Mosaic law in the sense of having to follow all of its prescriptions literally, in another sense they remained under obligation to practice the righteousness that the law prescribed, thus fulfilling the law's *purpose* or *spirit*. According to the Gospels, Jesus had taught that there were certain principles underlying the law, in particular, the principle of loving God and loving one's neighbor as oneself (Matt 23:36-40; Mark 12:28-34; Luke 10:25-28). This idea was not unique to Jesus: the idea that there is a central principle or "core" to the commandments is found in Judaism itself.[44] In Judaism, however, this idea is not employed as a basis for arguing that literal observance of the commandments can be set aside. In contrast, while Jesus agreed that at times it was necessary to adhere strictly to the letter of the law in order to fulfill it, at other times he apparently claimed that it was necessary to go *beyond* the law's letter and occasionally even go *against* it in order to fulfill the law's *spirit*. This is evident particularly in Jesus' treatment of the sabbath commandment, where he insists that true fulfillment involves meeting people's needs, doing good, and saving life (Mark 2:23—3:6). Similarly, he affirms that what truly makes a person impure is not the food that goes into that person's body but the evil that comes out of that person's heart (Mark 7:14-21). Even if the affirmation that Jesus "declared all foods clean" (Mark 7:19) is not considered historically accurate in an explicit sense, it is not difficult to see how his teaching could have led many to arrive at such a conclusion.

The claim that true obedience to the law involves fulfilling its purpose or spirit is found elsewhere as well in the teaching attributed to Jesus in the Gospels. Commandments such as those that prohibit murder and adultery are to be fulfilled not only literally but in a deeper, spiritual sense (Matt 5:21-27). What the law really demands is not simply literal fulfillment but justice, mercy, faith, and love of God (Matt 23:23; Luke 11:42). On this basis, Jesus criticized the Pharisees and scribes for oppressing others with the law, laying unbearable burdens on their shoulders and practicing injustice in relation to widows and even their own parents (Matt 23:4; Mark 7:9-13; 12:40); while they may have observed the law's letter, they violated its spirit. For this reason, Jesus tells his followers that their righteousness must exceed that of the scribes and Pharisees (Matt 5:20).

Thus, while Jesus remained in continuity with Jewish thought in teaching that it was necessary to practice righteousness, he redefined this righteousness in terms that had to with the *spirit* of the law. Undoubtedly, the same emphasis found in Jesus' teaching on the need to fulfill the spirit of the commandments by practicing justice and mercy is found in the law itself, as well as in the prophetic writings and Jewish teaching in general. However, Jesus seems to have gone further than others in his willingness to lay aside the letter of the law as traditionally interpreted in order to focus on its spirit. This led to conflict with many of the Jewish leaders who defined observance of the law in different terms.

In Jesus' teaching on divorce, he also seems to argue that the Mosaic law was a temporary and imperfect dispensation given to the Jewish people because of their sinful nature. When the Pharisees tell Jesus that Moses allowed a man to divorce his wife, Jesus responds, "Because of your hardness of heart he wrote this commandment for you. But from the beginning of creation, 'God made them male and female'. . . . Therefore what God has joined together, let no one separate" (Mark 10:5-6, 9). In Matthew's version, Jesus responds, "It was because you were so hard-hearted that Moses allowed you to divorce your wives, but from the beginning it was not so" (Matt 19:8). Both versions clearly imply that God gave at least part of the Mosaic law on account of Israel's sinfulness and therefore as a provisional dispensation. This means that, at least to some extent, Jesus did not teach that the Mosaic law represented God's eternal and unchangeable will. Furthermore, Jesus' teaching on the subject of divorce is presented as a return to what God intended from the beginning of creation. This means that for Jesus there was an original "law" or "order" in creation that was distinct from and superior to the Mosaic law.

Thus Paul's teaching that the law was given "on account of sin" as a provisional measure in order to restrain Israel's sin until the Messiah might come to restore God's original plan seems to be rooted in the teaching attributed to Jesus in the Gospels.[45] Paul also follows Jesus in teaching that true fulfillment of the law has to do with fulfilling the commandment to love others: "the one who loves another has fulfilled the law . . . love is the fulfilling of the law" (Rom 13:8-10; cf. Gal 6:14). When Paul speaks of fulfilling the "law of Christ" (Gal 6:2; 1 Cor 9:21), he seems to have this spiritual interpretation of the law in mind.[46] On this basis, Paul affirms that those who are "physically uncircumcised" may "keep the just requirements (*dikaiōmata*) of the law" and thus "keep the law" (Rom 2:26-27; my translation). Similarly, in 1 Cor 7:19 he teaches that neither circumcision nor uncircumcision matter but only "keeping the commandments of God in everything," thus claiming that one can keep the law without obeying the commandment found in that same law regarding circumcision. These statements would sound self-contradictory to most Jews, since the law commanded that one be circumcised; thus no one could keep the law without being circumcised. For Paul, however, fulfillment of the commandment regarding circumcision as well as the rest of the commandments had to do with practicing justice and righteousness: "For a person is not a Jew who is one outwardly, nor is true circumcision something external and physical. Rather, a person is a Jew who is one inwardly, and real circumcision is a matter of the heart—it is spiritual and not literal" (Rom 2:28-29). For this reason, Paul can accuse even Jews who were most zealous about a strict literal observance of the law, such as those who opposed him in Galatia, of failing to observe the law: "Even the circumcised do not themselves obey the law, but they want you to be circumcised so that they may boast about your flesh" (Gal 6:13).

In the same context in which Paul affirms that obedience to the law has to do with observing its spirit and that uncircumcised Gentiles can fulfill the law, he also affirms that such observance is necessary and that all people will be judged on the basis of their observance of the law. In fact, for Paul obedience to the law is a requirement for justification: "it is not the hearers of the law who are righteous in God's sight, but the doers of the law who will be justified" (Rom 2:13). Thus, while the Mosaic law is no longer binding on believers, they are still under obligation to keep the "just requirements" of that law by practicing the justice or righteousness that it prescribes (Rom 2:26; 8:4). In a literal sense, believers like Paul are "not under the law," though in another sense they are "not free from God's law" but "under Christ's law," since they must still fulfill the spirit of God's law as taught by Christ (1 Cor 9:20-21). In light of what we have seen above, however, it can be concluded that for Paul the justice and righteousness prescribed by the natural law written on the hearts and in the consciences of all people is the same justice and righteousness that the Mosaic law ultimately mandates. The same might be said of Jesus' teaching regarding the need to love God and neighbor, which can also be associated with the natural law or the principles underlying the Mosaic law. Thus, while believers are not required to observe literally all of the commandments of the Mosaic law, they, together with all people, are expected to practice the love, justice, and righteousness on which the Mosaic law is based and will be judged by God on the basis of whether they have done so.

In principle, the recognition that most of what Paul says about the law has to do with the Mosaic law rather than a natural law written on the heart of all human beings calls into question the Scriptural basis of much of the Lutheran teaching regarding the law. When Paul writes in Galatians that "no one will be justified by the works of the law" (2:16), that those who rely on the works of the law are under a curse (3:10), that the law was "added because of transgressions" (3:19), and that it was "our disciplinarian until Christ came" (3:24), he is speaking throughout of the *Mosaic* law. The same is true regarding his affirmations in Romans that "through the law comes knowledge of sin" (3:20) and that he would not have known sin had it not been for the law (7:7). These passages have formed the basis for the Lutheran teaching regarding the uses of the law to restrain sin (first use) and to convict people of their sin (second use). In reality, however, all of these passages refer only to the Mosaic law and not to a natural law lying behind the Decalogue and written on human hearts. Thus, for example, Paul's idea (and perhaps that of Jesus as well) was that the Mosaic law had been given to restrain or curb *Israel's* sin due to their hardness of heart and not that its purpose was to restrain the sin of Gentiles, who never received the Mosaic law. Likewise, in Paul's thought, it is the *Mosaic* law that reveals sin and points people to Christ rather than a natural law. The promises of salvation as well as the threats of curse were also associated with the law of Moses rather than being tied to the natural law given to humanity as a whole, though of course the fact that Gentiles did not observe the Mosaic law meant that they had no access to the promises and might be understood to be under the curse pronounced by the law on those who did not keep it.

Nevertheless, Paul's teaching regarding the natural law in Romans 2 does seem to provide some basis for associating divine promises with obedience to the law written on human hearts as well as associating divine punishment with disobedience to that law. Because all people, both Jews and Gentiles, will be judged on the basis of their actions and there will be "anguish and distress for everyone who does evil" but "glory and honor and peace for everyone who does good" (Rom 2:9-10), salvation and justification do in fact depend on fulfillment of the natural law in Paul's thought. The law written on people's hearts as well as their conscience also can be said to accuse them of sin: "their conflicting thoughts will accuse or perhaps excuse them" (Rom 2:15). In both of these cases, however, it appears that Paul is teaching that the law does not only accuse and condemn but can constitute a basis upon which people can also be "excused" and justified. Thus, while Paul's words in Romans 2 provide a basis for relating the second use of the law with the natural law, they also present a challenge for Lutheran thought.

The natural law can, of course, also serve to restrain sin and thereby fulfill the task of the law's first use. This happens not only when governments and authorities enact and enforce laws that are in accordance with the natural law but when one's conscience leads one to abstain from doing wrong and instead moves one to do good. For this reason, even though most of the New Testament texts generally cited by Luther and Lutheran theologians in speaking of the first two uses of the law in reality refer to the Mosaic law rather than the natural law and therefore cannot properly be used as a basis upon which to ground Lutheran teaching regarding the law's uses, this teaching can still be considered to be in essential harmony with New Testament thought.

CHAPTER 3

Justification and the Work of Christ

For Luther as well as Paul, at the heart of the gospel lies the affirmation that Jesus "died for our sins in accordance with the Scriptures" (1 Cor 15:3). Everything revolves around the cross: *crux sola est nostra theologia*—"the cross alone is our theology." While in principle most Christians would agree with Luther on this point, many have found his understanding of the way in which Christ's death leads to the justification and salvation of believers problematic on both theological and biblical grounds. In fact, it is not only the teaching of Luther on this point that raises serious difficulties but that of the Christian tradition as a whole.

Christ's Death and Justification in Lutheran Thought

Central to the traditional Lutheran understanding of Christ's death is the idea that on the cross Christ delivered human beings from the punishment to which they were liable on account of their sins by making satisfaction to God's justice. This idea developed out of Anselm's teaching on the cross found in his 1098 work *Cur Deus homo*.[1] By Luther's day, the idea that Christ had saved human beings by making satisfaction to God for their sins had become firmly established in Western theology. Nevertheless, Roman Catholic theologians generally followed Anselm in maintaining that in his death Christ had obtained on behalf of believers only "absolution from all *past* guilt"; if believers sinned again after receiving this pardon, what Christ had done would be efficacious for them only if they were "willing to make an acceptable satisfaction and thereafter to mend their ways."[2] This meant that, in addition to the satisfaction already made by Christ, it was necessary for believers to make *further* satisfaction for their sins by means of a variety of penitential rites and religious acts prescribed by the church.

Luther was convinced that the idea that believers themselves had to make satisfaction for their sins was oppressive in that it ultimately made their salvation depend on their own efforts as well as their submission to the church. By constantly demanding that believers make satisfaction for their sins through confession, fasts, alms, acts of penance, prescribed prayers, and other supposedly pious practices, the church maintained control over their souls and thus over many other aspects of their life as well.[3] For this reason, Luther instead insisted that in his death Christ had made satisfaction for *all sins*. Therefore, no further satisfaction whatsoever was required on behalf of believers in order for them to be saved; all that was necessary was that they trust in Christ for their salvation. This belief lay at the heart of his understanding of justification: God declared believers righteous, not because of anything they had done or any works of their own, but only because Christ had died for their sins. According to Luther, "there is no repentance, no satisfaction for sins, no grace, no eternal life, except by faith alone in Christ, faith that he has given full satisfaction for our sins, won grace for us, and saved us."[4]

Luther also departed somewhat from the teaching of Anselm and Roman Catholicism in affirming a doctrine of penal substitution. In Anselm's thought, Christ had *made satisfaction* for human sins but had not endured the *penalty* for human sins on the cross. Satisfaction and punishment were regarded as *alternatives* so that, if satisfaction was made to God, punishment was no longer necessary: "*either* satisfaction *or* punishment must follow upon every sin."[5] Luther, however, equated satisfaction with the punishment of sins, affirming that God's justice was satisfied when the punishment or penalty human beings deserved for their sins was inflicted on Christ as their substitute: "Christ, the Son of God, stands in our place and has taken all our sins upon his shoulders. . . . [H]e is the eternal satisfaction for our sin and reconciles us with God the Father."[6] According to this understanding of Christ's death, human beings were under God's wrath on account of their sins but, by enduring that wrath on the cross in their stead, Christ has delivered them from it, thus propitiating God: "in his suffering" Christ "made satisfaction and merited propitiation for those who believe in him."[7]

For Luther, of course, this understanding of Christ's death was rooted in the Scriptures themselves. He looked to the idea of penal substitution to interpret the numerous New Testament passages that speak of believers being justified, redeemed, ransomed, and reconciled to God through Christ's blood and his death on the cross. At the same time, however, Luther also claimed to find in many of these passages another idea found in the Christian tradition he inherited, generally labelled the *Christus Victor* idea, according to which Christ had delivered human beings from the powers of sin, death, and the devil through his death and resurrection. Generally, he combined this idea with that of penal substitution to speak of these three powers, along with the law, as manifestations of God's righteous wrath which Christ endured on the cross so that human beings might be delivered from their power.[8]

Luther also understood Christ's work in terms of a "joyous exchange" between Christ and believers, who through faith are joined to Christ so as to become "as one person" with him.[9] In this exchange, their sin and its punishment are transferred to Christ, while Christ's righteousness is transferred to them. Luther spoke of this righteousness as an "alien righteousness" in that it did not originate in believers themselves but outside of them in Christ.

While at times Luther appears to have spoken of both sin and righteousness as actual entities or substances that are exchanged between Christ and believers, this exchange has more commonly been understood in a *forensic* sense, according to which the sin of believers is *reckoned* to Christ for him to endure its punishment and the righteousness of Christ is in turn reckoned or imputed to believers; on this basis, they are accepted by God as righteous. This understanding of Christ's work is stated particularly clearly in the Apology to the Augsburg Confession, composed by Philip Melanchthon: "Christ has taken into himself the right of the law to accuse and condemn those who believe in him, because he himself is the atoning sacrifice for them, on account of which they are now reckoned righteous. . . . '[T]o be justified' here does not mean for a righteous person to be made out of an ungodly one, but to be pronounced righteous in a forensic sense."[10]

This forensic understanding of justification met with resistance among not only Roman Catholic theologians but some Protestants as well. The penal substitution interpretation of Christ's death also encountered widespread rejection. Many of the liberal Protestant theologians of the nineteenth and early twentieth centuries, for example, regarded Christ's death as salvific through the example and inspiration it provides for believers as well as what it reveals to them about the nature of God, humanity, and the world.[11] Ideas such as these have generally been associated with Abelard, who questioned Anselm's teaching regarding Christ's death only a few years after the appearance of *Cur Deus homo*. In recent years, many Protestant theologians have proposed as an alternative to all of these views an understanding of Christ's work that revolves around the idea of participation in Christ's death and resurrection.[12] This view looks to Paul's language about dying and rising with Christ, an idea which was also important for Luther.

Although there are many differences among these various understandings of Christ's work, they share in common the idea that what God did in Christ constitutes the basis upon which people are justified, that is, declared righteous by God. Generally, it is maintained that Christ's death and resurrection had some type of salvific "effect" upon God, human beings, or the forces of evil, such as sin, death, and the devil. In other words, some type of change or alteration in the human situation is said to have taken place when Christ died and rose. It is also claimed that it was not possible for this change or alteration in the human situation to have been brought about in any other way and therefore that Christ's death was *necessary* for human salvation. In fact, it is usually maintained not only that Christ needed to suffer and die on the cross in order for human beings to be saved but that he had to be both fully divine and fully human in order for his sufferings and death to save humankind.

Closely associated with these ideas concerning Christ's death is a distinction commonly made in Protestant theology between an *objective* and a *subjective* justification or salvation. According to this distinction, in some sense what God has done in Christ is sufficient to effect the salvation of humanity *as a whole*. Christ paid for the sins of the *entire world*, endured the penalty due to *all human beings*, and delivered *humankind collectively* from sin, death, and the devil. Salvation, redemption, forgiveness, justification, and reconciliation with God are thus said to be *objective* in that Christ obtained these things for all people universally. Nevertheless, all of this can only become an actual reality for each person when that person appropriates it *subjectively* through faith.

Justification and Forgiveness in the Hebrew Scriptures and Ancient Judaism

Throughout the Hebrew Scriptures and ancient Jewish writings, salvation has to do first and foremost with the redemption of Israel as a whole. It is a *collective* salvation embracing an entire people and in this sense can be spoken of as "objective." To some extent, this salvation had already been accomplished in the past when God chose the people of Israel, redeemed them from their bondage in Egypt, gave them the law through Moses, and introduced them into the promised land. In Jewish thought, even the future generations that had not yet been born had participated in these events, since God had carried them out not only for the sake of those who were alive in the days of Moses and Joshua but for all the descendants of Israel as well, who would benefit from all that God had done for their forebearers.[13]

Yet although Israel had been redeemed in a sense in the days of Moses and Joshua, that redemption had not been definitive or complete.[14] As noted previously, many Jews looked forward to a new age when all oppression and suffering would come to an end for God's people. The fact that in Jesus' day they had still not experienced that salvation in its fullness led them to conclude that they had not yet become truly obedient to God in the way that God desired. For that reason, God was continuing to test, purify, and refine them through suffering so that they might become more obedient. In this sense, God had not yet forgiven Israel's sins. Eventually, however, it was expected that, in spite of those sins, God would act to redeem the people of Israel and bring about in them the obedience and righteousness that the law demanded.

Therefore, while Judaism conceived of the salvation to come as an objective reality embracing all, that salvation depended on a subjective response on the part of the people. "All Israel" would be saved, yet only those who made the proper subjective response were counted as members of that Israel.

Even though the forgiveness of sins depended on God's being gracious and merciful toward those who repented of their disobedience to God's law, it also depended on their following the prescriptions the law laid down regarding atonement for sins. This involved making reparation for any wrongs committed against others, presenting sacrificial offerings, and participating in the annual Day of Atonement rite. In later rabbinic thought, it was claimed that almsgiving, suffering, death, and the study of the law also made atonement for sins and obtained divine forgiveness.[15]

While the people of Israel were to do collectively what God had ordained, it was of course also necessary for each member of Israel to do what God had ordained on an individual basis. Those who did were "justified," that is, counted as belonging to the community of the "righteous," in contrast to those who did not, who were labeled "sinners." Strictly speaking, justification was not *equated* with salvation but was a *pre-requisite* to salvation: one had to be accepted as righteous by God in order to be saved. Of course, in order to be counted among the righteous, one actually had to *live* righteously and be committed to the commandments. Nevertheless, there was also an element of forgiveness in justification, since all the members of God's people were imperfect and inevitably sinned. As long as one repented and manifested that repentance in the ways prescribed by God, however, one was forgiven and one's imperfect righteousness was accepted as sufficient. Justification, then, was not merely a forensic declaration, nor was it synonymous with forgiveness; rather, it was based on the actual righteous behavior of each person.

Like Israel as a whole, individuals and particular communities belonging to God's people might experience salvation to some degree even in the present age. This present salvation consisted of different types of well-being: a long, healthy life in the company of one's loved ones, an absence of suffering and oppression, the satisfaction of one's material needs, and a general experience of wholeness in body and soul. Just as God could bless or chastise Israel collectively, so also could God bless or chastise individual members of Israel, depending on what they did. When people experienced difficulties or hardships, it was often thought that God was punishing or disciplining them for their sins and thus that they needed to repent and do what the law prescribed, especially by taking part in the sacrificial worship carried out at the Jerusalem temple.

The temple was the place where God had chosen to make God's name dwell, that is, the place in which God's people might have access to God's presence. For the vast majority of the people, this access was not direct but had to be mediated through the priests that God had designated as intermediaries as well as through the sacrificial offerings that the people gave to God by means of those priests. On occasions such as the Day of Atonement and certain festivals, the people came before God to ask for divine forgiveness and blessings collectively. However, individuals could also go to the temple to seek for themselves blessings on a personal basis, such as the restoration of health, deliverance from other types of hardships, and the satisfaction of various physical and spiritual needs. This inevitably involved seeking God's forgiveness as well, since the hardships from which people suffered were seen as divinely ordained in order to correct, discipline, purify, and test them. However, forgiveness was not an end in itself, nor was forgiveness understood merely in abstract or spiritual terms; instead, it was all about being restored to God's favor so that God would grant material, concrete blessings in one's life. The objective was not merely to find some spiritual "peace with God" or assurance of eternal salvation in an other-worldly realm but to experience God's salvation and blessings in *this* world. As long as people were counted among the righteous, obeying the commandments as best they could and repenting and making atonement when they sinned, they could expect that God would not take their sins into account and would listen to the prayers they offered at the temple.

This was, in fact, the primary significance of the temple in the Hebrew Scriptures and ancient Jewish thought: it was a "house of prayer" (Isa 56:7; cf. 1 Kgs 8:30, 33, 44-48). Christian interpretations of the Jewish temple and sacrificial system have tended to overlook this point, ascribing primary importance to the sacrificial offerings themselves rather than the prayers that accompanied those offerings and gave them meaning. This has often included viewing sacrifices in magical or mechanical fashion, as if the mere shedding or offering of blood or the killing of animals in itself produced some salvific effect, making atonement or procuring the forgiveness of sins.[16] Thus it has been common for scholars to inquire as to how sacrifice "worked," what "mechanics" were involved, how sacrificial blood "effected" atonement, what the relation was between the killing of animals and the forgiveness of sins, and the precise manner in which sin was thought to be washed away or covered up by sacrifices.

While most biblical scholars and theologians have recognized that in ancient Hebrew and Jewish thought it was necessary for sacrifices to be presented with a right heart, a commitment to righteousness, and a spirit of repentance in order to obtain divine favor and forgiveness, many have continued to combine this idea with the claim that sacrifices were believed to "work" in some way to "effect" atonement. This involves an attempt to establish an *intrinsic* relation between the sacrifices and the forgiveness of sins, so that forgiveness resulted *automatically* as a consequence of a sacrifice properly offered. In order to make this claim, it is necessary to affirm that God had set up some type of self-ordered system that functioned by itself independently of God so that no divine decision was needed as to whether a sacrifice was acceptable; this would be to posit an *extrinsic* relation between sacrifice and forgiveness once again.

The problem with attempting to establish an intrinsic relation between sacrifices and forgiveness is that it requires some type of objective, independent criteria that are able to determine on their own, independently of God, whether one's faith, obedience, and repentance are sufficient for the sacrifices to "work." This can be done only by quantifying these things in some way so that no divine decision is necessary as to whether they are sufficiently present in the person offering the sacrifice. Furthermore, faith, obedience, and repentance end up being part of a "magic formula": when these things are present, the sacrificial rite automatically "works" to produce the desired "effect," but when they are lacking, the sacrifice accomplishes nothing. When it is said that faith, for example, is necessary for the sacrifices to effect forgiveness and make atonement, then faith simply becomes one more cog in the sacrificial machinery and saving faith is reduced to believing that the sacrificial mechanics "work," rather than trusting solely in God's grace and forgiveness.

All of this is extremely problematic. In reality, in biblical thought, only God can determine whether one is sincerely repentant or whether one's commitment to obedience is sufficient. In addition, because forgiveness is something personal and therefore requires a divine decision, no intrinsic relation can be established between the offering of sacrifices and divine forgiveness: it is *God* who must forgive sins, not some system established by God that works independently of God. To speak in such terms takes God out of the picture: God merely stands back and lets the sacrificial mechanics "work" on their own.

At times, rather than claiming that God set up some type of self-functioning, independent system in which sacrifices had an intrinsic power to effect atonement in themselves, some have argued that, in the covenant God established with Israel, God bound God's self to granting forgiveness when sacrifices were properly offered. Thus, for example, it might be said that sacrificial blood had some power to obtain forgiveness from God, not because by nature blood had any power over God, but because for the sake of human beings God had graciously *granted* sacrificial blood the power to effect atonement and obtain divine forgiveness. Once again, however, the problem is that some type of divine decision was necessary. If the proper repentance or commitment to obedience was not present, then the sacrificial blood did *not* have power to effect atonement; yet only God could decide whether the proper repentance or commitment to obedience was present. This destroys any type of intrinsic relation between sacrifice and forgiveness or atonement, which still ultimately depended on what God saw in the heart of those offering sacrifices rather than the rites themselves.

Another way to attempt to establish an intrinsic relation between sacrifice and atonement is to define atonement, not in terms of forgiveness, but in terms of some actual change brought about in the condition of the person who offered sacrifice or the person on whose behalf it was offered. For example, it can be argued that sin was thought to be some type of malignant substance that was transferred from the individual to the sacrificial victim, perhaps by the laying-on of hands, or that sacrificial blood was viewed as a "ritual detergent" that washed away the sins that adhered to God's holy house as stains are removed from some substance or surface.[17] In this way, God's people were actually cleansed and freed from their sin and were consequently accepted as clean and pure before God. In other words, people first had to *become* pure through a sacrificial rite and then on that basis were *declared* pure by God.

In this regard, a distinction is often made between expiation and propitiation. Expiation involves cleansing or purification, such as that just described, whereas propitiation involves placating God's wrath at sin. In reality, however, in Hebrew thought sacrifices in themselves could accomplish neither of these things. Sacrifices could not *cleanse* the worshipers so that God then had to *accept* them as clean, since a proper disposition on their part was necessary and only God could determine whether that disposition was present; thus it was this disposition of repentance and a commitment to obedience rather than the rite itself that could cleanse and purify people from their sins. For the same reason, sacrifices could not in themselves take away God's wrath, since God's wrath was taken away only by a proper disposition, not by the sacrificial rites themselves. This means that ultimately *it was only the proper disposition* that could make people clean or pure before God, just as only a proper disposition could appease God's righteous wrath at sin.

For all of these reasons, it is incorrect to affirm that in ancient Jewish thought sacrifices were believed to "effect" atonement. God could not be bought or manipulated by sacrifice, nor could any sacrificial rites "work" to obtain God's favor and forgiveness. In order to please God, atone for one's sins, and obtain divine favor and forgiveness, it was necessary for one's heart and life to be acceptable to God; this was the determining factor. When this was not the case, then no sacrifice could be pleasing to God nor obtain God's blessings and forgiveness. This means that those rites were not understood to be magical or mechanical, automatically and inevitably accomplishing their objective when performed in the way prescribed by the law. Of course, if one was confident in one's heart that one was truly repentant and followed the divinely-prescribed atonement rituals to which God's promise of forgiveness had been attached, one could rest assured that one's sins were forgiven. But this assurance lay, not in the conviction that the sacrificial rite itself had been performed properly or that the sacrificial mechanics had worked, but in *what was in a person's heart*, that is, true repentance and a commitment to obedience.

It would be incorrect, therefore, to speak of some type of *necessity* for sacrificial atonement in order for God to forgive sins in Jewish thought. The Jewish view of God's sovereignty precludes the idea that there is some type of law or justice to which God is subject that does not allow God to forgive sins without atonement being made. Of course, this raises the question of why sacrificial worship existed at all in Israel: If repentance and a commitment to obedience were all that was necessary for God to forgive sins, why should God have commanded the people to offer up sacrifices?

Although the Hebrew Scriptures do not offer any clear answer to this question, it seems best to see the sacrificial worship prescribed there as symbolizing and expressing in visible and palpable ways important aspects of the relation between God and God's people. Thus, for example, by presenting to God various types of offerings—it was the act of *offering* that constituted the central idea and defining moment of sacrificial worship, rather than the killing of animals which was done to make the offering possible—the people were able to manifest in concrete fashion their love for God and their submission to God as their sovereign Lord, approaching God with gifts that expressed their spirit of thanksgiving, penitence, and adoration. Like Christians do today when they present monetary offerings to God, people offered up to God not only what was most precious to them or the fruit of their labor but *their very own selves*; this did not involve presenting a sacrificial victim *instead* of themselves as a substitute, however, but offering themselves up to God *through* the sacrificial offering and *together* with it. The use of sacrificial blood in various ceremonies reinforced the idea that life belonged to God alone as the sovereign Lord and Creator of all that has life and underscored the gravity of the offenses they had committed. The high costs involved in presenting sacrificial offerings also reminded them that there was a high cost to worshiping and serving God and making reparation for their sins; these costs gave value to the spiritual actions they carried out in the temple.

At the heart of all of this, however, was the idea of *prayer*.[18] Sacrifices were in a sense enacted prayers, since they involved thanking and worshiping God, seeking forgiveness, and making petitions to God. The way that the smoke and incense rose up to God symbolized the way that the people's prayers ascended to God's presence. There is overwhelming evidence from ancient Jewish sources that the idea of prayer was believed to lie at the heart of Israel's sacrificial worship. When the high priest went into the Holy of Holies on the Day of Atonement to sprinkle sacrificial blood, for example, he was presenting prayers to God through a symbolic act, asking for God to be favorable to God's sinful people who acknowledged their sin. Even the scapegoat rite carried out on the Day of Atonement must be seen as a symbolic act, representing the way that the people's sins laid upon the goat were taken away, far out of God's sight. Yet the fact that this was merely a symbolic act and did not actually effect some type of actual transfer of Israel's sins (as if sins were substances that had an objective reality of their own and could thus be passed from one living being to another) becomes evident when it is recalled that, when the people were not truly repentant for their sins nor committed to obeying God, the Day of Atonement rites did not "work" or "effect" atonement. Thus, once again, it was repentance and obedience, not the performance of rites, that made atonement for sin. Undoubtedly, there was an objective aspect to the Day of Atonement rites, in that God was believed to forgive the sins of the people as a whole when the rites were performed; but what ultimately mattered was the subjective aspect: only those who were truly repentant as they came before God imploring God's forgiveness actually attained it. Furthermore, even though the rites carried out on that day were regarded as necessary, this was not because there was some inner need in God or God's nature that made it impossible for God to forgive sins without those rites. Rather, the rites were necessary because God had commanded them for Israel's own benefit on account of the meaning and symbolism that were associated with them; the people could hardly be said to be committed to obeying God's will in general if they did not carry out the rites God had prescribed for them.

Finally, it is important to note that the Jewish belief that forgiveness and salvation were available only to those who repented and were committed to obeying God's law excluded from the community of the righteous not only unrepentant, non-observant Jews but Gentiles as well. Gentiles did not have full access to the blessings promised by God's law to faithful Jews. While it was common to maintain that there were righteous Gentiles who would have some share in the age to come when Israel's redemption arrived, their participation in that redemption was limited unless they came to submit fully to God's law and the covenant God had established with Israel.[19] Therefore, the idea of an objective salvation or redemption embracing humanity as a whole was foreign to Jewish thought; there was no sense in which it could be said that all human beings had been delivered from sin, death, and divine condemnation, even in principle. The objective atonement associated with the Day of Atonement rites, for example, included only the repentant members of God's people Israel and not all human beings. Only those living in the covenant had full access to God and God's blessings of forgiveness, because the only means God had defined for approaching God were those stipulated in the Mosaic law, which mandated not only keeping the commandments but participating in the sacrificial worship associated with the temple.

Christ's Death and Justification in the New Testament

Throughout the New Testament, redemption, justification, reconciliation with God, and forgiveness of sins are associated with Jesus' death or blood. This is particularly true with regard to the letters traditionally ascribed to St. Paul. Paul speaks of Jesus' death as being "for our sins" and "for our trespasses" (Rom 4:25; 1 Cor 15:3; Gal 1:4) and attributes justification, forgiveness of sins, redemption, and reconciliation with God to Christ's death and blood (Rom 3:24-25; 5:9-10; Gal 2:21; 3:13; Eph 1:7; 2:16; Col 1:14, 19-22; 2:13-14; cf. 2 Cor 5:18, 21). These ideas are particularly stressed throughout the Letter to the Hebrews (1:3; 2:17; 9:11-14, 26, 28; 10:10-11, 14, 19; 13:22) and are present in many of the other New Testament writings as well (1 Pet 1:2; 2:24; 3:18; 1 John 1:7; 2:2; Rev 1:5; 5:9). In the Synoptic Gospels and Acts, Jesus' death is spoken of as a ransom for many (Matt 20:28; Mark 10:45; cf. 1 Tim 2:6), while his blood is said to have been "poured out for many for the forgiveness of sins" (Matt 26:28) and is regarded as a price paid to obtain the church (Acts 20:28).

Although the New Testament writings repeatedly relate Jesus' death to salvation, redemption, justification, and the forgiveness of sins, nowhere do they provide any type of explanation as to precisely *how* Jesus' death was thought to bring these things about. Instead, we repeatedly find brief formulas that are open to a wide variety of interpretations. For example, it is possible to read all kinds of theological ideas back into the affirmations that Christ "died for our sins" (1 Cor 15:3), "gave himself as a ransom for all" (1 Tim 2:6), "bore our sins on the tree" (1 Pet 2:24), "offered for all time a single sacrifice for sins" (Heb 10:12), and "freed us from our sins by his blood" (Rev 1:5). At least since the time of the Reformation, however, passages such as these have been interpreted primarily by looking to ideas associated with the satisfaction and penal substitution understandings of Christ's death already considered above.

The New Testament also affirms that in some sense believers are one with Christ. This language is particularly characteristic of the Pauline letters. Paul frequently speaks of being "in Christ" as well as of Christ being in believers and even affirms: "it is no longer I who live, but it is Christ who lives in me" (Gal 2:20; cf. 1 Cor 6:17). The idea that believers suffer, die, and rise with Christ in some sense is also found repeatedly in the letters ascribed to Paul (Rom 6:1-12;

8:17; Gal 2:19; Eph 2:4-6; Col 1:24; 2:12-13; 2 Tim 2:12-13; cf. Rom 8:17; 2 Cor 4:14; 5:14; 1 Pet 4:13). Once again, however, the New Testament offers no explanation as to precisely how this union with Christ and with his death and resurrection is to be understood.

Satisfaction Views and Their Difficulties

The basic premise of the Anselmian understanding of Christ's work is that God's justice or righteousness does not allow God to forgive the sins of human beings freely out of mercy: "for this kind of divine mercy is utterly contrary to God's justice, which allows only for punishment to be requited for sin. Therefore, as it is impossible for God to be at odds with himself, so it is impossible for him to be merciful in this way."[20] Anselm argued that God's ultimate concern was not for God's own self but for human beings and the "order and the beauty of the universe":[21] if God simply ignored or condoned sin without condemning and punishing it, then sin would spread unchecked throughout the world. For this same reason, God needed to defend God's honor, since when human beings fail to honor God by obeying God's will, the result is sin and chaos.

For Anselm, however, God's justice allowed for an alternative to punishment: if satisfaction were offered to God by repaying to God the honor and obedience due to God, then punishment would no longer be necessary. This is the work of Christ, who makes satisfaction for human sin through the honor and obedience he gave to God in his passion and death. On this basis, no punishment is inflicted either on Christ or on human beings for human sin.

The penal substitution understanding of Christ's work that arose in the centuries following Anselm is also based on the premise that God cannot freely forgive sins and remain holy, just, and righteous. In contrast to Anselm, however, a penal substitution view insists that God *must* punish sin with death, both physical and spiritual. While the word "satisfaction" is still used, it is not viewed as an *alternative* to punishment but is identified with the punishment itself: God's justice is satisfied only when the punishment due to human sins is endured by Christ. Once this has occurred, that punishment no longer must be inflicted on sinful human beings themselves. Thus, whereas for Anselm it is the honor and obedience Christ rendered to God in his death that satisfies God's justice, in penal substitution views it is Christ's death or blood itself. Luther, for example, claimed that "just one drop of [Christ's] innocent blood would have been more than enough for the sin of the whole world."[22]

One of the most common criticisms of penal substitution views is that they seem to present God as the one demanding Christ's death in order to remit sins and as the one who must pour out the divine wrath on Christ in order to be appeased. This seems to make God the executioner who is satisfied only by an act of violence and has led feminist theologians to criticize this view of Christ's work as divine child abuse.[23] The idea that God was ultimately responsible for Christ's death is not resolved by affirming that God merely sent the Son to die without requiring that he do so, as Anselm argued;[24] after all, Christ was obeying God in offering up his life and in the end it was God who delivered Christ up (Rom 8:32). This means that Christ's death was ultimately God's will and not that of Christ alone (Mark 14:36).

In order to address these problems, theologians have often sought to remove God from the picture so as to speak of God's *justice* or *law* requiring the death of Christ if human beings are to be forgiven, rather than God personally.[25] This is an attempt to establish an *intrinsic* relation between Christ's substitutionary death and human deliverance from the punishment of sin, so that God does not intervene directly; God merely sends the Son to fulfill a requirement inherent to the system of divine law or divine justice that God has established, which now functions on its own independently of God. It is this system and not God personally that demands that sin be punished and is then satisfied when that punishment is endured by Christ.

Because penal substitution views maintain that God's justice is satisfied not by Christ's obedience per se but by Christ's death or blood, they require that a distinction be made between Christ's *active* and *passive* obedience.[26] Christ's active obedience consisted of his life of perfect righteousness in which he fulfilled the law in every detail without ever committing sin. This was necessary in order for Christ to be qualified to die in the stead of others; had he not been perfectly holy, innocent, and sinless, he would have had to die for his own sins and thus could not have died for the sins of others. Strictly speaking, however, what delivers human beings from the punishment due to them is Christ's *passive* obedience in which he allowed that punishment to be inflicted on him by giving himself up to death on the cross. This constitutes a point of difference between Anselm's understanding of Christ's work and that found in penal substitution views: for Anselm, human beings are saved by the *active obedience* that Christ rendered to God by remaining committed to justice all the way to his death, while in penal substitution views it is Christ's *passive* obedience that delivers human beings from the punishment due to their sins. His active obedience only makes it possible for his passive obedience to be redemptive.

Views of Christ's work such as these have been heavily criticized, not only for presenting God as the one who demands Christ's death, but also because they pit God's justice against God's mercy. In God's mercy, God *wants* to forgive sins freely but God's justice will not allow it. Ultimately, it appears that we are faced with "God against God," as Luther affirmed:[27] through Christ, God must save us from God's own self. Human beings must be delivered, not so much from sin, but from God's *wrath* at sin: we must "get God off our backs," since God or God's perfect righteousness constitutes the problem that must be overcome.[28] Salvation thus consists merely of being spared divine punishment. Furthermore, in such views it is a misnomer to speak of the forgiveness of sins, since in reality nothing is forgiven; each and every human sin is punished and paid for by Christ in his death.

Particularly problematic, however, is the claim that it was not possible for God to remit human sins justly and thereby save sinful human beings without Christ's death.[29] As noted above, this claim constitutes the main premise upon which such views of Christ's work are based. This argument for the necessity of Christ's death requires that God be subjected to a law or standard that is above God and will not allow God to forgive human sins freely.[30] Generally, it is argued that this is the law of God's holy and righteous nature, which cannot be compromised.[31] In this case, God's nature dictates to God what God can and cannot do; God is bound by God's own justice and righteousness, so that God is no longer free to do whatever God pleases, such as exercising mercy to sinners by freely overlooking their sins. This would be to act contrary to justice and thus unjustly, which by nature is not possible for God. Of course, as noted above in discussing sacrifice, it is often claimed that God has voluntarily bound God's own self to the system of justice and laws that God has established and thus has willingly limited God's own freedom. Yet, from God's perspective, it is not clear what God would gain from placing limits on God's own self in this way; nor is it possible any longer to speak of Christ's death as an absolute necessity, since it is only necessary because God chose to limit God's own freedom by submitting to a system established by God's own self.

The argument for the necessity of Christ's death is also problematic in that it requires that some equivalency be established between the satisfaction rendered by Christ to God or God's justice and the debt or penalty to which sinful human beings were subject. In a satisfaction view such as that of Anselm, what Christ pays to God must be greater in value than what human beings owe to God in order for God's justice to be satisfied and God's honor restored. But how can the obedience and honor paid to God by a single man, even if he is divine, make up for the debt of obedience and honor that billions of human beings throughout human history have owed to God due to their disobedience to God? Anselm attempted to resolve this by ascribing infinite value to the obedience and honor rendered to God by Christ in his death: "The life of this man was so sublime and so precious that it can suffice to make payment for what is owed for the sins of the whole world—and even for infinitely more [sins than these]."[32] Yet it would seem that such a determination can be made only by God, who must *regard* Christ's death as greater in value than what was owed to God by human beings. This ends up undermining the argument for the necessity of Christ's death, since God could have regarded *any* price paid as sufficient payment for the debt owed to God by human beings.

These difficulties are even more pronounced in a penal substitution view, which requires that some equivalency be established between the punishment Christ endured in his death and the punishment to which humanity as a whole was subject.[33] How can the punishment endured by one man be considered equivalent to the punishment to which countless sinful human beings of all times and places were liable collectively? It might be said that God could *accept* what Christ suffered as equivalent to the punishment to which humanity as a whole was liable. However, this undermines the argument for necessity once more, since Christ's death is equivalent only because God voluntarily chose to accept it as such.

Further complications arise when it is argued that Christ's death made satisfaction for human sin not to God personally but to God's law or God's justice, since then the equivalency between what Christ suffered and what human beings had to suffer must be established by the system put in place by God: According to what law, legal system, or system of justice can the punishment endured by one man, even if he is divine, be considered equivalent to the punishment due to billions of human beings of all times and places? In itself, such a system or law functioning independently of God is unable not only to establish such equivalency but to determine that it is right, just, and legally permissible for one righteous and innocent individual undeserving of death to undergo the punishment due to countless others, while those who are guilty go free. All of this seems clearly to *contradict* justice rather than upholding it, so that justice ends up being satisfied by an injustice. To say that because Christ voluntarily accepted such a death it was not unjust does not resolve the difficulty, since the injustice lies not in Christ volunteering to die for others but in either God or God's law accepting Christ's death as just and equivalent to what human beings deserved. The problems associated with the attempt to establish some equivalency between what Christ paid to God and what human beings as a whole owed to God led to the doctrine of acceptilation (*acceptilatio*), according to which God merely *accepted* as equivalent the payment made by Christ in his death even though it was not *inherently* equivalent.[34] Yet, as just noted, this undermines the argument for the necessity of Christ's death.

In addition, if the penalty due to human sin consists of enduring physical death, then it cannot rightly be said that Christ endured this in the place of sinners, since all people continue to die physically and thus experience this penalty for sin. People also continue to experience spiritual anguish when they die and thus it is difficult to argue that Christ endured this in their stead. If the penalty instead is said to be eternal death and condemnation, then it can hardly be said that Christ endured this in the stead of others, since he did not suffer eternal condemnation in hell; and to claim that Christ *did* suffer the torments of the damned in hell after he died is problematic, not only because those torments were not eternal in duration, but because then it is what Christ suffered *after he had died* that satisfied God's justice rather than his passion and death themselves. In that case, any type of death would have sufficed for Christ to pay the penalty for human sin, since what was necessary was not that he die on a cross but that he descend into hell to suffer there. Proponents of penal substitution views often look to the beatings and mistreatment Christ endured during his last hours and his physical and spiritual sufferings on the cross as salvific, claiming that these sufferings were of infinite proportions, but these can hardly be identified with the penalty for human sin if that penalty is said to be eternal condemnation *after* death. In fact, in reality, the sentence dictated by God's law for human sin was not a certain amount of *suffering* but simply *death*. Ultimately, then, the problem of acceptilation arises here once more: the penalty endured by Christ is sufficient for God to remit sins, not because of any inherent sufficiency, but only because God accepted it as sufficient. But this involves a personal decision by God, so that neither God's law nor God's justice can be said to determine the sufficiency of Christ's death in themselves.

While satisfaction and penal substitution understandings of Christ's death claim to be faithful to the New Testament witness, in reality there is no firm evidence to support them there. The New Testament never speaks of Christ making satisfaction to God, putting an end to God's wrath against sin (which in biblical thought continues in force until the final judgment, Rom 2:5, 8; Eph 5:6), dying as humanity's substitute, or undergoing divine judgment or condemnation. While the New Testament speaks of the necessity for Christ to die in order that the Scriptures might be fulfilled, it never affirms that his death was necessary for God to forgive sins; in fact, both the Scriptures and ancient Jewish thought maintain that God is able to accept repentant sinners freely, rather than affirming that there is something in God's nature that prevents God from forgiving sins or from accepting those who are not absolutely perfect into God's fellowship. The Gospels do not present Jesus as dedicating his life to attaining a perfect level of righteousness so that he might be qualified to die for the sins of others; and while the Passion narratives allude very briefly to Christ's anguish, suffering, and bloodshed, these are not the center of focus. Much less is it ever implied in the New Testament that Christ suffered something such as the "pangs of hell" in his death. There is no reason to read such an idea back into

Christ's cry of dereliction on the cross (Matt 27:46; Mark 15:34), especially since that same cry was originally that of a Psalmist (Ps 22:1); this means that Jesus was not the first or the only one in history to feel abandoned by God. Although several New Testament passages allude to the idea that Christ descended into the place of the dead (1 Pet 3:19; 4:6; Rom 10:7; Eph 4:9), it is never said that he suffered there but only that he proclaimed the gospel there. Finally, it has often been noted that the New Testament speaks of believers being reconciled to God, rather than God being reconciled to human beings (Rom 5:10; 2 Cor 5:18-19; Eph 2:16; Col 1:20). This implies that the basis for reconciliation lies in a change in human beings rather than in God. Thus, while it is no doubt possible to read back into the New Testament ideas associated with satisfaction and penal substitution views, particularly in the case of the brief formulaic passages that allude to the redemptive nature of Christ's death, the New Testament offers no explicit and clear evidence that Christ's death was understood along the lines of a satisfaction for human sin made to God's justice.

Satisfaction Views and the Doctrine of Justification

Most of the preceding criticisms of satisfaction and penal substitution views are nothing new; in fact, they have been made for centuries and, as many would agree, they admit of no satisfactory solution. In spite of this, Protestant theologians have continued to adhere to such views primarily for one important reason: they supposedly make it possible to affirm that justification depends entirely on God's work in Christ rather than on anything human beings do. This was what pleased Luther, for example: one could have full certainty regarding one's salvation and justification since this depended solely on what Christ did *outside of* us (*extra nos*), rather than any change occurring *in* us (*in nobis*).[35] Christ's death is thus regarded as providing the *objective* basis for justification.

Upon closer examination, however, it is not actually true that in Protestant thought the basis upon which believers are justified lies *outside* of them in Christ's death. Once it is claimed that only those who respond properly to God are justified and saved, this subjective response becomes the determining factor and constitutes the basis upon which people are justified. Whether this proper and necessary response is defined in terms of faith alone or obedience to God's will as well, without it one's sins are *not* actually forgiven and one remains under divine condemnation. In that case, it is not true that justification depends solely on the work of Christ, since if people do not have faith, what Christ did ends up being of no avail for them and they are *not* justified. This means that forgiveness and salvation do indeed depend on a change taking place *in* people, namely, the change from unbelief to faith. Thus it is not Christ's death that provides certainty of salvation for believers but their faith.

For this reason, once a subjective response is said to be necessary, the idea of an objective redemption or salvation embracing all people universally loses all sense and meaning. Generally, the claim that all people have been saved through Christ's death is qualified in some way by affirming that this salvation has taken place "in principle" or "potentially":[36] all people now *can* be saved. Nevertheless, this salvation must still become "actual" or real by being accepted through faith. Later Protestant theologians affirmed that Christ's death was "sufficient" for all but "efficient" only for the salvation of those who come to faith.[37]

However, once faith is deemed necessary for salvation, then it cannot rightly be said that in his death Christ put away or exhausted the wrath of God at human sin once for all, delivered humankind from God's judgment and condemnation, and made sufficient atonement for the sins of the whole world. God's wrath at human sin is *not* put away or exhausted but remains on those who do not come to faith and will finally be manifested at the last judgment; that wrath is put away only by their faith, not by Christ's death. Unbelievers are still under God's judgment and condemnation and have not in fact been saved from these things by Christ; they must and will pay for their sins in spite of the payment for sins already made by Christ. It is not the event of the cross that delivers people from judgment and condemnation but their faith. Christ's death is thus *not* sufficient to save all people from their sins, since without faith it is *insufficient* for human salvation. To affirm otherwise requires that we speak of a "double payment" for the sins of unbelievers: Christ paid their debt and suffered the penalty for their sins, yet they will also have to pay that debt and suffer that penalty themselves following the final judgment.

For the same reasons, it is senseless to speak of an objective salvation accomplished through Christ's death. If it is said that Christ's death has put away God's wrath at human sin and saved humanity as a whole "in principle," as the objective doctrines of Christ's work affirm, then all that can be said is that the situation of human beings has been changed from one of being "*not* saved in principle" to one in which they now "*are* saved in principle" (though not in actuality). Proponents of these views ultimately end up affirming that if people do not come to believe, the wrath of God that Christ supposedly put away "once for all" comes back into force. Thus unbelief must be said to nullify what Christ did, "de-reconciling" people who had previously been reconciled to God by Christ's death or "unredeeming" and "unsaving" those whom Christ had redeemed and saved. The affirmation that in his death Christ did "all that was necessary for the salvation of all humankind" is shown to be false, since the faith of human beings is necessary and that faith only becomes a reality in the present.[38]

Among some Reformed theologians, these problems have been addressed by positing a limited atonement, according to which Christ died only for the sins of the elect.[39] This apparently makes it possible to resolve the problem of a double payment for sins and avoid the idea that Christ died in vain for some, namely, those who would not come to faith and therefore not obtain the benefits of his death. According to such a view, however, in reality the objective basis for the justification of believers is not Christ's death but God's eternal election: ultimately, they are saved and justified, not because Christ died for them, but because in eternity God elected them for salvation. In fact, here the cross ends up being a mere formality and it can no longer be maintained that Jesus' death was necessary for God to save human beings and forgive their sin justly. Once God had determined to save those whom God had elected, God could have used any means to accomplish that end, including some means other than Christ or the cross. For the same reasons, faith can no longer truly be regarded as the subjective basis for their justification, since ultimately they are justified not because they come to faith but because God determined ahead of time to create faith in them. It is thus their election rather than Christ's death or their faith that constitutes the basis upon which they are declared righteous by God.

In similar fashion, Christ's death is reduced to a mere formality when a universalistic doctrine of salvation is maintained, according to which *all* people are ultimately saved independently of whether or not they come to faith. While in principle this might seem to make it possible to affirm that Christ's death is the basis upon which all are justified and saved, in reality the basis for their justification is not Christ's death but God's decision to save all people universally. As in a doctrine of limited atonement, God could just as easily have chosen any means other than the cross to save humankind collectively once God had determined to do so.

Protestant thought has generally sought to maintain the necessity of both Christ's death *and* human faith for salvation by seeing Christ's death for sins as the *object* or *content* of saving faith. In this case, it is not sufficient to believe in God or in Christ in a general sense in order to be saved; rather, one's sins can only be forgiven if one believes that Christ's substitutionary death is the sole basis upon which one's sins are forgiven. In this case, however, Christ's death was necessary for human salvation only because, for no intrinsic or necessary reason, God determined that faith in the sufficiency of Christ's death would be the condition upon which people would be saved. God could have defined the content of saving faith in any way God desired, since what ultimately saves is faith rather than its object or content. For example, God could have made belief in Christ's divinity, his miracles, or his resurrection the condition for salvation. Even simple faith in God such as that which God's people Israel had prior to Christ's coming and which many non-Christians have could in principle have been sufficient for salvation. For some reason, however, God chose to make both Christ's death and faith in that death the conditions for salvation, even though in principle God could have determined to save human beings without either of these things.

In satisfaction and penal substitution views, therefore, what has changed as a result of Christ's death is that people can now be justified and saved by faith, whereas previously they could not. In order to sustain the argument that Christ's death was necessary for salvation, it must be affirmed that, in former times, even if people came to faith and repentance, God was not able to save and forgive them because God's righteousness would still not allow it; now, however, Christ's death has made it possible for God to do something that God could previously *not* do. Christ's death has thus effected a *change in God*.[40] This means that Christ's death satisfied *a divine need* rather than a human need; while undoubtedly human beings could not be saved without it, the ultimate obstacle to their justification lay not in them but in *God*, since that obstacle was not their sin but God's inability to accept their sin. Therefore, Christ needed to die so that God might be changed from a God who could not accept sinners even if they had faith into a God who *can* accept sinners who have faith—though for some reason Christ's death did not succeed in enabling God to accept sinners who do *not* have faith.

According to interpretations of Christ's death based on the idea of satisfaction, therefore, what ultimately interests God is not that there be any change in human beings or the world but only that satisfaction for sin be rendered to God's justice or that the penalty for human sin be inflicted on someone, whether this be Christ or sinful human beings themselves. Satisfaction or punishment is *an end in itself*, since if its purpose were to bring about some change in human beings or the world, God would not be satisfied or propitiated until that change took place. This undermines Anselm's argument that God demanded satisfaction for sin in order to uphold the order and beauty of the universe. This order and beauty can only be a reality when *all people* practice justice and righteousness, not when one righteous person does so in their place; thus, if this were God's ultimate concern, what Christ did could not be regarded as sufficient to restore the universe's order and beauty. Similarly, if God's ultimate concern in threatening human beings with punishment for their sin were that they stop sinning or that evil be done away with, it would be senseless for God to accept Christ's enduring the punishment prescribed by God's law as sufficient to revoke the punishment of humanity as a whole. Sin and evil in the world are not put away by one man enduring their penalty. On the contrary, it could be argued that God has given free rein to sin and evil by no longer threatening those who practice them with punishment, since by virtue of Christ's substitutionary death they supposedly need not be concerned about being punished for their sins. Ultimately, then, if Christ's death is said to be the sole basis for the justification of believers, then God does not take into account anything believers do when declaring them righteous; and consequently, any moral change in them is superfluous, since they are never held accountable for their actions as long as they have faith.

Roman Catholicism seeks to avoid this difficulty by affirming as Anselm did that, even though Christ made satisfaction for their sins, when believers fall back into sin, this satisfaction needs to be complemented by further acts of satisfaction on their part. Thus their salvation depends not only on what Christ did but on what they continue to do as well. At the same time, these two ideas are brought together by affirming that, because the satisfaction believers make for their sins is inevitably imperfect, it can only be rendered acceptable to God on the basis of the satisfaction Christ made in his death: as the Council of Trent affirmed, the satisfaction offered up by believers for their sins is made in and through Christ, whose satisfaction in essence makes their insufficient satisfaction sufficient.[41] At first glance, this seems to make forgiveness depend on what believers do and thus to place the burden for obtaining forgiveness on them. In reality, however, once it is said that Christ's perfect satisfaction renders their own imperfect satisfaction acceptable to God, then it seems that no matter how inadequate, insufficient, or feeble their own satisfaction may be, it is still made acceptable to God through Christ. In that case, what ultimately satisfies God is what Christ did rather than anything believers do, since they can always rely on the satisfaction made by Christ to make up for whatever their own satisfaction is lacking.

Underlying all of these problems is the claim that satisfaction must be made to God for human sin. This claim is common to both Roman Catholic and Protestant theology, though they differ over the question of whether Christ alone made satisfaction for human sin or believers must also make satisfaction. Yet once it is argued that the satisfaction rendered by Christ to God or God's justice was necessary for human beings to be forgiven, then Christ's death must be seen as responding to a divine need and God's concern can only be that of preserving God's own righteousness, rather than seeing righteousness brought about in human beings themselves. This means that, when satisfaction views of Christ's death are made the basis for the doctrine of justification, justification must ultimately be only about God desiring to *declare* people just but not being concerned about whether they actually *become* just; whether they do or not, God is ultimately satisfied by Christ's death alone and not what human beings do.

The Alien Righteousness of Christ as the Basis for Justification

Following Luther, Protestant theologians have generally taught that the righteousness of Christ is reckoned or imputed to believers. Luther referred to this as an "alien righteousness," since it comes from outside of believers; it is Christ's righteousness that avails for them before God, rather than any righteousness of their own.[42]

In Protestant thought, the idea that God justifies believers because they are clothed or covered with the righteousness of Christ imputed to them has traditionally been combined with the idea that Christ made satisfaction to God or God's justice in his death.[43] In reality, however, these constitute two distinct and even conflicting ideas. According to the latter idea, it is Christ's *passive* righteousness that is reckoned to believers: because Christ endured the penalty of human sin in their stead, they are no longer subject to that penalty; it is as if they had already suffered it themselves. According to the former idea, however, what is reckoned to believers is Christ's *active* righteousness, that is, the perfection that is his as a result of his obedience to God's law throughout his life, passion, and death and as a result of his resurrection and exaltation to God's right hand. In other words, what took place in Christ's life, death, resurrection, and exaltation served to bring about in him a righteousness that he may now share with believers from heaven as they are joined to him by faith. This is how Luther generally seems to have understood the imputation of Christ's righteousness to believers: as they are united to the living, exalted Christ by faith, he shares his righteousness with them.

The problem with combining these two views is that, when taken together, one or the other becomes redundant. If what Christ did in obeying the law and living a life of perfect righteousness is reckoned to them, then believers must be regarded by God as having kept the law perfectly and being righteous now themselves; in that case, the penalty for sin is no longer in force, not because Christ himself endured that penalty, but because those who are perfectly righteous are not subject to any penalty. Thus it would not be necessary for Christ's passive obedience to be reckoned to them; in fact, it would seemingly not even be necessary for Christ to have died on the cross, since the active righteousness he attained in life would be sufficient for believers to be declared righteous by God once that righteousness is reckoned to them. But if the suffering Christ endured as the penalty for human sin (his passive obedience) is reckoned to them as if they themselves had suffered it, then there is no need for his active obedience to be reckoned to them as well, since once they have been delivered from the punishment for their sins their own lack of righteousness is no longer an obstacle to their salvation.

The idea that the righteousness of Christ is reckoned to believers raises many of the same problems as the penal substitution view of Christ's death. If God wished to regard believers as righteous in a forensic sense, it would seem that God could simply have done so independently of anything done by Christ. The traditional argument is that it would be unjust for God to do this, since believers *are not* actually righteous (much less perfectly so); and since by definition God cannot act unjustly and cannot tolerate imperfection, it is impossible for God to freely accept the unrighteous as righteous. Yet, as already noted above, this places the problem on the side of God, who must be enabled to see the unrighteous as righteous. Christ's death is also thereby seen as having the objective of making it possible for God to do something that God wished to do but found impossible by nature, thus satisfying a divine need.

If Christ's perfect righteousness is said to be reckoned to believers, then it would appear that God's justice or righteousness is maintained by an apparent *injustice* or a legal fiction. It is as if salvation and justification were all about God deciding to see things that are not really true: God sees believers as righteous, when they really are not, and sees Christ as a sinner, which he is not. In essence, Christ's work consists of throwing a cover over God's eyes or over believers themselves so that God no longer sees reality, namely, that believers are *not* righteous but sinful.

It is often countered that in reality there is no legal fiction because, by *declaring* people righteous, God actually *makes* them righteous.[44] But it is not clear what this might mean: Are those declared righteous by God *actually transformed* into people who are truly righteous in their behavior, so that they are no longer sinners, merely by God's declaration that such is the case? This appears to be equivalent to God waving a magic wand to transform them into something else. It also raises the question of why God does not just make people righteous in that way *before* declaring them righteous. However, if the affirmation that God's declaration that believers are righteous actually *makes* them righteous is taken to mean that when God declares something to be true it actually *becomes* true, this is also problematic in that it seems that God can make things that are false to be true simply by declaring them such.

In addition to the theological difficulties raised by the idea of Christ's righteousness being reckoned to believers, there is also the problem that the New Testament never speaks in those terms. It does, of course, speak of Christ being righteous, of Christ's act of righteousness leading to the justification of others

(Rom 5:18), of the faith of believers themselves being reckoned by God as righteousness (Rom 4:1-11, 22-25), and of believers having a righteousness that comes from God rather than from themselves or their own actions (Rom 10:3; Phil 3:9). However, to affirm that the righteousness of believers originates outside of them (perhaps through the activity of God or the Holy Spirit) and that their own faith is reckoned by God as righteousness is not the same as saying that the righteousness reckoned to them is that of Christ himself.

Like the satisfaction and penal substitution understandings of Christ's death, the idea that Christ's righteousness is imputed to believers implies that God is not concerned about them attaining any real righteousness of their own; because at the final judgment God will not consider whether they lived righteously or not, it ultimately makes no difference to God if they actually become righteous to some extent. Similarly, to speak of Christ obeying the law in the stead of believers implies that God did not care *who* kept the law but simply that *someone* do so. If God were truly interested in human beings practicing justice and righteousness, then Christ's imputed righteousness would not be able to satisfy God, since only a change in human behavior could accomplish that. When looking at human beings, God does not care *whose* righteousness they have or if they are actually righteous but only that they have some righteousness on the basis of which God can justify them without compromising God's righteous nature. If God desired and demanded that human beings practice righteousness *for their own sake*, that is, so that there might be justice and well-being for all in this world, then it would be senseless for God to reckon the righteousness of Christ to believers; in reality, this would be counterproductive, since people could then sin freely without worrying about practicing righteousness before God.

As noted above, the idea that Christ made satisfaction for human sin can be combined with the idea that believers must also make satisfaction without laying the burden of their salvation on them by maintaining that their own satisfaction is rendered acceptable to God by virtue of the satisfaction made by Christ. In similar fashion, the idea that the justification of believers depends on the imputation of Christ's righteousness can be combined with the idea that their justification also depends on their actually *becoming* righteous. In fact, Luther himself combined these two ideas by asserting that the imputation of Christ's righteousness to believers is only temporary and provisional until they actually *become* fully righteous through death and resurrection. At present, even though they continue to sin, they have a "beginning of righteousness" and God accepts this righteousness in view of the fact that one day it will become complete. They are like sick people who are already in the process of being cured and, because of this, they can be considered righteous even now; they are righteous "in hope" (*in spe*) even though they are not yet righteous "in reality" (*in re*). Until that happens, Christ intercedes on behalf of believers, imploring God to accept them as righteous and tolerate their sin at present until the day when they become perfectly righteous.[45] This intercession can be understood as taking place in the past, when Christ died on the cross, and in the present as well, as Christ asks God mercifully to forgive the sins of believers from his position at God's right hand. In this case, their justification is based not only on what Christ did in the past and does in the present but what he will do in the future when he makes them perfectly righteous.

In reality, this idea raises the same basic problem mentioned previously with regard to the idea that the satisfaction of believers is rendered acceptable to God by virtue of the satisfaction made by Christ. If believers do not actually grow in righteousness, it makes no difference, since no matter how much or how little righteousness of their own they attain in this life, Christ will make up for it. Thus even though their "beginning in righteousness" at present and their perfection in righteousness at the *eschaton* contribute to their being declared righteous by God, ultimately their justification depends solely on what Christ has done and will continue to do *in* them and *for* them, rather than any moral activity of their own, which ends up being superfluous.

The "Joyous Exchange"

Perhaps the primary conceptual difficulty regarding Luther's idea of the "joyous exchange" between Christ and believers is the question of whether this exchange should be understood forensically or in terms of an actual exchange of substances or realities. According to a forensic understanding, at the same time that Christ's righteousness is reckoned to believers, their sin is reckoned to Christ, who expiates it by enduring its penalty. However, both Christ's righteousness and human sin can also be understood in an ontological sense as some type of actual substances or realities that are communicated or transferred between Christ and believers.

When understood forensically, the idea of a joyous exchange is an attempt to combine the idea of the imputation of Christ's righteousness to believers with that of a substitutionary understanding of Christ's death. This raises once more the problem of why both of these things should be necessary. If the sin of believers is reckoned to Christ, then they are without sin and thereby righteous; in that case, they have no need of Christ's righteousness. But if Christ's righteousness is reckoned to them, then this covers their own sin and they are no longer liable to punishment for that sin, since it has disappeared from God's sight; there is thus no need for their sin to be reckoned to Christ.

The notion of a joyous exchange between Christ and believers also raises problems for the penal substitution understanding of Christ's work in that, if the sins of believers are not reckoned to Christ until they become one with him through faith in the *present*, then it is not clear how it can be said that those sins were already assumed by Christ *in the past* when he endured their penalty on the cross. If Christ took "all the sins of all men" and women upon himself when he died,[46] then this took place independently of any faith union between them and Christ, and such a union is not necessary. In other words, a penal substitution view maintains that the sin of *all people* was transferred to Christ *in the past* when he died on the cross, whereas according to the idea of a joyous exchange, strictly speaking, only the sin of *believers* is transferred to Christ and this takes place *in the present* as they are united to Christ by faith. When Luther says of Christ and the soul, "let faith come between them and sins, death, and damnation will be Christ's, while grace, life, and salvation will be the soul's," it is clear that this joyous exchange takes place only where there is faith.[47]

Luther's idea of the joyous exchange can be understood not only in a forensic sense but in a literal, real, or ontological sense. In this case, both sin and righteousness are seen as some type of substance or power that can be transferred from one person to another. When Luther says that alien righteousness "is not instilled all at once" but that "it begins, makes progress, and is finally perfected at the end through death," it appears that this righteousness here cannot simply be understood in a forensic sense as something merely *accounted* or *imputed* to believers but is something *imparted* to them.[48] Similarly, when Luther speaks of Christ "absorbing" the sins of believers into himself,[49] his words imply that these sins have some objective reality of their own and are thus capable of being transferred from believers to Christ so as to be absorbed in some way into his being, where they are subsequently devoured or disappear.

This kind of understanding of the joyous exchange has recently been defended by a number of Finnish Lutheran scholars headed by Tuomo Mannermaa. For Mannermaa, who looks to the Eastern Orthodox doctrine of *theosis* to interpret the idea of a joyous exchange, Luther's doctrine of justification revolves around the notion that "faith denotes a real union with the person of Christ."[50] In this union, Christ is really and ontologically present: "Luther regards the ontological nature of the presence of Christ as absolutely real . . ."; "the union between the believer and Christ is so complete that these two become 'one person'."[51] Through his union with human beings, Christ takes upon himself their sins in an actual sense: "Christ has and bears the sins of all human beings *in a real manner* in the human nature he has assumed. The sins of humankind are not only imputed to Christ; he 'has' the sins in his human nature."[52] At the same time, because Christ is divine and thus possesses in himself all the divine attributes, including righteousness, those who are united to him share in those attributes: "The presence of Christ in faith is real, and he is present in it with all his essential attributes, such as righteousness, blessing, life, power, peace, and so forth."[53] Thus, because "the person of Christ *is*, in an ontologically real manner, righteousness,"[54] his righteousness is not only *imputed* to those who are joined to him by faith but actually *imparted* to them. Justification thus involves receiving not only the grace of being *accounted* righteous in a forensic sense but the gift of an actual righteousness that transforms the believer ontologically; according to Simo Peura, a Finnish Luther scholar closely associated with Mannermaa, "Christ himself is the grace that covers a sinner and hides him from God's wrath, and Christ himself is the gift that renews the sinner internally and makes him righteous."[55]

It is questionable, however, whether such an interpretation of the joyous exchange is faithful to Luther's thought. Luther may perhaps have regarded things such as righteousness, justice, grace, life, and perhaps even sin as "substances" having an ontological reality of their own that would enable them to be transferred between Christ and believers, yet this is not by any means certain. As we shall see in the next chapter, such an understanding of the joyous exchange appears to be more in continuity with the Roman Catholic teaching that Luther sought to replace, in which grace and righteousness are something "infused" into human beings. In fact, according to this interpretation, Christ himself, or his divinity, seems to constitute some type of magical, mysterious substance that transforms people through their contact with it. There are other ways of understanding the idea of Christ's presence rather than in substantial terms. Christ might be said to be present, for example, through the *activity* he carries out in believers or the influence he exerts on them in some way.[56] It is also possible to understand Christ's presence in a mystical fashion that may be distinguished from an ontological union of substances or essences. Exactly how Luther conceived of this presence is not clear.[57]

Precisely what meaning and purpose Christ's life and death have according to such an idea is also problematic. If all that were necessary were the uniting of the divine and human natures or substances, the incarnation of God's Son would have been sufficient to accomplish this. How do Christ's life and death contribute to producing in him this righteous, divine substance that he can now communicate to those who believe in him? Did he not already possess this "ontologically real" righteousness at birth by virtue of his being divine? Or is it instead something he had to accumulate or acquire over the course of his earthly life and then more fully in his death and resurrection? Is this righteous substance some entity that can be quantified, so that he had more at the end of his life than he had at the beginning? In fact, it is not even clear why the incarnation was necessary: If the Holy Spirit is divine, and if God can pour out the Holy Spirit into the hearts of human beings even *before* the incarnation of God's Son and independently of it (as the Old Testament attests), what need was there for God to become human in order to unite human nature to the divine nature? And if it is faith rather than the incarnation that unites believers to Christ in the present, then it is what the living, exalted Christ does *now* that saves them, since it is only at present that he communicates this divine, righteous substance to them and absorbs their sinful substance into himself. The only meaning that Christ's life, death, and resurrection can then have is that, without those events, it would have been impossible for Christ to do what he does now by sharing his righteousness with believers and absorbing their sin into himself. Those events must therefore be interpreted as having had the aim of building up in him some righteous substance that he might then communicate to believers from heaven as they are joined to him by faith.

Similar questions arise with regard to the sin of believers. When people sin, does some type of sinful substance or ontological reality build up in them? Can this substance or ontological reality then be transmitted in some way to another person, such as Christ? Does Christ somehow "absorb" or "neutralize" this substance or ontological reality and, if so, does he do so by virtue of his divinity, which should itself be understood as some type of substance? Is all of this analogous to some type of chemical reaction? Once this sin has been communicated to Christ to be absorbed by him, does it cease to exist in believers? Does it begin to develop and accumulate once more when they sin again? The idea that the sins of believers are "absorbed" by Christ also raises the question of when this happens, that is, the same question noted previously with respect to the forensic interpretation of the joyous exchange: How can the sins that believers commit or accumulate at present be "absorbed" by Christ in the past? It seems to be the "present Christ" who absorbs sin now, rather than something Christ did when he died.

The Finnish interpretation of the notion of a joyous exchange is also problematic in that it confuses the idea of an objective union of natures between Christ and all people by virtue of the incarnation with that of a subjective union of persons between Christ and believers through faith. As noted above, Luther appears to understand the union as something that takes place only where there is faith. In Eastern Orthodox and patristic thought, however, the idea is that, by assuming the human nature common to all people, God's Son becomes joined to all human beings universally; thus he takes upon himself or absorbs into himself the sin of all, while communicating the qualities of his divine nature to all. If this is understood in the sense of an exchange of substances such as sin and righteousness between Christ and human beings, then this exchange takes place *prior* to faith and *independently* of it.

While Luther undoubtedly spoke of Christ taking on himself the sins of all humanity, he seems generally to have understood this in terms of taking on himself the *guilt* and *punishment* of the sins of all people, rather than some type of sinful substance. For example, in the same sentence that he affirms that Christ "has and bears the sins of all in his body," he says that he took these sins "in order to make satisfaction for them with his own blood."[58] It also seems that for Luther Christ takes the sins of humanity upon himself *at his passion and death*, rather than when he assumed human nature at the incarnation, as in Eastern thought and Mannermaa's interpretation of Luther.[59] In addition, Luther seems to have followed the Western idea that Christ's human nature had to be *sinless* so that he might be qualified to die for the sins of others, rather than the Eastern idea that Christ assumed *sinful*, diseased human nature at the incarnation so as to heal it from within.[60]

A more serious problem, however, is that if Christ is said to have assumed into himself the sin of all humanity at the incarnation, then are not all human beings without sin independently of whether they come to faith or not? And if Christ joined the divine nature to the one human nature in which all people share, then are not all people one with him so as to receive the righteousness he communicates? In other words, why is a subjective response necessary for these things to take place? If faith is necessary in order for one to be one person with Christ, then it must be said that the union of *all* people with Christ either exists only "in principle" or "potentially" but not "actually," or that when people who have already been united to Christ by virtue of his incarnation do not come to faith, they are "dis-united" from him. The same problem is evident when it is claimed that "[a]fter the Logos has become flesh and is immersed (*submersus*) in all sins, all sins are immersed in him, and there is no sin anywhere else that is not in his person":[61] When people do not come to faith or fall from faith, are their sins *transferred back* to them so that they are no longer immersed in Christ? And does the righteousness that they received from Christ by virtue of the fact that he united the divine nature to the human nature revert back to Christ so that it is no longer theirs? Or was it never actually theirs in the first place? A similar problem arises with regard to baptism when it is said that "through the sacramental act of baptism God binds himself ontologically to a sinner and is one with him through his whole earthly life, if he adheres to Christ in faith":[62] If one *does not* adhere to Christ in faith or falls back into unbelief, is the ontological union with God undone or terminated? Or did it perhaps never exist in the first place? In either case, baptism seems to be understood magically as effecting an ontological union with Christ, yet without a subjective response of faith it has no effect or loses that effect.

Eastern theologians have generally sought to address these problems by speaking of a process in which the divine nature permeates the human nature shared by all people like leaven gradually permeates dough: "From the one man Jesus divine life can spread to all human persons because of the ontological interconnectedness of humankind. Our Lord, St. Paul, and following them St. Gregory the Theologian compare humankind to a single lump of dough. In the human Jesus divine life is introduced into this dough-like leaven and spreads from that one point to permeate the whole lump."[63] Once more, however, it is not clear what role faith plays in this, since the process appears to take place automatically: just as dough does not need faith in order to be gradually transformed by the leaven, so "all human persons" apparently do not need faith in order to be transformed by the divine nature that has been introduced into their own nature.

A further problem arises when it is claimed that Christ's righteousness is something that is *both* imputed *and* imparted to believers by Christ. If that is the case, is it the righteousness imputed to them forensically that ultimately constitutes the basis for their being declared righteous by God or the actual righteousness imparted to them and instilled in their hearts? The Finnish theologians, for example, seek to maintain both of these ideas in speaking of Christ and righteousness as both favor (or grace) and gift,[64] yet how these two ideas are to be combined is not clear. If the righteousness of Christ reckoned to them forensically constitutes the basis for their justification, then they have no need for the actual righteousness of Christ to be imparted to them in order to be justified; this imparted righteousness thus ends up being superfluous. To say that they need this imparted righteousness in order to be justified would mean that the righteousness of Christ imputed to them is insufficient for their justification and that it needs to be supplemented by another righteousness that is not merely forensic.

However, if believers are justified on account of the actual righteousness of Christ that is imparted to them, then it is not clear why they should also require the forensic righteousness of Christ. In this case, it must be argued that, because this actual righteousness is incomplete, Christ's righteousness must be reckoned to believers at present until they are perfected in righteousness. Yet rather than reckoning *Christ's* righteousness to them, God may simply reckon to them at present *their own future righteousness*, which will some day be perfected. In this case, they have no need for the imputation of Christ's righteousness in order to be justified.

For all of these reasons, Luther's idea of a joyous exchange is extremely problematic. Yet it becomes even more problematic when it is read through the lens of the Eastern Orthodox doctrine of *theosis*, as the Finnish Lutheran theologians have done.

Justification and a Revelational Understanding of Christ's Work

In light of the many problems raised by the satisfaction and penal substitution views of Christ's work and the many difficulties arising from the effort to make these the basis for the doctrine of justification, many Protestant theologians have developed other understandings of Christ's work and incorporated these into their teaching on justification. As noted at the outset of this chapter, some have adhered to the view of atonement commonly attributed to Abelard, according to which Christ's death saves human beings by providing them with an example or model to imitate or inciting them to greater love. The problem with making this the basis for justification, however, is that it seems to make justification depend on the moral renewal that Christ's death brings about in believers. This would stand diametrically opposed to the Protestant view of justification by faith alone and thus would seem to be irreconcilable with it.

This difficulty was resolved by some Protestant theologians by arguing that justification is ultimately based not on Christ's death but on God's mercy, love, and favor alone, which are for *all* people. In this case, as the liberal Protestant theologians never tired of insisting, God did not need to be reconciled to human beings through Christ's death, nor was God wrathful toward them. Thus it was not necessary for Christ to obtain forgiveness or propitiate God's wrath on the cross. God is *always* willing to forgive and God's justice is not opposed to God's mercy.

This was essentially the teaching of Albrecht Ritschl. Ritschl rejected outright the idea that God was wrathful at human sin and thus needed to be appeased through Christ's death in order to forgive that sin or remit its penalty.[65] The problem was not that God had to be made willing to forgive but that human beings were unprepared to receive this forgiveness and believe in it.[66] According to Ritschl, the basis upon which human beings are forgiven is merely the love, grace, and mercy of God, which are for *all* of humanity. In order to be justified, all that is necessary is that human beings come to believe in God's love for them and God's acceptance of them in spite of their sins: "The ground of justification, or the forgiveness of sins, is the benevolent, gracious, merciful purpose of God to vouchsafe to sinful men the privilege of access to himself. The form in which sinners appropriate this gift is faith, that is, the emotional trust in God. . . . Through trust in God's grace the alienation of sinners from God, which was essentially connected with the unrelieved feeling of guilt, is removed."[67] Thus it is not *God* who must be changed but *human beings*, since human guilt is a problem not for God but for human beings themselves, whose feelings of guilt distance them from God: "Justification, then, signifies the bringing back of the sinner into nearness with God, the removal of the alienating effect of the existent opposition to God and the accompanying consciousness of guilt."[68]

For Ritschl, Christ and his death manifest God's love to human beings and reveal that fellowship with God is possible. Christ's objective in life and death, therefore, was to live in a new relationship with God and with others so that others might come to live in the same relationships.[69] Christ is "the bearer of the perfect revelation of God" and the content of this revelation is "the love of God to sinners."[70] Christ's death only saves people in the sense that it brings about a change, not *in God*, but *in them*, turning them away from sin and to God: "the death of Christ serves to beget in us the new life, through the power which this event exercises upon the heart, inasmuch as by it sin is broken at the very heart of the life of this world."[71]

In more recent years, a similar view of the role of Christ and his death has been put forward by Gerhard Forde. Like Ritschl, Forde questions the Anselmian and penal substitution understandings of Christ's work, insisting that God is by nature only merciful and forgiving and does not need to be propitiated.[72] God is characterized by "unconditional and universal forgiveness" that is "full and free with no strings attached"; God's love is also "radical and unconditional."[73] Nevertheless, because human beings desire to ascend to God by keeping God's law but find this impossible, they see God as "a threat and a terror" and experience God as wrath.[74] This wrath is "the alienation, the guilt, the lostness. . . which we feel and experience"; "it is the reality of God's absence from us, as the *deus absconditus*," as well as "the inescapable reality of God's omnipresence as the God of law."[75] God has decided "not to be for us the God of wrath," yet in our alienation we "are bound to have it so," insisting that God be this God.[76] Due to our view of God as wrath, we cannot "actually receive this God and trust this God's self-giving"; for this reason, "God is not the problem, we are."[77]

According to Forde, however, God has also made this problem God's own so as to destroy the barrier and put an end to the separation.[78] God does this by coming to us in Jesus in order to rescue us "from our insistence on having a God of wrath."[79] Jesus "opened a new vision of God for those who accepted him" by manifesting God's love.[80] Above all, he announced God's forgiveness to all and actually said to others, "I forgive you in God's name."[81] "God gives himself in Jesus because he will not be a God of wrath."[82] Yet because we human beings could not accept this, "we killed him. We would not have it."[83] Jesus' death was thus the price God had to pay for choosing to be a God of mercy for us: "God will not be known other than as a God of mercy. The cross is the price God, in mercy, pays to be concretely for us. . . . The cross is the price of mercy. It is not paid to God; however, it is paid *by* God. . . . The cross is what it costs God to be who he will be for us, rather than the one we insist on."[84] At the same time, Jesus' resurrection is his vindication, proving that "he was right and we are wrong."[85] This makes it possible for the word of forgiveness to be communicated to all: "What Jesus won for us on the cross is precisely the right to say the saving word of forgiveness to all universally, and he commissioned his followers to *do* so."[86]

All of this means that, for Forde, what is necessary is that God be changed from wrath to mercy, not in God's own self, but in the way that human beings perceive and experience God. It is in this sense that Jesus puts away God's wrath, that is, our separation from God. Forde insists that "God is not changed in the sense of being *made* merciful by the historical event. The event takes place because God *is* merciful and desires to be so concretely *for us* in spite of our opposition and bondage."[87] Against this background, Forde *is* willing to affirm that the cross changes God but only in the sense that "God serves notice that he will not be any more the absent one, the hidden one, the naked God of wrath. In the cross God becomes 'other,' the God of mercy for us. God comes. God says no to being a God of wrath; God dies to that."[88]

Forde also speaks of Jesus' death as necessary for human salvation, yet this necessity is rooted in the fact that human beings reject God's love and mercy. "Jesus had to die because God is forgiving and because God insists on being so. Jesus died precisely because he said, 'I forgive you in God's name.' He died because we would not have it."[89] "The necessity for the cross roots in God's decision to be a God of mercy in spite of our bondage and rejection."[90] Atonement is thus something done *to us* rather than to God. "Atonement occurs when God gives himself in such fashion as to create a people pleasing to God, a people no longer under law or wrath, a people who love and trust God. When God succeeds in that, God is 'satisfied'."[91]

Although views such as these are distinct from that generally attributed to Abelard, primarily in that the objective of the cross is not merely to provide an example for human beings or kindle love for God in them, they revolve around the notion that Christ and his death are salvific through *what they reveal*. This revelation may be concerning the nature of God or some divine attribute, such as the extent of God's love and mercy and God's willingness to freely forgive and accept sinners, or it may be about the nature of human beings or the world:

Christ's death reveals "the nature of human life on earth," shows believers "the costs of human sin," "unmasks the violence of the scapegoat mechanism," or demonstrates "that the objectives of the reign of God are not accomplished by violence."[92] This revelation may be *descriptive* in the sense that it communicates some knowledge that human beings did not previously have or *prescriptive* in that instructs human beings as to what they should do.

What distinguishes this revelational understanding of Christ's work from others is that it does not posit any type of objective salvation according to which all humanity has been saved from sin and its penalty or reconciled to God; only those who are brought to faith and repentance by what Christ did are saved. The purpose of what has taken place in Christ is to bring about a proper subjective response in human beings, that is, to change *them* rather than changing God.

At times this revelational view of Christ's work is combined with ideas from other views, such as those to be considered below. In fact, while this view has commonly been considered antithetical to satisfaction and penal substitution views, in reality they can also be seen as complementary. Often, for example, proponents of satisfaction and penal substitution views affirm that Christ's death reveals the gravity of human sin as well as God's condemnation of that sin and that Christ's resurrection reveals that God has accepted Christ's sacrificial death on behalf of others.[93] Once Christ's death and resurrection are said to be salvific through what they reveal, however, the question arises as to whether human beings are ultimately saved by those events themselves or only by the revelation they bring. It must also be asked whether the purpose of those events was to effect some change in God or in human beings. In other words, it would appear that it is no longer Christ's life, death, and resurrection in themselves that reconcile people to God but the subjective response these events make possible through what they reveal; in this case, it is this response which constitutes the basis for justification rather than Christ's death per se.

In a sense, however, it is still possible to speak of an objective justification embracing all people when it is affirmed that God's forgiveness is open to all unconditionally. In this case, *all* are justified, even unbelievers, though the basis for this justification is God's universal love rather than Christ's death. From God's side, there are no obstacles to accepting sinners and apparently there is no divine wrath at sin either. While some would see this as a strength of this view, it raises the problem that God ends up accepting sin, evil, and injustice just as readily as God accepts goodness and righteousness, since in God there is no real condemnation of wrongdoing. Naturally, it can be said that God wants human beings to refrain from sin, evil, and injustice for their own well-being; but if they do not, God apparently does not act to put a stop to these things or to punish those who insist on practicing them. This seems to represent a *lack* of love and mercy on God's part, in that God does nothing to bring oppression and injustice to an end by acting on behalf of those who suffer these things.

A number of other criticisms have been made of the revelational type of interpretation of Christ's death. Feminist theologians have claimed that it still ascribes a positive value to suffering and violence, since these continue to be seen as redemptive.[94] When people, especially women, are called to follow Christ's example of self-sacrifice, the result can be injustice, victimization, and the glorification of violence. Some theologians have criticized the fact that this revelational view of Christ's work does not regard his death as absolutely necessary for salvation, though others would regard this as a virtue rather than a problem. An argument for necessity is possible, however, if it is claimed that what was revealed through Christ and the cross could have been revealed in no other way or that the only way human beings could be changed and brought to repentance in the way God desired was through these events. Naturally, this argument is problematic, especially since it seems that much of what was revealed through Christ and his death is not entirely new or unique. Many have also argued that this view of Christ's work fails to do justice to the New Testament teaching, which seems clearly to relate Christ's death or blood with the forgiveness of sins. The New Testament speaks of Christ not only relating to human beings on behalf of God but also relating to God on behalf of human beings; this vicarious aspect of his work is often lost when the objective of his life and death is defined primarily or exclusively in terms of bringing about some change in human beings by means of what these events reveal.

Justification and the *Christus Victor* Idea

Thanks especially to the publication of Gustav Aulén's book *Christus Victor* in 1931, it has become widely recognized that the so-called "classic" idea of redemption is particularly prominent in Luther's thought. According to this idea, "Christ—Christus Victor—fights against and triumphs over the evil powers of the world, the 'tyrants' under which mankind is in bondage and suffering, and in him God reconciles the world to himself."[95] Often overlooked is the fact that this understanding of Christ's work appears in three different forms that correspond to ideas already considered in this chapter: the "victory" obtained by Christ can be understood *forensically*, *ontologically*, or in a *revelational* manner.

The forensic form of the *Christus Victor* motif affirms that the devil lost his rights over human beings when he took Christ's life, since he had no right to do so due to Christ's being perfectly righteous and innocent. This idea is found in the writings of many of the church fathers.[96] It was also developed by Luther,

who viewed not only the devil but sin, death, and the law as "tyrants" oppressing human beings. The law, for example, "accused, intimidated, and condemned" Christ even though it had no jurisdiction over him, since he was
innocent; and because it overstepped its limits, "it loses its jurisdiction not only
over Christ—whom it attacked and killed without any right anyway—but also
over all who believe in him."[97] Similarly, "when death overcame him and slew
him, without however having any claim or cause against him, and he willingly
and innocently permitted himself to be slain, death became indebted to him,
having done him wrong and having sinned against him"; thus Christ "has an
honest claim against it" and in this way death no longer has any rights over
human beings.[98]

Once it is understood, however, that it is *God* who has subjected human
beings to the powers of sin, death, the devil, and the law as punishment for their
sins,[99] it becomes clear that there is no real difference between this view and the
penal substitution view: by voluntarily submitting to the punishment imposed by
God's justice on sinners as their substitute, the righteous and innocent Christ
delivers them from that punishment. This involves saving human beings from
God's righteous wrath, which for Luther is counted among the powers hostile
to sinful human beings: "our Lord Jesus Christ is the one and only Victim with
which satisfaction has been made to the wrath of God."[100] The fact that here
and elsewhere Luther readily combines the idea of satisfaction with that of
Christ's victory over the various powers that are expressions of God's wrath
makes it clear that, rather than constituting an *alternative* to the penal substitution
view of Christ's work, this understanding of the *Christus Victor* idea is simply
another expression of it: once Christ has endured God's righteous wrath in the
form of the personified powers of sin, death, and the law, God's justice is
satisfied and that wrath is exhausted.

For this very reason, however, the forensic understanding of the *Christus
Victor* idea raises most of the same problems as the penal substitution understanding of Christ's work. God appears to be subject to God's own justice, so
that God cannot act contrary to that justice by simply delivering human beings
from the powers that oppress them through an act of divine omnipotence.
When these powers are personified, it appears that God's justice makes it
necessary for God to respect their rights over human beings, rather than
snatching human beings from them by force. From patristic times, many have
criticized the idea that God had to respect the devil's rights, arguing that the
devil had in fact subjected human beings to himself by deceiving them; others,
however, responded by claiming that human beings had voluntarily subjected
themselves to the devil. In the latter case, it appears that human beings are saved

by Christ *against* their will, since they have chosen subjection to the devil over subjection to God.

An *ontological* understanding of the *Christus Victor* idea is somewhat different from the *forensic* one in that, whereas in the latter the evil forces such as the devil lose their *legal rights* over human beings, in the former these forces are *overpowered* by Christ by virtue of his divinity. This idea is also found in Luther in combination with the forensic idea: "sin, death, the curse of the Law, and the wrath and judgment of God" were "savage monsters" that "could not be overcome by any human power. . . . For to conquer the sin of the world, death, the curse, and the wrath of God in himself—this is the work, not of any creature but of the divine power. Therefore it was necessary that he who was to conquer these in himself should be true God by nature."[101] Some of the church fathers taught that God had offered Christ to the devil as a ransom in exchange for the human beings under his power and that the devil had accepted this deal, not realizing that hidden under of the veil of Christ's humanity was his divinity; like a fish that swallows a baited hook, the devil was unwittingly overcome when Christ rose from the dead by virtue of his divinity. In this way, the devil lost his power over both Christ and human beings. This same basic idea is found in Luther as well.[102]

In principle, the idea that the devil is overpowered by Christ's divinity can be understood both in the sense that the devil no longer has the power to inflict death on human beings and in the sense that the devil has lost his power to incite human beings to sin. This latter idea, however, is not characteristic of Luther's thought, since believers continue to struggle against the devil throughout their life on earth and remain under the influence of sin as a power. Furthermore, human beings must be said to sin of their own free will and not only due to the activity of the devil or the presence of the power of sin in their hearts; otherwise, once the power of the devil or sin in them had been broken, they would cease to sin. To claim that believers are declared righteous because sin and the devil have lost their power to incite them to sin would also be problematic for Protestant thought in that it would involve basing justification on the moral change that takes place in believers as a result of Christ's victory over the devil. For this reason, a *Christus Victor* understanding of Christ's work generally only claims that human beings have been delivered from the power of *death* and not of *sin*. The difficulty, however, lies in determining whether to see death as a punishment inflicted on sinners by God in God's justice or as the work of evil powers such as the devil that act independently of God and perhaps even *against* God's will.

Both a forensic and an ontological interpretation of the *Christus Victor* idea are regarded by most people today as overly mythical. Few would want to interpret literally the idea that the devil has been defeated by Christ in an actual face-to-face struggle or as the result of a commercial transaction. It is also problematic to speak of sin, death, the law, and God's wrath as if these were personal beings with a mind and will of their own in the way that Luther does. The *Christus Victor* idea also raises the same difficulties as other interpretations that posit an objective redemption accomplished by Christ affecting humanity as a whole. In addition to the fact that it seems to contradict reality, in that human beings appear to be just as much under the powers of sin, death, and evil as they were prior to Christ's death, it raises problems once faith is regarded as necessary for salvation. Those who do *not* come to faith must be said to remain subject to those powers and *not* to have been liberated from them by Christ, unless it is claimed that their unbelief results in their becoming enslaved to those forces once more after they had initially been liberated from them. Ultimately, it seems that *faith* is what delivers people from these powers and not Christ directly. Christ's victory only appears to make it *possible* for those who have faith to be saved from sin, death, and the devil, which implies that previous to Christ it was *not* possible for people to be saved from these things, even if they did have faith. The *Christus Victor* view also conceives of salvation in terms of being liberated from evil powers, rather than being forgiven or declared righteous by God, so that it is difficult to combine with the doctrine of justification. As noted above, Luther was able to base justification on the *Christus Victor* view only by seeing sin, death, the devil, and the law as expressions of God's righteous wrath against sinners and, in this context, defining justification not so much in terms of being declared righteous but being delivered from the punishment for sin imposed by God's justice.

While a revelational understanding of the *Christus Victor* view has never been prominent in Lutheran thought, in recent years it has become common in some theological circles. J. Denny Weaver, for example, has proposed a "narrative *Christus Victor* motif" in which "the death and resurrection of Jesus definitively reveal the basis of power in the universe, so that the invitation from God to participate in God's rule—to accept Jesus as God's anointed one—overcomes the forces of sin and reconciles sinners to God." Those who identify with Jesus in his death and resurrection therefore "have life in the reign of God."[103] Similarly, David Seeley has argued that in Paul's thought Jesus overcame sin and death in the sense that "sin exercised no rule over him. He was and remained free from it." Believers therefore can also be delivered from sin's power by re-enacting Jesus' death: "When Jesus' sinless death is re-enacted, it thus frees the re-enactor from Sin's hold. . . . The re-enactment of Jesus' death frees the believer from Sin and establishes him or her in righteousness. . . . As Jesus' obedience kept him free from

Sin's power, so also the believer who re-enacts that death is released from Sin and becomes obedient 'from the heart'."[104]

Like the other revelational views considered above, this understanding of the *Christus Victor* idea cannot serve as the basis for a doctrine of objective justification. Christ's work does not in itself actually deliver human beings from the powers of sin and Satan; it only helps to make it possible for them to be delivered as they learn from and are transformed by the revelation coming through Christ and his death and resurrection. Forgiveness is not a problem, since it is available to all prior to and independently of Christ's life and death. What matters is that human beings struggle against sin and evil through their own efforts, inspired, empowered, and illuminated by what has taken place in Christ. Of course, to the extent that salvation is made to depend on a moral response to what Christ did, such a view is in conflict with the Protestant doctrine that human beings are saved by faith alone.

Justification and Participation in Christ

As noted above, the idea of a personal union with Christ was particularly characteristic of Luther's thought. John Calvin also spoke in these terms.[105] In the early twentieth century, however, greater attention came to be focused on this idea thanks especially to the work of Pauline scholars such as Adolf Deissman and Albert Schweitzer, who argued that Paul conceived of the relation between Christ and believers in mystical terms.[106] At the same time, the History of Religions school came to claim that the ancient Greek mystery religions and Gnostic thought had exerted an important influence on Paul's understanding of Christ and salvation. On this basis, it was argued that Paul not only spoke of a mystical union between Christ and believers but taught that believers mystically participated in the event of Christ's death and resurrection. Salvation was thus understood in terms of dying and rising with Christ. Eventually, due especially to the work of E. P. Sanders, this understanding of Christ's work was labeled a "participatory" understanding. According to Sanders, the basic idea is that "by *sharing* in Christ's death, one dies to the *power* of sin. . . ."[107] This constitutes the basis for one's justification and forgiveness, since when "one dies with Christ to the power of sin and lives in the Spirit . . ., one stops (and is acquitted of) sinning and produces the fruit of the Spirit."[108]

The idea of participating in Christ's death can be understood in a *forensic*, *ontological*, or *ethical* sense. According to a forensic understanding, God looks on believers *as if* they had died and risen with Christ. This is actually a form of the penal substitution view: because Christ underwent the penalty for human sin on the cross, God looks on all those who are joined to Christ by faith as if they had undergone that penalty as well; they "died in God's sight in Christ's death."[109] In this way, they are delivered from that penalty and are no longer subject to death. While this understanding of participation can therefore serve as a basis for the doctrine of justification, it raises the same problems as the penal substitution view of which it is an expression.

The notion of participation can also be understood in an ontological manner. While Sanders does not use the word "ontological," he does insist that Paul's words should be understood in a "real" and literal sense. Yet Sanders himself was at a loss to explain how this should be conceived, and ultimately concluded that "what Paul thought cannot be concretely appropriated by Christians today."[110] Mannermaa claims that such an idea of participation is found in Luther's thought as well: "When participating in Christ, the believer shares in an ontological and real manner in what is 'death to death' (i.e., life)" and "'sin to sin' (i.e., righteousness)."[111]

While this real or ontological union with Christ in his death can be understood to take place only when one comes to faith, it can also be viewed as embracing all human beings independently of any faith on their part. Karl Barth, for example, looked to the patristic idea of a union between Christ and humanity as a whole by virtue of Christ's assumption of human nature in order to claim that all people died with Christ when he did. "For then and there, in the person of Christ taking our place, we were present, being crucified and dying with him. . . . We died: the totality of all sinful men. . . . His death was the death of all."[112] For Barth, faith does not effect this union with Christ in his death but is merely a recognition that one has already died with Christ by virtue of the fact that one shares the same human nature with him. Barth combined the ideas of participation and substitution in affirming that, because all have died with Christ, Christ can be said to have died in the place of all because they must no longer die.[113]

According to an ontological understanding of participation in Christ's death, salvation involves first and foremost the transformation of sinners. While believers are forgiven and justified, the basis for this is the ontological change effected in them rather than what Christ did for them per se: they are forgiven because they have been transformed, rather than being transformed because they have been forgiven. Undoubtedly, this transformation can be understood as an act of God in which believers play only a passive role and thus can be said to take place by faith alone. However, this implies that the ontological transformation takes place magically, mechanically, or automatically in believers simply by virtue of their union with Christ. Faith appears to be necessary only in that, without it, the magical or mechanical process does not "work." Questions also arise as to whether this dying with Christ is to be regarded as something that takes place over time or as a one-time event. The relation between the ontological dying with Christ and a life of obedience and righteousness is also not clear: Is this new life brought about automatically as a result of an ontological change in a person, so that when one "dies with Christ to the power of sin," one actually stops sinning, as Sanders affirmed?[114] And does the forgiveness of sins depend in some way on the progress one makes in righteousness and obedience or does God forgive and justify a person simply because God has effected an ontological change in that person?

As I have argued at length elsewhere,[115] this kind of participatory understanding of Christ's death raises not only serious conceptual difficulties but historical ones as well. It therefore appears quite doubtful that it represents faithfully the thought of Paul. For this reason, it seems best to understand his language about dying with Christ in an ethical sense, in which believers consciously identify with Christ in his death. They choose to die with him in the sense that they "crucify their flesh" and consider themselves dead to sin, no longer letting it exercise dominion over them, as Paul affirms (Gal 5:24; Rom 6:11-12). This does not involve any type of ontological or forensic participation in the event of Christ's death but merely taking up one's cross in faith to follow Christ in serving others (Mark 8:34; 10:43-45). Yet, rather than constituting the basis upon which they are justified, this can be seen as an expression and consequence of their faith.

Reconsidering the New Testament Teaching regarding Christ's Death and Justification

To understand the relation between Jesus' death and justification in the New Testament, including especially the Pauline letters, it is necessary to see Jesus' death against the background of the aims of his ministry as a whole.[116] According to the Gospels, Jesus saw himself as God's chosen instrument to bring God's blessings of salvation and wholeness into the lives of others. He did this in many ways: through his teaching and healing activity, by calling others to follow him in living according to God's will as he defined it, and by preparing disciples to carry on his same work. In general, his way of relating to people on various levels had as its objective the wholeness or *shalom* of those people themselves as well as that of others through them.

As noted above, in Jewish thought the blessings of salvation and wholeness depended on God's people observing God's law and approaching God through the means established by that law, including especially the worship that revolved around the Jerusalem temple. As a result of Jesus' ministry, however, many came to believe that those blessings were now mediated *through Jesus*. This belief then led to the conviction that what was offered through Jesus was greater than what was offered through the law and the temple.[117] This idea could be interpreted both in the sense that Jesus was *above* the law and temple and thus superseded them and in the sense that Jesus constituted the *fulfillment* of the law and temple, which pointed to him. In the latter case, Jesus was not seen as *abolishing* or *replacing* the law and temple; rather, the law and the temple provided the background against which Jesus' work was interpreted and, in this way, both his ministry as well as the law and temple were filled with new meaning.

The Gospels repeatedly present much of Jesus' work as being aimed at those who were believed not to have access to God and God's blessings for various reasons.[118] Many were regarded as impure either because of some physical ailment, such as leprosy or a flow of blood, or because of their activities, such as collecting taxes or dedicating themselves to other tasks that prevented them from maintaining ritual purity. There were also the poor, who could not participate in the temple worship as fully as those who were better off economically due to the costs involved in traveling to Jerusalem and presenting sacrifices; many have interpreted Jesus' "cleansing" of the temple as a protest against a system carried out in God's name that contributed significantly to the enrichment of some and the impoverishment of others. Jesus was also criticized for having fellowship with the "sinners" who did not keep the law. In fact, to some extent, all of these different groups of people could be regarded as sinners, since the common belief was that, if one suffered physical ailments or poverty, this was a sign that one was under God's judgment for one's sins.

As observed in chapter 2, in both his teaching and his practice, Jesus was viewed by many as calling into question the traditional interpretations of the law: for him, true obedience to the law involved fulfilling the principles underlying it. Because in Jewish thought righteousness was defined on the basis of the law, this involved a reinterpretation not only of the law but of righteousness. Righteousness was to be defined no longer simply in terms of observance of the law but of obedience to what Jesus taught and exemplified in word and deed. This also involved redefining who belonged to the community of the righteous, that is, the community of those "justified" by God: many of those considered "sinners" were now included in that community, while many of those generally regarded as righteous were no longer counted as members.

According to the Gospels, these aspects of Jesus' teaching and practice led to conflicts with the religious authorities. These conflicts reached their head in Jerusalem. The Gospels present Jesus going up to Jerusalem expecting to suffer and die there in order that the Scriptures might be fulfilled (Matt 16:21; Mark 8:31; Luke 9:22). The idea of the fulfillment of Scripture is prominent throughout all of the passion accounts (Matt 26:24, 31, 54-56; 27:9, 35; Mark 14:49;

Luke 18:31; 24:26-27, 44-47). When Jesus' death is spoken of as "necessary" in many of these passages, this necessity has to do with the fulfillment of the Scriptures. Never is it said or implied that Jesus' death was necessary because it was the only way God could forgive sins and still remain righteous or because it was impossible for God to save the world in any other way. This fulfillment of the Scriptures had to do, not only with certain passages or prophecies that pointed to Jesus' passion and death, but with the law in a broader sense, including what the law prescribed about access to God through the system of sacrificial worship at the temple as well as the promises of salvation to which the law pointed.

The words ascribed to Jesus at the Last Supper regarding the new covenant in his blood or the blood of the (new) covenant must be understood against this background (Matt 26:28; Mark 14:24; Luke 22:20; 1 Cor 11:25). By giving up his life and consequently being raised and exalted to God's right hand, a new covenant centered on Jesus would come into place. In this new covenant, people would have access to God and God's blessings *through Jesus*, who would constitute the new mediator. As the Letter to the Hebrews affirms, like the priests of the first covenant on the Day of Atonement, in his death Jesus had gone before God imploring God's forgiveness for the members of the covenant people; yet rather than taking the blood of animals, he had offered up his own blood as well as his own self or body (Heb 5:1-7; 9:11-14, 24). In this way, he had entered into God's presence and had become established as the one through whom all could now draw near to God (Heb 4:14-16; 10:19-22; cf. Eph 2:18; 3:12). God's blessings of salvation and forgiveness would now be given to those who lived under the new covenant established through Jesus' death. Entrance into this new covenant community would be on the basis of faith in Jesus as God's Son rather than on the basis of obedience to the Mosaic law.

The first believers interpreted Jesus' death and resurrection against the background of the idea that virtually everything found in the first covenant with Israel prefigured and pointed to what had taken place in Jesus. In Luke's Gospel, the risen Jesus is presented as interpreting to the disciples on the road to Emmaus everything written about him in the Scriptures, "beginning with Moses and all the prophets" (Luke 24:27), and then telling the rest of the disciples the same day: "These are my words that I spoke to you while I was still with you—that everything written about me in the law of Moses, the prophets, and the psalms must be fulfilled. . . . Thus it is written, that the Messiah is to suffer and to rise from the dead on the third day, and that repentance and forgiveness of sins is to be proclaimed in his name to all nations, beginning from Jerusalem" (Luke 24:44, 46). As in Matthew's Gospel, the apostles are sent out not just to the Jews but particularly to the "nations" or "Gentiles," who through faith and baptism are to be incorporated into the community of believers; there they are to await the final redemption that will take place at Jesus' second coming (Matt 28:19-20; Acts 1:8; cf. Mark 13:10).

According to this understanding of Jesus' work, it is not *his death in itself* that saves or redeems people but *all* that has taken and will take place through him. His death is salvific only because of what preceded and followed it and it must not be isolated from that context. It does not "effect" anything, such as a change in God or the world in general; nor did it have as its purpose that of revealing something previously unknown to human beings or changing human hearts. Jesus did not die in the place of others as their substitute, nor did his death or blood make satisfaction for human sins to God, God's justice, or God's law. In New Testament thought, God's judgment and God's wrath against human sin did not come to an end when Jesus died but remain in force until the final judgment. Human sin was not "transferred" to Christ at his incarnation or in his death in either a forensic or an ontological sense. Human beings of various times and places did not participate in the event of the cross, nor can they participate in that event now; they were not and are not mysteriously or ontologically joined to Christ, so that what happened to Christ thereby happened to them as well. Christ did not attain some type of righteousness by virtue of his incarnation, life, death, and resurrection that is now imputed to believers; nor is Christ's righteousness imparted, transferred, or communicated now to human beings, as if they might "participate" in it in some way. The biblical writers never affirm that Jesus' death was necessary because it was impossible for God to remit sins, justify sinners, overcome evil, or change human beings in any other way; nor do they speak of his death ushering in a new age or effecting some change in the human condition. *All of these ideas so deeply engrained not only in Christian theology but biblical scholarship are simply foreign to New Testament teaching and have been read back into the New Testament.*

What the New Testament *does* affirm is that people are saved *through* Jesus' death or blood (Rom 3:25; 5:9-10; Eph 1:7; 2:13, 16; Col 1:20, 22; Heb 13:12; Rev 1:5). This is not the same as affirming that his death or blood itself justifies them, redeems them, or reconciles them to God, as if it had some such "effect." Their justification, redemption, and reconciliation with God constituted Jesus' objective as well as that of God not only in Jesus' *death* but throughout his ministry, as he laid the foundation for people to live in a new relation with God and experience God's blessings by his teaching and example, by founding a community of followers, and by preparing his disciples to carry out the same kind of ministry he did. When his work in this regard led to conflict and the threat of the cross, he did not shrink from such a death but remained faithful to his mission until the end, offering up his life to God in obedience to God's will.

Jesus died trusting that God would bring to fulfillment everything to which Jesus had dedicated his life and in essence presenting such an implicit petition to God. God's response was to raise Jesus from the dead and exalt him to heaven so that he might pour out the Holy Spirit on the members of his community and might return some day to make the salvation of others for which he had lived and died a reality. In this way, by giving up his life in faithfulness to the mission given him, Jesus obtained for all those who by faith would come to form part of the new covenant community under him their justification, redemption, and reconciliation with God, since through Jesus they are accepted by God as righteous, live in peace with God and one another, and will one day be redeemed when Jesus returns.

In New Testament thought, there is both a *Godward* and a *humanward* aspect to what Jesus did in the past and continues to do at present until the end. Through his teaching and example he sought to bring about a new life in others, both those with whom he came into direct contact and those who would later come to form part of the community under him, so that they might relate differently to God and others, practicing righteousness and obedience to God's will; this is what Jesus did *in relation to human beings*. However, his work also has a Godward aspect in that he sought that God might accept those belonging to his community as righteous and forgive them their sins. This is what he sought from God as he gave up his life in faithfulness to the mission God had given him. He continues to intercede to God for others from God's right hand in heaven (Rom 8:34; Heb 7:25; 1 John 2:1) and also remains active in believers through the Holy Spirit, who guides and directs them on the basis of what Jesus did and said during his life (John 14:26; 16:13; Rom 8:14; Gal 4:6; 5:18—6:2; Tit 3:6).

For the New Testament writers, of course, because Jesus is God's Son and consistently acted out of obedience to God his Father, all of his work is *God's* work as well. God sent him to carry out a mission in the context of a divine plan, gave him over to death on the cross when Jesus' activity led to conflict, and finally glorified Jesus after his death and poured out the Holy Spirit through him. In this way, God established a new covenant through Jesus and his death, achieving the objective of having a community composed of both Jews and Gentiles who are committed to living as God's people as defined by Jesus.

The doctrine of election must be understood against the background of these ideas: the idea is not that God elected certain individuals but rather a *people* of which individuals can now come to form part. God's intention from the start was to establish a covenant not only with Israel but with people from all nations through Jesus (Rom 11:1-24; Gal 3:6-9; Eph 3:1-12; 1 Pet 1:2). According to the New Testament, the covenant God made with Israel under Moses prefigured, anticipated, and pointed to the new covenant God would make through Jesus (2 Cor 3:1-18; Heb 8:1-13; 9:15-28). For this reason, Jesus is consistently seen as the one who fulfills the Scriptures in many ways, including especially through his passion and death. However, the founding of the church, the ministry of the apostles, and the inclusion of people from all nations were also said to fulfill the Scriptures, since all of this constituted just as much a part of the divine plan as that which took place in Jesus (Acts 13:26-41; Rom 1:1-5; 4:9-25; Gal 4:21-31).

All that the New Testament affirms regarding the saving significance of Jesus' death must be understood against the background of these ideas. Jesus died for others and for their sins, not in the sense that his death enabled God to do something God could previously *not* do or satisfied some divine requirement for forgiveness, but in the sense that *Jesus gave up his life to establish the new covenant community in which people might now find salvation and the forgiveness of sins.* The relation between Jesus' death and forgiveness is thus not a *direct* one, as if forgiveness resulted directly from Jesus' death, but an *indirect* one, in that Jesus' death led to a community in the context of which forgiveness of sins is offered. He was given up on account of their trespasses (Rom 4:24-25) in that the trespasses committed both by those under the Mosaic law and by the nations made it necessary for a new and different covenant to be established in which people from both groups might find salvation; and in order for this covenant to be established, God gave Jesus over to death and then raised him up so that people might be justified as they live under him in this new covenant. Those who previously did *not* have access to God because of their sins now *do* have access to God thanks to Jesus and to the fact that he gave up his life so that such access might be available to them. He bore the sins of others in the sense that he went to his death seeking that others might obtain salvation and forgiveness through him in the context of the community that would be brought into being through his death. This was analogous to the way in which the high priest went before God on the Day of Atonement bearing the sins of God's covenant people in the sense of imploring God to accept and forgive them (Heb 9:26-28; 1 Pet 2:24).

As noted previously, in biblical thought it was not actually the blood or sacrifices themselves that obtained God's forgiveness and acceptance of those who repented but *the petitions of the priest who went before God with the blood and sacrifices on their behalf.* In the same way, *it was not Jesus' death or blood itself* which made expiation for sins but the implicit petition he offered up to God on behalf of others through his death; and in this way, he obtained from God for all of those who would live in faith, obedience, and righteousness under him the full forgiveness that had been promised under the Mosaic covenant but had not become a reality. Furthermore, because this forgiveness, acceptance, and justification are now available, not only to those living under the Mosaic covenant, but to people from all nations who live under Jesus in the new covenant established through his death, the New Testament affirms that he is the expiation or propitiation for others and that his blood (that is, the giving up of his life) cleanses and redeems them (Rom 3:25; 1 John 1:7; 2:2; 4:10; cf. Heb 1:4; 2:17). They are now accepted by God by virtue of the fact that Jesus gave up his life in order to obtain their inclusion among this new covenant people. In this sense, he offered himself up as a "ransom for many" (Matt 20:28; Mark 10:45; 1 Tim 2:6): in exchange for giving up his life in obedience to God's will, he obtained their redemption, forgiveness, and salvation, all of which is now to become a reality through him. His death is sacrificial in that he gave up his life and allowed his blood to be shed by those who put him to death so that others might be brought into fellowship with God and attain salvation as members of his community the church.

Of course, those living as members of the new covenant people are not perfect and continue to sin. Nevertheless, God accepts them on the basis of Jesus' intercession on their behalf. This intercession is based on the fact that as Jesus' disciples they are committed to the way of life that he taught and embodied. Yet the basis for the justification of those who form part of this new covenant community is not the righteousness of Christ imputed or imparted to them but *their own righteousness*;[119] though it always remains imperfect, this righteousness is brought about by Christ, both through his teaching and example in the past as well as what he continues to do in them now through the Holy Spirit in the context of the community of believers. In this sense, their righteousness may be spoken of as "alien" in that its origin is not in anything they have done but in what Christ and the Spirit do in them.

The reason that Christ's own righteousness does not need to be imputed to them is that in biblical thought God does not require perfection from people in order to justify them; in fact, such perfection is not even considered a possibility. Because believers are being transformed into new people through their relationship with Christ and the Spirit, God *simply forgives their sins without imposing any penalty for those sins either on them or on Christ*. Neither God nor God's law nor God's justice require that their sins be punished or that satisfaction be made for their sins. While they are no longer under God's wrath and condemnation, the reason for this is not that Jesus endured that wrath and condemnation in their stead but simply that, by virtue of Christ's past, present, and future activity in relation to them and in relation to God on their behalf, God puts away God's wrath and no longer threatens them with condemnation. There is free forgiveness on God's part, which in no way is considered to contradict God's justice. In Christ, *God accepts them as they are*, knowing that through Christ and the Spirit they are becoming the people God wants them to be *for their own good and for the good of others whom God also loves*. This is the only thing that could ever "satisfy" God, not the death of an innocent victim; God did not simply want one representative individual to be obedient or righteous but wants this from *all* people. For the same reason, God could not be pleased merely by reckoning the righteousness of Christ to others; God wants *all* to actually *become* righteous. Christ's righteousness is thus not imputed or imparted to believers, nor did his righteousness qualify him to die in their stead; rather, the commitment to righteousness and obedience of which his death was the greatest expression has led to a new situation in which they can be included among those justified as members of the new covenant community established through his life, death, and resurrection. This is what it means to affirm that Christ's "act of righteousness leads to justification and life for all" and that his obedience results in many being made righteous (Rom 5:18-19): through his obedience unto death in seeking to bring a new, righteous people into existence, what he sought has become a reality.

As believers follow Jesus in faith, because they leave behind their old way of life and begin a new life, they can be said to die with Christ; that is, they identify with him in being "dead to sin and alive to God" (Rom 6:11). They were buried with him and their old self was crucified in the sense that, by becoming committed to the same cause that Jesus was, they have ceased to be the people they were, crucifying their flesh and in essence taking up their cross to follow him (Rom 6:3-8; Gal 5:24); they are thus crucified to the world (Gal 6:14), since they no longer identify with this world and the sin and evil that characterize it but with the world to come.[120] As a consequence of this and their commitment to righteousness and justice, they face rejection and even persecution in this world as Jesus did and in this sense can be said to suffer together with him; they trust, however, that by suffering with him, they will one day also be raised together with him, that is, transformed into the same glorious condition in which he finds himself (Rom 8:17; 2 Cor 4:14; Phil 3:21). Nevertheless, none of this involves any type of ontological or mystical union with Christ, nor do they actually "participate" in Christ or in the past events of his death and resurrection. Rather, it is a matter of identifying with Christ in what he lived and died for, as well as with the new resurrection life he attained by means of his faithfulness unto death.

Precisely because such a subjective response is necessary in order for people to benefit from what God has done in Christ, it would be incorrect to posit some type of objective salvation embracing humanity as a whole effected by Christ's death. While he can be said to have died for all, this is not because his death saved the whole world in some sense or transformed the human condition in general, but because he gave up his life seeking that people from all over the world might be brought into the community that would be established through his death in order to find forgiveness of sins and salvation there. In New Testament thought, Jesus' death did not effect some type of mysterious transformation in the world or human nature, nor was humanity delivered from the oppression of evil powers or from its sinful condition. The transformation and redemption of the world as well as of human beings still lies in the future; while in a sense it can be said that believers have already been saved, this involves being saved "in hope" (Rom 8:24).

Jesus' death, then, results in the justification of believers, not because it enables God to forgive or acquit them, but because it has led to the establishment of a new covenant community where people can find forgiveness and justification in Christ. In reality, in Christian thought, those who live in this new covenant community are justified on the same basis upon which people were said to be justified under the Mosaic covenant: they are included as members of God's covenant people through their faith. This faith is expressed in a commitment to righteousness, justice, and obedience to God, and is inseparable from these things. Even though they inevitably sin in spite of that commitment, they recognize that they are sinners, repent of their sins, and ask God for forgiveness. What distinguishes this new covenant people from those who live under the Mosaic covenant is that they define obedience to God's will in terms of following Jesus rather than literal observance of the Torah and seek forgiveness and justification through the mediation of Jesus their Lord rather than in the ways prescribed in the Mosaic law. For them, Jesus is the fulfillment, objective, and perfection of that law, and the divine blessings promised in that law are now to be found in him.

CHAPTER 4

Grace, Faith, and the Gospel

In Lutheran teaching, the gospel is defined as "the promise of the forgiveness of sins and justification on account of Christ" or the "proclamation of the grace and favor of God because of Christ."[1] Of course, in order to actually receive this grace, favor, and forgiveness from God, people must respond to the gospel in faith. Although such an understanding of the gospel and salvation may seem simple and straightforward, in reality it raises a host of problems that have been the subject of endless debate not only among Lutherans but among Christians in general. These have to do primarily with the manner in which grace and faith are to be understood, the question of whether God's grace and forgiveness must be merited in some way, and the relation between the forgiveness of sins and the transformation of believers in righteousness.

Grace and Faith in Lutheran Thought

Luther's teaching on grace and faith was in large part a reaction to the Roman Catholic teaching of his day. According to Roman Catholic thought, while in one sense God's grace was offered to all people freely, in another sense people needed to continue to *merit* grace by *cooperating* with the grace already given them in order to ultimately be saved and justified by God. This understanding of grace was combined with the claim that God had chosen the church—that is, the clergy—as God's means to communicate this grace, especially by means of the sacraments. Those who wished to continue to have access to God's grace, then, had to receive the sacraments from the hands of the clergy and perform the "works" commanded by the church, which in Luther's day had to do not simply with doing good to others but participating in things such as masses, fasts, vigils, tithes, processions, pilgrimages, the veneration of relics, the purchase of indulgences, and the monastic life. For the most part, these activities did not profit the poor or those in need but the church, especially as they provided the means by which the church obtained its wealth of material and human resources.

The Roman Catholic understanding of faith was also intimately tied to the church, the works it mandated, and its sacramental system. The faithful were called to believe that the church had divine authority to communicate grace and grant the forgiveness of sins and that the sacraments were efficacious in this regard. Although faith was undoubtedly regarded as necessary for salvation, it was only a first step: in order not to lose their justification, believers had to do their best to fulfill the commandments given by God as defined by the church and, when they failed, seek forgiveness of sins through the means prescribed by the church, particularly the sacrament of penance.

For Luther, this understanding of grace, faith, and justification gave the church a monopoly over salvation and led to the corruption and oppressive practices that had come to characterize it. In effect, the Roman Catholic teaching established the church as the mediator of God's salvation on earth, so that access to God and God's blessings in this world and the world to come could only be had through the church and its hierarchy: "outside of the church there is no salvation" (*extra ecclesiam nulla salus*). To affirm that the church, and especially its head the pope, spoke for God and Christ was in essence to make the church and the pope God on earth. In his *Letter to the Christian Nobility of the German Nation*, for example, Luther affirms that to claim that the pope is subject to no human authority, is the sole interpreter of Scripture, and is above any church council is ultimately to "raise the pope above God" and make him "higher than Christ," since it implies that the word of the pope is indistinguishable from the word of God and Christ.[2] Luther thus sought to reverse the situation in which the church stood over the gospel as the sole channel of God's grace, forgiveness, and salvation by instead subjecting the church to that gospel. He did this by positing a direct relationship between believers and Christ: through faith, Christ came to dwell in the heart of believers. This meant that believers had direct access to Christ through faith in God's word and thus to God and God's grace as well.[3]

Luther also called into question the Roman Catholic understanding of grace as something infused into human beings by God, defining it instead simply as God's favor and mercy toward sinners in forgiving them their sins and thereby justifying them.[4] Undoubtedly, this idea of grace as divine forgiveness was found in Roman Catholic thought as well, yet there forgiveness was made to depend on the way believers responded to the grace infused into them by God: one had to cooperate with that grace in order to obtain God's forgiveness. Christ's work was understood in terms of meriting the grace that was communicated to believers through his death, as well as meriting that the imperfect repentance and acts of satisfaction of believers might be acceptable to God. Nevertheless, believers still had to merit God's grace and forgiveness through their own works as well, so that these things were merited both by Christ *and* by believers themselves.[5] Curiously, Luther did not question the idea that God's grace must be merited; he merely affirmed that Christ alone had merited or obtained that grace and thus that nothing was required of human beings in order to be justified and saved other than that they come to faith.[6] Of course, Luther insisted that such faith cannot remain idle but will inevitably manifest itself in acts of obedience toward God and love toward one's neighbors; through faith, believers receive a new heart and it is this which pleases God and makes a new life of righteousness possible. For Luther, however, even though the works done by believers are pleasing to God, those works do not constitute the basis upon which they are justified, since justification is by grace alone through faith alone.

Grace, Merit, and Faith in Ancient Jewish Thought

Just as Luther's emphasis on justification by grace through faith was drawn from Paul's letters, so also his critique of the Roman Catholic teaching was based on parallels that Luther saw between his Roman Catholic opponents and the "Judaizers" who appear as Paul's adversaries in his letters. According to Luther, his opponents were proclaiming essentially the same message previously proclaimed by those who had opposed Paul's inclusion of uncircumcised Gentiles in the early Christian community: namely, that justification before God depended on one performing to God's satisfaction the works commanded in God's law. This made it necessary for believers to strive their hardest to merit God's grace and forgiveness through their own actions. Such an understanding of justification would lead some to falsely boast that they had earned God's acceptance and forgiveness through their righteous behavior, while leading others to despair of their salvation knowing that they could never do enough in God's sight to merit their justification. According to Luther, this teaching was at the heart of both the Judaism of Paul's day and the Roman Catholicism of his own day.

As noted briefly in chapter 2, since the publication of E. P. Sanders' book *Paul and Palestinian Judaism*, this understanding of Judaism has been called seriously into question. As Sanders argued, the concept of grace was central to the Jewish faith, where it was constantly stressed that God had graciously chosen Israel as God's people through no merit of their own.[7] The law given by God through Moses was also an expression of God's grace, since it was to serve them as a guide (Torah) to attain life and *shalom*. When the people strayed from that law, God's grace was further manifested in that God sent them prophets and chastised them through punishments in order to correct them and bring them back to the way of life God had commanded them for their own good. In fact, even when God destroyed a large part of the nation in order to leave a small remnant in the hope that this remnant would be a purified people, this was considered to be gracious and merciful on God's part, since the alternative would have been to destroy the people entirely or simply abandon them to their own fate.[8]

Of course, in order for God's people to attain the salvation promised in the law, it was necessary for them to respond properly to the grace shown them by God. As noted previously, they had to be committed to observing the commandments and were to make atonement when they sinned. Yet even though in this regard it can be said that God's people had to be deserving of salvation and *merit* God's favor and blessings, they remained entirely dependent on God's grace. Any merit they might attain before God was a gracious gift, since the only reason that it was possible for them to obtain merits before God was that God had mercifully chosen them to be God's people, instructed them in the way they should walk, corrected and disciplined them when they strayed, and forgave them when they fell. In grace, God accepted their good intentions and efforts to obey as sufficient for them to be declared righteous even when these remained far from what God desired.

The idea that the people had to *merit* their salvation made it possible to maintain the doctrine of God's goodness, since when things went poorly for them, both as individuals and as a people, this could then be attributed not to a lack of grace and mercy on God's part but to their own sin and disobedience. In other words, to maintain that any suffering and hardships the people endured were not *God's* fault but *theirs*, it was necessary to see punishment as something merited by their actions, and this required that salvation and deliverance from such punishment also be seen as something merited by their actions. In order for the people to be saved by God from their plight, then, they had to return to God: not only did they have to become more obedient to God's commandments but a greater portion of the people had to come to practice that obedience. Nevertheless, this could only happen as they depended trustingly on God's grace, looking to God rather than to themselves for the obedience they needed.

The goal of every faithful Israelite, therefore, was to be counted among the righteous who would attain salvation, both in this world to some extent and ultimately in the world to come. Of course, because salvation was something that God alone could bring about, what mattered was attaining God's approval. Justification thus involved being declared righteous by God. This was not the same as being declared *innocent*, however, or being acquitted of one's sins, since even the righteous were guilty of many sins. What separated the righteous from the unrighteous was not that the former were innocent and the latter guilty but that the righteous recognized their guilt and imperfection, repented of their sins, and committed themselves to obeying God's law; in contrast, the unrighteous refused to do these things.[9] At the same time, of course, if one was truly committed to obeying God's law to the best of one's abilities, one would inevitably live righteously to some extent and thereby attain a certain level of righteousness in God's eyes through one's behavior. Justification thus involved a recognition on God's part that one had dedicated oneself to living righteously to the best of one's abilities; and because of this commitment to obeying God's will, God graciously forgave that person's sins.

Because justification depended on one's being committed to living according to God's will as revealed in the law, it might seem that the Lutheran idea that people are saved by faith alone would be foreign to Judaism. This is not necessarily the case, however. Naturally, if it was necessary to live faithfully and righteously as a member of God's covenant people in order to be saved, one would seek to live in this way only if one believed that the God of Israel was Lord and that this God had established a covenant with Israel, promising salvation to those who lived in that covenant. In fact, one could hardly be said to have faith in the God of Israel if one did not live in the covenant established by Israel's God. Thus faith was undoubtedly necessary for salvation.

Yet faith was also defined in terms of absolute trust in God. Such faith is evident in the Psalms, for example, where believers cry to God for salvation from their diverse plights yet wait trustingly on God to respond in whatever way God chooses; at the same time, however, those who cry to God repeatedly draw God's attention to their efforts to obey God and live righteously, often in contrast to their enemies.[10] Faith therefore assumed an *active* and a *passive* form: to trust fully in God meant actively striving to live in the way God had commanded in the law,[11] yet also passively resigning oneself to whatever God ordained. When God ordained suffering, death, exile, and other calamities, faith involved submitting to God's will, trusting that eventually God would do justice for those oppressed, and at the same time examining one's own life to see what changes needed to be made in order to conform more fully to God's commandments.

Understood in this sense, it might be said that the Jewish people believed that they were saved by faith, though not necessarily by faith *alone*. Nevertheless, if faith is defined as living one's life trusting fully in God by striving to live as God has commanded, asking God for forgiveness when one sins, and accepting whatever God ordains, then it might even be said that people were saved by this alone. Ultimately, all God asked of God's people was that they trust fully in God; when they did so, they would inevitably strive to do God's will, since trusting God by definition meant attempting to do what God asked and commanded. Yet by doing so, they did not in any sense save *themselves* through their obedience; God alone could save.

Finally, it is important to note that in Jewish thought the ideas of grace and faith were intimately linked to the covenant. While it might be said that God was gracious to people from all nations, allowing them to enjoy the blessings found in God's creation and at times overlooking their sins, God's grace in its fullness was available only to those who lived in the covenant established through Moses; they were treated by God differently than other people. Thus, while those outside the covenant might experience salvation to some extent in this world and perhaps the world to come as well, only those who belonged to God's covenant people would experience that salvation fully. For that reason, there could be no saving faith outside of faith in the God of Israel.

Grace, Faith, and Justification in the New Testament

In developing their understanding of justification, Luther and the theologians of the Reformation who followed him looked primarily to the letters of Paul and especially his Letters to the Romans and Galatians, where the language of justification appears most prominently. There Paul insists that "a person is justified by faith apart from works prescribed by the law" and that God "will justify the circumcised on the ground of faith and the uncircumcised through that same faith" (Rom 3:28, 30); "we know that a person is justified not by the works of the law but through faith in Jesus Christ" (Gal 2:16); "by grace you have been saved through faith, and this is not your own doing; it is the gift of God—not the result of works, so that no one may boast" (Eph 2:8-9).

Undoubtedly, the idea that God graciously saves those who have no merits of their own and are undeserving of that salvation is found throughout the Hebrew Scriptures, as is the idea that one must trust in God for salvation and forgiveness rather than trusting in one's own strength or abilities.[12] In this sense, it can be said that the doctrine of justification by grace through faith is not merely a Pauline idea: the righteous are those who trust in God alone and not in themselves. In fact, Paul looked to the story of Abraham to argue that the idea that faith is reckoned as righteousness is a teaching of the Torah itself (Gen 15:6; Rom 4:1-25; Gal 3:6-18).

At the same time, however, the idea that one must live in conformity to God's will in order to be saved also runs throughout the New Testament as a whole. The righteous are defined as those who obey God's commandments faithfully and salvation and forgiveness are promised to them alone.[13] This clearly implies that, while salvation is by grace alone, human beings must also do what God asks in order to be saved and thus must be *deserving* of salvation.

Curiously, this apparent paradox is found in Paul's writings as well. Paul repeatedly insists that obedience is necessary and sees it as the objective of his ministry: "Circumcision is nothing, and uncircumcision is nothing, but obeying the commandments of God is everything" (1 Cor 7:19; Rom 1:5; 6:16-17; 16:26). He also follows Judaism and the rest of the New Testament in teaching that all people will be judged on the basis of their deeds (Rom 2:7-10; 2 Cor 5:10). He even seems to contradict his teaching that justification is not by the works of the law by affirming that "it is not the hearers of the law who are righteous in God's sight, but the doers of the law who will be justified" (Rom 2:13). Needless to say, these apparent inconsistencies in his thought have posed a problem for scholars of the New Testament.

In recent years, however, it has become increasingly clear that what Paul is rejecting is not the idea that believers must do God's will but that they must submit to the Mosaic law. In other words, when he writes that people are not justified by the works of the law, he is affirming that righteousness is not defined on the basis of adherence to the commandments of the Torah, such as circumcision and the observance of the Jewish festivals and dietary restrictions. Gentile believers do not need to become Jewish in order to be included as full members of the community of the righteous. As noted in chapter 2, however, Paul did insist that believers still needed to fulfill the law's *spirit* by practicing the righteousness commanded in the law; in this sense, they were still under the law. By redefining obedience to the law in this way, he seems to have been in continuity with Jesus' teaching regarding true observance of the law.

The New Testament also redefines grace and faith in relation to the Jewish view. God's grace is manifested in choosing believing Gentiles as well as Jews for salvation. All of those who form part of the church under Christ are God's chosen people (Romans 9–11). They are the children of Abraham in whom God's promises to Abraham are fulfilled (Gal 3:29) and can even be spoken of as the "Israel of God" (Gal 6:16) and the true circumcision (Phil 3:3; cf. Rom 2:28-29). In particular, God's grace is shown in the inclusion of "sinners" in the community of the righteous. They are incorporated into that community through faith and baptism, the new rite of purification. Saving faith involves not only recognizing the God of Israel as the true God but Jesus Christ as Lord and Son of God. In New Testament thought, because in Jesus the God of Israel has now sent the promised Messiah to fulfill the promises of salvation made of old, one can hardly continue to believe in God without believing in the one God has sent; rejecting Jesus thus involves rejecting the God who sent him as well as the salvation that will come through him.

The Doctrine of Justification
in Western Christian Thought

Throughout the history of Western Christianity, the doctrine of justification has been the subject of a great deal of theological discussion and debate. Much of this discussion has centered on the question of whether believers are first *declared* righteous by God in order then to *become* righteous or whether they must *become* righteous before being *declared* righteous. For a long time, Roman Catholic and Protestant scholars argued over whether the verb "to justify" in Paul's thought meant to "make righteous" or to "declare righteous." Most Roman Catholic biblical scholars now seem to agree with Protestant scholars that Paul understood justification in terms of being *declared* righteous, yet disagreements remain regarding the basis upon which this divine declaration is made.

Similar to what was noted in chapter 3, in order to understand properly the discussions over the doctrine of justification, it is important to distinguish between three different types of change that can take place with respect to those justified: forensic, moral, and ontological. Virtually all doctrines of justification maintain that God makes a forensic declaration with regard to those justified, accepting them as righteous in spite of the fact that they remain unrighteous, at least to some extent; this involves a change in their *status* before God or the way that God views them. All agree as well that a moral change takes place in those who come to faith and are justified: as a result of their faith, they begin to actually practice righteousness, though this righteousness remains imperfect. It is also common to posit some type of ontological change in believers, that is, a change brought about by God in their *being* involving a transformation of their heart, mind, or will. This ontological change must be distinguished from a moral change in that the latter involves conscious, deliberate activity on the part of believers, whereas an ontological change is something brought about by God rather than by human beings.

The disagreements over the doctrine of justification have had to do primarily with the question of how these three types of change are related to one another. According to traditional Lutheran teaching, justification involves first and foremost a *forensic* change: those sinners who come to faith are declared righteous by God, who is enabled to make such a declaration by virtue of Jesus' vicarious death on the cross or his righteousness that is imputed to them. The guilty are thus declared to be innocent and free of sin, that is, righteous, even though they are unrighteous.

A common criticism of this forensic understanding of justification is that it represents a legal fiction, since the justified are *not* actually righteous even though legally or forensically God accepts them as such. In response to this criticism, some have opted to speak of justification in terms of "acquittal."[14] This idea is slightly different in that, when a judge "acquits" someone, she does not necessarily declare that person to be innocent but merely drops any charges against that person, often on some other grounds. Thus, according to this view, believers are justified in the sense that they are "acquitted" of any charges against them, not because they are innocent of those charges but on the grounds of Christ's work in them or on their behalf. Whether justification is seen in terms of acquittal or a declaration that one is without sin, however, the basic idea is that one is spared divine punishment for one's sins.

Lutheran theology has often made a distinction between a *synthetic* and an *analytic* understanding of justification.[15] Forensic justification involves a *synthetic* judgment on God's part, since the person declared righteous is not actually righteous but is merely accepted by God as such on the basis of the alien righteousness of Christ that comes from *outside* of believers. In contrast, according to an *analytic* understanding of justification, God pronounces believers righteous on the grounds that they actually *are* or *will become* righteous. The basis for their justification thus lies *in* them rather than *outside* of them. This analytic understanding of justification has been rejected by many Lutheran theologians for making justification depend on a change in believers: if it is *their own* present or future righteousness rather than the alien righteousness of Christ that constitutes the basis for their justification, then they apparently are directed to look to themselves rather than to Christ for justification and can have no certainty regarding their salvation.[16] In contrast to such an idea, Lutheran theologians defending a forensic understanding of justification have generally insisted that justification cannot be based on any type of change taking place in believers; they are justified by the alien righteousness of Christ *imputed* to them but not by any quality or characteristic of their own that they actually possess.

In reality, however, once it is claimed that faith is necessary for justification, the basis for justification then becomes an actual change taking place *in* people: namely, their transformation from unbelievers to believers through the work of the Holy Spirit, who creates faith in them. Because this involves a transformation of their being, it can be seen as an ontological change, and this then constitutes the basis upon which God declares them righteous forensically. As a consequence of both the new heart they receive through faith and the forgiveness of sins that they receive, a moral change takes place in them as well; this change is generally referred to as "sanctification" in Lutheran theology. Nevertheless, their justification does not depend in any way on the change in their moral behavior, since in that case they would be under obligation to actually practice righteousness in order to be accepted as righteous by God. This would make their justification depend on what *they* do instead of depending on God alone.

In order to avoid the idea that the forensic declaration of justification depends on a prior change in human beings, some Lutheran theologians have insisted that justification *precedes* faith: God declares people righteous and forgives their sins *before* they come to faith. Gerhard Forde, for example, questions the notion that faith or repentance is a condition for justification, affirming that the gospel of justification is an "absolutely *unconditional* promise" and thus that justification itself is "entirely unconditional."[17] He rejects the idea that justification involves a movement of progression from sin to righteousness, arguing that people are justified solely for Christ's sake through imputation: "righteousness comes just by divine pronouncement," which involves God simply "declaring us righteous unilaterally, unconditionally for Christ's sake. . ."[18] Justification is thus of an "absolutely forensic character."[19]

Similarly, Carl Braaten follows Alister McGrath's criticism of seventeenth-century Lutheran dogmaticians who taught that "faith was logically prior to justification" and that "justification was dependent on a change in man," insisting instead that Luther "understood justification to concern the *unbelieving sinner*."[20] Braaten argues:

> It is important to grasp the objective validity of the forgiveness of sins offered on the part of God *prior* to the act of faith, and therefore also prior to repentance. . . . The free and full forgiveness of sins is proclaimed as an objective gift of God, on account of Christ, to sinners, not *because* they repent and believe but *in order that* they may believe and repent. . . . Justification is objectively prior to faith. Faith is subjectively the result of the creative impact upon the sinner of God's acceptance.[21]

The problem with claiming that justification precedes faith and takes place independently of it is that *all* people must therefore be said to be justified and forgiven, independently of whether they ever come to faith, know of Christ, or come to practice righteousness. This would result in a universal understanding of salvation, according to which God simply saves everyone and condemns no one. Such a view has often been associated with Karl Barth's teaching on justification. For Barth, all people are forgiven and justified but not all are aware of it; they must still be brought to the knowledge that God has already justified them.[22] The question, of course, is whether those who do *not* come to the knowledge that they have been justified actually remain in a justified condition. To answer in the affirmative would mean that all people are saved, yet to answer in the negative would mean that through their unbelief people who were already justified can become "un-justified" or "de-justified," so that God ceases to accept them as righteous and forgive their sins. In reality, however, this is the same as affirming that faith is necessary for justification. In this case, not all people are ultimately justified but only believers; salvation is thus not universal.

In order to speak of justification as being unconditional or prior to faith while nevertheless maintaining the need for faith for salvation, it is necessary to posit a *double justification*. This involves making a distinction between an initial or provisional justification embracing *all* people and a second or definitive justification that ultimately embraces only believers. Thus, for example, it can be said that all people are justified *in principle* but only those who come to faith are *actually* justified by God in the end, or that all people are initially justified *unconditionally* but must then be brought to faith in order not to lose their justification. Ultimately, however, only the second justification ends up really counting. The initial justification is not definitive since it can be reversed or negated through unbelief. Thus the second or definitive justification is *not* unconditional, nor is the justification that really matters *prior* to faith. *People must still come to faith in order to be justified in the end.*

It might be argued that the priority of justification over faith can also be maintained through a doctrine of election or predestination. In this case, God justifies those whom God predestines for salvation *before* they come to faith. However, because they are predestined not only to be justified but to have faith, in reality it is not entirely correct to speak of justification preceding faith. Instead, it is election that precedes both justification and faith, since from the start God intended to declare righteous and bring to faith only those whom God elected. As noted previously, in reality this reduces both justification and faith to mere formalities: what really saves people is neither that they are now graciously declared righteous by God or come to faith but that they were elected by God before creation.

Whereas Lutheran theology has generally regarded justification as depending on an *ontological* change in people (the change from unbelief to faith) but not a *moral* change, in Roman Catholic thought one's definitive justification has been seen as depending on *both* an ontological and a moral change. This moral change results from a prior ontological change brought about in believers: God pours God's love and grace into their heart and, as they respond favorably to this love and grace, they live in a righteous, God-pleasing way. On this basis, God continues to declare them righteous or justify them and forgives them their sins.

That this involves a double justification is clear from the Decree on Justification of the Council of Trent. According to this Decree, the initial justification depends on God's grace, which embraces what Christ has done for human beings as well as the gift of the Holy Spirit, who infuses justice and love into the hearts of believers. Nevertheless, only those who continue to respond properly to God's grace are ultimately justified and forgiven by God. Once they have been justified initially by being "made the friends and domestics of God," as they mortify their flesh and observe the commandments of God and the church by producing good works through faith, they "increase in that justice received through the grace of Christ and are *further justified*. . . ."[23] When they sin so as to fall from grace, the initial justification must be followed by a second one: "Those who through sin have forfeited the received grace of justification, can *again be justified* when, moved by God, they exert themselves to obtain through the sacrament of penance the recovery, by the merits of Christ, of the grace lost."[24]

The idea of a double justification has also been maintained explicitly by some Protestant theologians. The English Puritan Richard Baxter (1615–1691) taught an initial justification that was conditional or provisional and affirmed that one's final justification depended on one's works: those who have been "conditionally pardoned and justified may be unpardoned and unjustified again for their non-performance of the conditions."[25] The same basic view has been attributed to John Wesley.[26] While at times Wesley insists that justification is by faith alone, at other times he seems to include obedience as part of faith so that one cannot be justified without it. If this represents faithfully Wesley's thought, then his understanding of justification is essentially the same as that of Roman Catholicism, except that the works of obedience are defined differently, since in Roman Catholicism these works include those commanded by the Church.[27]

In reality, however, the idea of a double justification must be seen as characteristic not only of Roman Catholicism and certain forms of Protestantism but Lutheran thought as well. Virtually all agree in positing an initial justification or forgiveness of sins based on the reception of God's grace through faith and baptism. Yet this initial justification is not definitive: it depends on a *continuing response* on the part of believers. In other words, after "getting in" by sheer grace, one must still "stay in," to use E. P. Sanders' language.[28] The difference between the Lutheran and Roman Catholic views is that, in Lutheran thought, the response necessary to "stay in" is defined solely in terms of *continuing in faith*, whereas in Roman Catholic thought, one must not only continue in faith but also practice the moral behavior commanded by God. In fact, when the Roman Catholic and Protestant traditions have been said to be in essential agreement with one another on the doctrine of justification, as in the *Joint Declaration on Justification* or Hans Küng's study of Karl Barth's doctrine of justification, this agreement has actually had to do primarily with the *initial* justification rather than the final, definitive justification; Trent's teaching regarding a double justification is not addressed.[29] This is evident as well in the Roman Catholic teaching that, while believers cannot merit justification, they *can* merit eternal life.[30] From a Protestant perspective, to be justified and to attain eternal life are one and the same thing, since justification has to do with one's status at the final judgment. However, for Roman Catholics to claim that eternal life can be merited but justification cannot makes it clear that when they speak of justification, they generally have in mind the initial justification, and that the agreements reached have to do primarily with this justification rather than the second, definitive justification at the last judgment.

Reformed theology has often sought to avoid the idea of a double justification by affirming that the initial justification cannot be forfeited or lost due to the lack of a proper response. In reality, however, this is to equate justification with divine election: as noted above, in such a view it is not faith or one's behavior that actually leads to justification but the divine decree of election which is seen as irreversible.

The Roman Catholic and Lutheran understandings of justification each respond to a different concern and raise a different problem. The Roman Catholic idea that justification depends on a moral transformation in believers responds to the concern that believers actually come to practice the righteousness commanded by God. If believers can ultimately be declared righteous independently of any righteous behavior on their part, then that behavior is no longer necessary for them to be saved. This means that after they have initially been justified by faith, in principle they might simply continue in their sinful ways and make no effort to change their behavior, knowing that even if they choose not to do so, they will still be justified and saved.

Lutheran theologians have responded to this problem by insisting that, while justification is ultimately by faith alone and does not depend on any moral transformation taking place in believers, that moral transformation will inevitably take place as a result of one's justification. For Roman Catholic theologians, however, this affirmation is still not strong enough, since it provides no basis for *requiring* believers to live morally righteous lives: one can say that they *should* live righteously but not that they *must* live righteously to be saved. This makes the life of righteousness optional. To say that believers inevitably *will* live righteously implies that a righteous life follows automatically from faith. While in principle this might seem acceptable, it is contradicted by reality: many believers simply do not live morally upright lives as they should; thus it cannot rightly be said that the moral transformation that God desires to see in believers invariably and inevitably results from faith. People can only be obligated to live in a morally righteous manner if their salvation and justification are made to depend on this type of life.

According to Lutheran theologians, the problem with making justification depend on the moral behavior of believers is that the burden for their salvation is placed upon their shoulders. While in a sense their salvation depends on God, in another sense they must save themselves by doing what God commands. This undermines any certainty that they may have of salvation, which is the primary concern to which the Lutheran understanding of justification responds. Roman Catholic theologians, however, have considered the Lutheran view problematic in that, when one has certainty of one's salvation, one can easily grow morally complacent and see no pressing need to live a righteous life. Yet the Roman Catholic teaching is regarded as oppressive by Lutheran theologians, who claim that by keeping believers in a state of perpetual uncertainty regarding their salvation and incessantly making moral demands on them, Roman Catholicism deprives them of any real comfort and assurance regarding the future and instead directs them to look to themselves for their salvation; even though they are aided by God's grace in their attempt to live a moral life, ultimately their salvation depends on their own efforts. The same criticisms made of the Roman Catholic view of justification, of course, would apply to any Protestant or Evangelical view of justification that makes it depend on the moral behavior of believers.

Grace and Righteousness

No matter how the doctrine of justification is understood, divine grace is seen as playing a vital and indispensable role. Corresponding to the three types of change in human beings are three different understandings of God's grace and the human righteousness that results from it. When justification is understood *forensically* as a change in status before God, grace will be equated with the forgiveness of sins: God graciously accepts as righteous those who are sinners. Here grace provides the solution to the problem of sin understood as *guilt*. Righteousness is correspondingly seen as a right standing before God in which one is declared free of guilt. Grace can also be understood in terms of a divine revelation that instructs and motivates human beings to live righteously; in this case, God's grace is aimed at bringing about a *moral* transformation in believers by affecting their understanding through the new knowledge they receive and by altering their will as they are moved by the love shown to them. In this case, righteousness consists of moral behavior in accordance with God's will. Finally, grace may be viewed as some type of divine power, energy, substance, presence, or activity in believers by means of which an *ontological* change is produced in them. This may involve the creation of faith in them as well as the infusion of righteousness (*iustitia infusa*) and love into their hearts. In these latter two views of grace, it is seen as resolving the problem of sin understood as a *power* to which human beings are subject; this makes it possible for believers to possess an actual righteousness which is given to them by God but is nevertheless their own as well.

Similar to what we considered in the previous section, these three under-standings of grace and righteousness generally co-exist alongside one another. Grace as God's merciful forgiveness of human sin and guilt is generally regarded as being shown to believers throughout their life all the way to the final judgment, as long as there is a proper response on their part. This necessary response may be understood merely as having faith (as in Lutheran thought) or as living righteously as well. On the basis of this response, God accepts them as righteous. When grace is understood as that which produces an ontological change in believers, it is generally maintained that this is *accompanied* by the grace of forgiveness rather than constituting an *alternative* to it. In this case, believers are *accepted* as righteous on account of the ontological change God graciously brings about in them. The moral transformation that takes place in believers can be attributed not only to some type of gracious revelation or guidance given to them but to the other two expressions of God's grace: as they receive divine forgiveness, they respond in gratitude by mending their sinful life and seeking to obey God's commandments; and as a result of the ontological transformation brought about in them by God's grace, they are morally renewed and enabled to live more in accordance with God's will.

In virtually all Christian traditions, grace has been particularly associated with the activity of the Holy Spirit. In fact, in the Roman Catholic tradition, the Holy Spirit and grace have often been identified with each other, so that they are one and the same; this is referred to as uncreated grace.[31] Generally, however, a distinction is made between the two, so that grace is something given *through* the presence and activity of the Holy Spirit (created grace). In Eastern Orthodoxy, a distinction is made between the divine *essence* and the divine *energies*: through the Holy Spirit, God does not communicate God's *essence* to believers but only the divine *energies* that emanate from the divine essence. These energies are identified with God's grace and believers are called to cooperate with them.[32]

While Roman Catholicism does not associate grace with divine energies, it does speak of grace in terms of the infusion of righteousness and love into the hearts of believers. This is called "sanctifying grace."[33] To affirm that God infuses something into the souls of believers might seem to imply that God communicates some type of substance to them. However, Roman Catholic theologians have rejected the idea that grace is a substance, looking instead to the Aristotelian and scholastic distinction between substance and accident to speak of grace as an accident, habit, or quality inhering in believers created by the presence and activity of the Holy Spirit in them. This created grace is thus distinct from the uncreated grace identified with the Holy Spirit. This makes it possible to affirm that the good works done by believers are *their own* rather than something God works unilaterally in them. Such would not be the case if grace were a divine substance inhering in believers distinct from the substance of believers themselves or if grace were simply the Holy Spirit (uncreated grace), since then those works would be something produced by God in believers unilaterally rather than by believers themselves; in that case, those works could not be meritorious.

This understanding of grace has been criticized by Protestant theologians, who claim that it is foreign to the thought of the New Testament and is instead grounded in the philosophical thought of medieval Roman Catholic scholasticism.[34] Undoubtedly, Roman Catholic theologians would argue that this view of grace is in harmony with the New Testament teaching, yet one can hardly find any passages there where grace is explicitly understood as a quality, habit, or accident infused into believers. The same difficulty exists with regard to the distinction between uncreated and created grace. More importantly, however, when grace is seen as something infused into human beings, this implies some type of magical or mechanical process by which human beings are transformed. Justification then becomes a matter of God declaring believers righteous because the Holy Spirit has introduced into them some type of mysterious divine reality that transforms them.

Similar problems arise with regard to the Eastern Orthodox understanding of grace as divine energies. These energies are seen as working through some natural or supernatural process to produce some effect in believers, like leaven in bread dough, as if in themselves they had some inherent mysterious power to transform human beings. In this case, as in Roman Catholicism, believers are called to cooperate with some impersonal reality that has been transmitted to them by the Holy Spirit, namely, grace as an energy or quality. Faith then becomes a belief that whatever the Holy Spirit infuses in them actually "works" to produce the desired "effects." When it is claimed that the church through its ministers and sacraments is the means by which God imparts this mysterious transforming reality called grace, the church is then viewed as having some supernatural power to make that divine reality present. In essence, this makes the church quasi-divine, in that it can mediate God, and gives it power over believers, who must subject themselves to the church in order to receive into themselves the divine reality communicated by means of the clergy through the sacraments.

In contrast, Protestant scholars have generally followed Luther in insisting that grace should be understood solely in terms of God's favor and merciful acceptance of sinners, that is, a divine disposition toward human beings. Melanchthon, for example, defined grace as "the favor, mercy, and gratuitous goodwill of God toward us. . . . [G]race is nothing but the forgiveness or remission of sins."[35] In this case, rather than being something communicated by God to human beings or infused into them, it is merely the way in which God relates to them. In reality, however, Protestant scholars have often inadvertently advocated the same understanding of grace as some type of divine reality or entity transmitted to believers. In many cases, this has involved identifying Christ himself as a power infused into believers so as to transform them through the effects he produces in them.

This is evident, for example, in the way that Luther's teaching regarding believers being one with Christ has been interpreted by the Finnish Lutheran scholars. Tuomo Mannermaa affirms that through Christ God communicates to believers the "essential divine properties" such as love and righteousness.[36] Because for Mannermaa, the union with Christ is "real" and "ontological,"[37] the divine substance itself is communicated to believers through this union: "Christ himself *is* life, righteousness, and blessing, because God is all of this 'by nature and in substance' (*naturaliter et substantialiter*). Therefore, justifying faith means participation in God in Christ's person. . . . Because faith involves a real union with Christ and because Christ is the divine person, the believer does indeed participate in God."[38] Mannermaa rejects the Roman Catholic idea that grace is a habit, accident, or inherent quality given to believers, since this would mean that "the permanent and fundamental element constituting the human being's relationship with God is his or her own love." Instead, he proposes that for Luther the nature of divine grace

> is precisely that of a "substance." To rephrase, grace is God in Christ. This reality has its being in itself—not in or from something else. While it is true that the Christ present in faith is the real righteousness that is in the reality of the Christian's being, at the same time, this righteousness retains its "substantial" (being in itself) character. To rephrase once again, the *formalis iustitia* is Christ himself, and even when this righteousness is present in a human being, it remains what it is with respect to essence— namely, it remains God's *own* righteousness, of which the human being cannot boast.[39]

Thus the righteousness communicated to believers is, like grace, none other than Christ himself: "the person of Christ *is*, in an ontologically real manner, righteousness. . . ."[40] Mannermaa also insists on the "real, almost physically natural quality of the holiness that a human being, in Luther's view, receives in faith"[41] and sees this as comparable to the patristic and Eastern Orthodox idea of leaven permeating bread dough to make it rise. Progression in sanctification depends on the extent to which this "leaven" has advanced: in some Christians, "the 'leaven' has permeated the 'dough' of the flesh more thoroughly than in their fellow Christians."[42]

If grace is God's own self as we encounter God in Christ and the Holy Spirit, as Mannermaa affirms, then it would seem proper to speak of uncreated grace, as Roman Catholicism does, since obviously God, Christ, and the Holy Spirit are all uncreated. His understanding of Christ and divine grace and righteousness as some type of ontological reality communicated to believers is also clearly analogous to the Roman Catholic idea of an infused righteousness. The difference is that this righteousness is viewed as a divine substance rather than an accident or quality and is identified with Christ himself: together with the Spirit, Christ produces the same kind of transforming effect in believers as leaven in a mass of bread dough, either by virtue of some mysterious power he possesses or else through something analogous to a chemical or biological reaction. If both grace and righteousness are understood as substances and identified with Christ, then apparently Christ himself is a substance communicated to believers and this constitutes his saving value. *Gratia infusa* is nothing other than *Christus infusus*. This is slightly different from the idea that grace and righteousness are communicated *through* Christ (an idea also affirmed by Mannermaa), since in this case they must be distinguished from Christ himself. In either case, the question arises as to how believers receive this substance or power from Christ. Do we require some theological understanding of Christ's human nature or body in order to regard it as the means by which Christ's righteousness is imparted to believers? Do human beings come into contact with this righteousness through the human nature that they share with Christ, as in Eastern Orthodox thought? How does that human nature "work" to communicate this substance or power? Is this righteousness instead something believers obtain by entering into contact with Christ's risen body that is ubiquitous? Is there actually a physical or material union with Christ or his body? Should we speak of a mystical union and, if so, what would that mean? Or do we need a certain theological understanding of the sacraments so as to regard them as the means by which this grace and righteousness are communicated to believers?

Often the indwelling of Christ in believers is said to be effected by the Holy Spirit. Calvin, for example, spoke of the Holy Spirit as "the bond by which Christ effectually unites us to himself."[43] This type of language, however, runs the risk of depersonalizing the Holy Spirit rather than Christ, so that the Spirit simply becomes some type of "glue" or link joining two persons, Christ and the believer. In this case, the Holy Spirit tends to be regarded as an impersonal extension of Christ, a "some*thing*" rather than a "some*one*" who relates to believers as a divine person distinct from Christ himself. When this impersonal understanding of the Holy Spirit is associated or even identified with divine grace, then justification is once more seen as being based on the infusion or transmission of some type of divine power, energy, or substance rather than God's gracious acceptance and forgiveness of sinners.

The affirmation that the Holy Spirit creates faith in believers can be problematic for the same reasons when this is viewed as taking place in some mysterious or quasi-magical manner. In this case, what is infused into human beings is *faith* rather than righteousness, although when faith is identified with righteousness then righteousness can be said to be infused into believers as well. Because this faith inevitably produces love of God and neighbor in believers, this can also be regarded as the infusion of love into their hearts. Thus, while Protestants have generally rejected the Roman Catholic idea of infused grace or righteousness, they have often adopted the same basic idea in a different form. Some new reality is said to be infused into believers or created in them so as to bring about an ontological transformation in them; this transformation is then viewed as the basis upon which God justifies and forgives them, as well as renewing them morally.

Although the idea of a moral change in believers brought about by God's grace has often been closely associated with that of an ontological change in them, in reality it is possible to posit a moral change that is not the result of any ontological change. In this case, God's grace is understood primarily in terms of God's activity in relation to believers and the world; it embraces not only the mercy and favor shown to human beings but what God has done and will continue to do through Christ and the Holy Spirit, teaching and guiding human beings through God's word and moving them to live in love and righteousness. Believers are transformed as God relates personally to them rather than by God imparting to them some type of divine energy, power, or substance.

Grace and Merit

To speak of grace being merited may sound like a contradiction in terms, particularly when grace is defined as God's undeserved love and mercy. Once it is said that grace must be earned or merited, it would appear that we are no longer talking about grace.

The idea that grace must be merited, however, is found in both the Roman Catholic and Protestant traditions. Undoubtedly, both traditions speak of some type of general or universal grace given freely to all people due to no merit on their part. While Lutheran theology usually reserves the word "grace" to denote God's favor and forgiveness, other Protestant traditions have spoken of "common" grace, as Calvin did, or "prevenient" grace, as Wesley did.[44] Roman Catholicism also speaks of "prevenient" or "actual" grace (*gratia gratis data*). At times this universal grace is made to depend upon what Christ has done for others, particularly in his death when he obtained divine grace for all, while at other times it is seen as something given naturally by God throughout the created order. In both Protestant and Roman Catholic traditions, however, this grace is not sufficient for human salvation; something further is needed. The problem consists in determining precisely what else is required: Is it necessary for *God* to do something else, giving further grace in addition to the grace given to all universally? Or is it necessary for *human beings* to do something, responding properly to the grace already given them?

Generally, both of these ideas are maintained. In Protestant thought, it is taught that because of original or inherited sin and the fallen human will, it is impossible for human beings to respond properly to God's grace. Therefore, a further act of grace is required, namely, that God forgive their sins so that they may be saved. Yet because of God's perfectly righteous nature, strict justice must be maintained; God cannot be gracious to human beings by forgiving them and being favorable to them until Christ has endured the punishment for human sins in the place of sinners. Thus God's grace must be *merited*, yet because sinners cannot do this, Christ must do it for them. Luther, for example, repeatedly affirms that Christ "won," "purchased," "acquired," "obtained," and "merited" God's grace for believers through his blood or death.[45] Of course, the fact that God sent Christ to merit grace for human beings by his death is itself seen as an act of grace on God's part. Thus, it might be said that, while God's grace must be merited, it is God in Christ who merits that grace for human beings who cannot merit it themselves. In other words, *God's grace moves God to merit God's own grace for us in Christ.*

At the same time, this is still not enough for human beings to be saved, since they must come to faith, accepting the forgiveness offered by God through Christ. As was argued in chapter 3, Christ's death becomes a mere formality once it is maintained that faith is necessary, since ultimately only those who come to faith are justified and saved; those who do not come to faith are condemned, even though Christ died for their sins as well. A further act of grace is therefore necessary, namely, that God create faith in their hearts and renew them through the Holy Spirit. Here God's grace no longer consists merely of forgiving them their sins but working an actual change in them as well. In both Protestant and Roman Catholic thought, it has been common to affirm that

Christ merited not only the forgiveness of sins for believers but also "merited that the Spirit be given to us."[46] When the Holy Spirit is associated with God's grace, then this once more involves Christ meriting grace for human beings.

In Roman Catholic teaching, it is affirmed that Christ also merited grace for believers in the sense that he merited the infusion of grace. Because in Protestant thought grace is not something that can be infused in believers, this idea is rejected there. Roman Catholicism also differs from Protestantism in affirming that believers themselves must merit grace. Undoubtedly, the Roman Catholic tradition has for the most part been careful to avoid affirming that God's grace can be merited by human beings, since this can easily be understood in the sense that the initiative lies on the side of human beings rather than God. This idea is rejected in Roman Catholic teaching, which instead emphasizes that God's grace is always a free and unmerited gift. Human beings, however, must *respond properly* to the grace they receive from God and this response merits *further* grace.[47] In other words, it might be said that in Roman Catholicism, believers must merit God's grace but can only do so on the basis of the grace that God has already given them as a free gift; that is, *they must be aided by grace to merit grace since they cannot merit grace unaided.* This ensures that the initiative always remains on the side of God rather than on the side of believers.

According to Roman Catholic teaching, in order to be justified, human beings must respond properly to the prevenient grace given by God to all people.[48] The Council of Trent affirmed that, while in adults the beginning of justification proceeds from God's "predisposing grace" through which they are called "without any merits on their part," nevertheless through God's "quickening and helping grace" they must "convert themselves to their own justification by freely assenting to and co-operating with that grace" rather than rejecting it; yet they can do this only by depending on God's grace.[49] Once justified, believers must increase in the righteousness they receive through the grace of Christ so as to be "further justified."[50] When through sin they forfeit the grace they have received, they must "exert themselves to obtain through the sacrament of penance the recovery, by the merits of Christ, of the grace lost."[51] They must also do good works to preserve and increase their justice or righteousness, yet can only do them by depending on God's grace.[52] The idea that grace must be merited by believers is reflected in the phrase used by some of the medieval scholastic theologians: "To the one who does what is in oneself, God does not deny grace" (*Facienti quod in se est, Deus non denegat gratiam*). While many Roman Catholic theologians have questioned the use of this phrase, most would find it acceptable as long as it is stressed that one can only do "what is in oneself" by depending on the grace already received. Either way, however, if one must do what is in oneself in order not to be denied grace, then clearly that grace must be merited.

This understanding of divine grace and human merit is reflected in the Roman Catholic distinction between operative and cooperative grace.[53] Operative grace, which is essentially the same as prevenient grace (*gratia gratis data*), is given to all people and makes it possible for them to be disposed to be converted by God and justified by the infusion of sanctifying grace. Once this initial justification takes place, however, believers must cooperate with the sanctifying grace infused into them in order to continue to be justified; this involves cooperative grace (*gratia gratum faciens*).

The Roman Catholic distinction between congruous and condign merit serves the same purpose of maintaining the initiative on the side of God while nevertheless insisting on the need for human merit.[54] Only Christ was capable of meriting the salvation of believers *de condigno* because no sinful human being could offer up to God a perfect sacrifice that truly merited God's favor and grace. Through his death, Christ merited from God not only divine forgiveness and the infusion of grace but also that the believers' imperfect works of obedience and satisfaction should be accepted by God as sufficient for them to be justified through those works. Believers can only merit their salvation *de congruo*, since their repentance and works are still imperfect and not truly deserving of salvation. Yet God accepts them as meritorious on the basis of the condign merit of Christ. In Roman Catholic thought, therefore, believers must merit grace understood both as an infused quality and as divine forgiveness by responding properly to the grace already received.

Although in Lutheran thought the idea that human beings themselves can merit any type of divine grace from God is rejected outright, once faith is regarded as necessary for justification, the question arises as to whether believers in reality merit justification by their response of faith, as if faith were the one "work" God required. Even when it is recognized that God is the one who graciously creates saving faith in believers through the Holy Spirit, it can be asked whether people must do something to merit or deserve God's creating faith in them. Lutheran and Reformed theologians have generally rejected such an idea, yet this rejection raises the question of why God chooses to create saving faith only in *some* people but not *all*.

Both the Lutheran and Reformed traditions have looked to the doctrine of election to address this question: from the beginning, God elected some human beings for salvation and determined to create saving faith in them. This doctrine, however, is problematic in several regards. Above all, it appears to contradict biblical passages such as 1 Tim 2:4, which affirms that God desires that *all people* be saved. Among Lutheran theologians, this idea continues to be affirmed, although it is not clear how this can be reconciled with the teaching that God did not choose all for salvation but only some and that the cause of this election lies not in human beings but in God.[55] In Reformed thought, 1 Tim 2:4 has often been interpreted to mean that God desires all *kinds* or *classes* of people to be saved but not all people universally.[56]

The idea that God determined what would happen before creating the world seems to destroy free will on the part of human beings, since only what God predetermined can take place. The distinction commonly made between God merely *foreknowing* the future (*praescientia*) and *predetermining* the future (*praedestinatio*) also raises problems:[57] God can only have foreknowledge of the future if the future is already determined. Thus, in order to elect particular individuals for salvation, God would first need to know all the details of history, including the circumstances in which each person would be born, raised, and live and everything that each human being would do, since all of this influences greatly whether one will be a Christian or not. It would be necessary for God to have knowledge of precisely which individuals would be born into Christian families, for example, or live in a time and place where Christianity would be practiced. This knowledge would only be possible if the future was already determined *before* God elected some individuals and not others for salvation; and since this had to have been determined before human beings actually existed and made any conscious or deliberate choices, only God could have determined it. For this reason, it is logically impossible to maintain that God merely *foreknew* the future when God created the world but did not *predetermine* it. Nor is there any basis for affirming that only some things in the future are determined while others are not, since those that are not determined would inevitably alter those that are; in that case, many details of human history would change and it would not be possible for God to have had the foreknowledge of human history necessary to elect some but not others for salvation.

While at times it has been maintained that God elected for salvation those whom God foresaw would come to faith,[58] such an understanding of election has generally been rejected by the Lutheran and Reformed traditions on the grounds that it makes justification depend once more on a human decision: ultimately, salvation depends on human beings electing God rather than God electing human beings, since God elects those who will come to faith. This is also to make justification depend once more on human merit: those who will choose to come to faith are elected because this choice means that they are more deserving of salvation than others. In that case, the ultimate cause of their election lies in them rather than God.

Thus, in order to affirm that salvation does not depend on human merit or a human decision, it must be maintained that God did not take into account what God foresaw that human beings would do in the future when electing some but not others for salvation. In addition to the fact that this is logically impossible, as just noted, it is also problematic in that, from a human standpoint, it seems obvious that among both believers and unbelievers, some individuals live in greater conformity and obedience to God's will than others. If God did not make God's election on the basis of how obedient each person would be—in which case election would have depended on one's merits—then God must have chosen for salvation many who would be relatively *less* obedient over others who would be relatively *more* obedient. This would clearly seem to be unjust on God's part.

This problem came to be addressed in some Protestant circles by affirming a doctrine of "total depravity," according to which all human beings can do no good whatsoever.[59] While it is generally recognized that people can attain a certain level of civil righteousness independently of any faith on their part, it is also affirmed that absolutely nothing human beings do in their natural state can be considered good and righteous in the sight of God. By affirming that none are more righteous than others since all are equally sinful, the notion that God elects some who are less deserving of salvation over others who are more deserving can be avoided. Of course, many have found it problematic to affirm that in their natural state human beings are totally depraved or even that nothing they do is good or God-pleasing; to them such a view of human nature seems overly negative and pessimistic.

Even when it is maintained that all are equally undeserving of salvation, however, the idea that God elects some and not others for salvation appears to make God arbitrary and unjust. Those who have defended such a doctrine of election have generally responded to this problem by arguing that it is not unjust for God to condemn eternally those not elected for salvation, since they are deserving of their fate due to their sins.[60] Such a response, however, overlooks the problem that what is unjust is not that some people be condemned for their sins but that God not treat all people in the same way: if all are equally deserving of condemnation, then justice would require that God either condemn all or deliver all from that condemnation but would not allow for God saving some and not others, since this would involve acting arbitrarily by showing partiality to some over others.

In spite of all of the problems raised by the doctrine of election and the rejection of the idea that human beings can do anything to merit their salvation, Protestant theologians have continued to adhere to this doctrine because this seems to be the only way to make it possible to affirm that believers can be certain of their salvation. Once it is affirmed that human beings *can* be deserving of salvation in some way, then it follows that they *must* be deserving in order to be saved, doing whatever is necessary to gain sufficient merits in God's eyes. This would undermine any assurance of salvation they might have and leave them in a state of perpetual uncertainty, since they could never know for sure if they had done enough to be deserving of salvation. This was the condition of Luther in the monastery, constantly striving his best to be fully obedient to God and free from sin but never achieving that goal; this led him into depression and despair.

Because of the problems related to this Protestant view, among Protestants themselves it has been common for the idea that salvation must be merited to creep in the back door. This can be done several ways. For example, it can be said that God grants forgiveness initially to those who come to faith but from then on any further forgiveness depends on their way of life. As noted above, this involves a doctrine of double justification in which the only justification that really ends up counting is the second one, which is dependent on human works; thus such a view ultimately maintains that salvation must be merited by works.

The Protestant discussions regarding the *ordo salutis* or order of salvation were also an attempt to resolve this problem. It was affirmed, for example, that God's grace liberated the human will so that one could come to faith; yet once liberated, it was still up to the individual to believe or not. Therefore one's salvation depended on one's own decision or choice.[61] In reality, however, this involves salvation by merit: those who come to faith are deserving of salvation but those who do not are condemned for their unbelief. At times, the desire to affirm that salvation depends on a human response while at the same time maintaining that salvation depends on God alone has led others to claim that justification depends on one *not resisting* God's grace.[62] Yet this is ultimately to assert salvation by merit once more, since those who do not resist are deserving of salvation while those who do resist are not.

In Roman Catholic thought, the idea that salvation can and must be merited by human beings is generally not considered problematic. It is taught that perfection is not required; on the contrary, on account of Christ, God is willing to forgive those who do their best or do "what is in themselves." When they sin, they need only repent of their sin and manifest this repentance through the sacrament of penance, which has as its objective not merely atoning for one's sins but drawing closer to God. Because salvation must be merited, faith alone is not enough for salvation, as it is in Protestant thought; rather, that faith must be manifested in concrete actions of doing good. Yet as long as one tries one's best, one can be relatively certain that this is sufficient for salvation in God's eyes. All of this puts Roman Catholicism in close continuity with Judaism, where the same basic ideas are maintained.

Nevertheless, this view is problematic in that it is not clear what "doing one's best" involves. In a sense, cannot all people be said to have done their best, given the amount of grace they received? Who can make this judgment? Are there not many complex factors that play a role in human behavior, factors that are often beyond our control? Can people always be blamed for the wrongdoing they commit, for example, when they have been raised in a problematic environment where they were never taught right from wrong or when they suffer from something such as chronic depression due to genetic, biological, or chemical causes? At times, it might be claimed that even those who do many good things for others have not done their best because they could have done much more given the wealth of resources at their disposal. Furthermore, must not the intentions behind one's actions be taken into account? Precisely because of all of these complexities, it seems difficult not only for human beings but for God to determine who has done their best and who has not.

The apparent advantage of the Roman Catholic view on these questions is that it seems to uphold divine justice, in contrast to the Protestant view where God seems unjust for arbitrarily electing some over others. When it is said that God rewards those who are good with salvation and punishes those who are evil with condemnation, then God appears to be acting justly, giving every human being what he or she deserves.

In reality, however, the Roman Catholic view also presents problems for upholding the justice of God. Clearly, all people are born into circumstances that vary greatly from one person to the next; sometimes these circumstances are favorable while at other times they are not. Together with the conditions in which people are born and raised, both nature and nurture play a role in determining what they will do, how they will live, and the decisions they will make. By nature, some people seem more open to the Christian faith and can even be said to have greater interest in spiritual matters, while others by nature appear to be less interested. The way people are raised and the environment in which they are placed also determine a great deal about their life; some are surrounded by nothing but vice and corruption throughout all of their early life and never experience true love from others, often experiencing instead only abuse and disdain. If this is all they ever know, it is difficult to expect them to leave these things behind. All of this means that all people are *not* created equal; in reality, there is no such thing as a "level playing field" in which all start out on the same basis. And because God is the one who has created this world, it seems clear that God must still be seen as having acted arbitrarily, showing favoritism to some over others by placing some in circumstances in which they would tend to come to faith and obedience while failing to place others in such circumstances.

Of course, it is usually countered that we live in a fallen world and that this inequality is the fault of human beings rather than God; God created a good world in which there was originally justice and equity. Even so, however, if the world's present condition is the consequence of human sin, then God should have ensured that all experienced the consequences of the fall equally rather than allowing some to enjoy much more favorable circumstances than others; or, at the very least, God should take this inequality into account at the final judgment.

Ultimately, then, both the Protestant and the Roman Catholic doctrines present problems for maintaining that God is just in saving some and not others. Of course, to affirm that God will save all universally also raises problems for God's justice in that those who do greater evil in this life will attain the same fate as those who do greater good. It thus seems clear that any position on these questions remains problematic.

In the end, however, as long as salvation is seen as something brought about by an act of God, it must be ascribed either to God's grace alone or to human merit as well. As Gerhard Forde and Carl Braaten have both noted, no matter how much one may emphasize God's grace, as soon as it is maintained that salvation depends on a human response that originates in human beings themselves of their own will, then the determining factor will be this response and the ultimate basis for justification will lie in human beings themselves rather than God.[63]

Justification and Faith

Virtually all of the Christian traditions agree that faith is necessary for salvation and that faith must lead to a new life of righteousness. Difficulties arise, however, when it is claimed that justification is *by faith alone*, as in Lutheran teaching, since this implies that it is not necessary to actually practice righteousness in order to be declared righteous by God.

This problem can be addressed only by defining what is meant by faith. Faith can be understood in terms of an intellectual assent to doctrines, that is, believing that something is true. Naturally, such a faith is necessary for salvation in Christian thought; one will not look to God or to Jesus for salvation if one does not believe that God exists or that Jesus is God's Son, for example. Yet faith can also be understood in a more *existential* sense as trust (*fiducia*) in God and Christ.

Often the affirmation that justification is "by faith alone" (*sola fide*) has been interpreted on the basis of the first understanding of faith, that is, an intellectual understanding of faith, both by those who defend that phrase and those who reject it. The *content* of what is to be believed can vary quite a bit between different traditions. In Protestant and Lutheran thought, in addition to a basic belief in God and Christ, it has often been affirmed that in order to be saved, one must believe that Jesus' death atoned for human sins, that justification is by grace alone through faith alone, that God is triune, and that Christ is both fully human and fully divine. Only those who accept these doctrines as true can be saved. Roman Catholicism also affirms the need for believers to assent to certain doctrines, called "dogmas." The Athanasian Creed reflects these ideas, affirming that "[w]hoever wants to be saved must, above all, hold the catholic faith. Whoever does not keep it whole and inviolate will doubtless perish eternally." Thus, after presenting a certain understanding of the doctrine of the Trinity, the Creed affirms: "who wants to be saved should think thus about the Trinity."[64]

According to this understanding of faith, what is necessary for salvation is correct belief. Thus, justification by faith alone becomes justification by *orthodoxy of belief* alone.[65] If justification by faith alone is interpreted in these terms, the implication is that all that God demands in order to save and justify people is that they accept certain doctrines as true. Believers are justified, then, *on account of their faith (propter fidem)*, that is, simply because they have orthodox beliefs. Faith also becomes a *work* that saves them. In this case, the only thing God demands of people in order to save them is that they accept the right doctrines as true and perhaps reject other erroneous doctrines as false. If they do this, nothing else is required of them.

While at times such an understanding of justification by faith has been maintained by some Protestants, it has been criticized and rejected not only by Roman Catholics but by most Protestants as well, and rightly so. This is not what Luther originally understood when he spoke of justification by faith, nor can such an understanding be regarded as being in harmony with biblical thought. Furthermore, this would involve proclaiming a rather strange God who saves some people for no other reason than that they believe true doctrines and reject false ones and who condemns others simply because they do not have the right beliefs. There would be no intrinsic relation between faith and salvation, nor between faith and a new life of righteousness, unless it could be argued that only those who have orthodox beliefs can live righteously. Even in that case, however, once it is maintained that justification is by faith alone, how one lives is irrelevant for salvation; God only takes into account what one believes. Thus, if one has orthodoxy of belief, it does not matter if one practices unrighteousness and injustice, since this will not be considered by God when one is judged.

When faith is understood in this way, it is natural for people to reject the idea that justification is by faith alone and instead argue that both faith *and* a life of righteousness and good works are necessary for justification and salvation. This has been the Roman Catholic view, though some Protestants have embraced it in some form as well. Yet this makes justification ultimately depend once more on one's works rather than one's faith, which is merely a first step toward producing the works necessary for salvation.

The Lutheran doctrine of justification by faith alone, however, must be understood with regard to the *second* definition of faith mentioned above. People are justified by *trusting entirely in God*, depending on God alone for salvation. This is all that God desires of people and demands of them *for their own good*: that they place themselves entirely in the hands of God and God's Son, looking to God and Christ and not to themselves for salvation. Of course, one will only do this if one first has intellectual faith. One must not only believe in God and Christ but believe that God is a gracious, loving, merciful God who in Christ accepts sinners just as they are. In this sense, of course, one must have an orthodox belief in God. If one merely believes that God is a wrathful, vengeful God who demands perfection and wishes only to condemn those who do not attain that perfection, one will certainly not place one's trust in that God and throw oneself at that God's feet, asking for mercy.

The Lutheran teaching concerning justification by faith, therefore, *does* posit the need for a correct belief in God and Christ but does not claim that this kind of belief or faith is what justifies. Both Luther and James, for example, insist that even evildoers and the devil believe in God, yet this does not mean that they are saved.[66] What is necessary is that one come to faith in the sense of placing one's trust and confidence in God alone (*fiducia*). As Friedrich Mildenberger observes, "Justifying faith is not only the knowledge of facts (*notitia historiae*); rather, it is the intentionality of the whole person who trusts the gospel."[67]

Once again, however, it is important to note that even when faith is understood as trust, justification is not *on account of faith alone* (*propter fidem*) but *by means of faith alone*. The phrase *sola fide* is in the ablative case in Latin, which means that faith alone is the *means* or *instrument* by which one is justified. Luther's thought is therefore that the only thing necessary for one to be declared righteous by God is that one trust fully in God, clinging to God's Son Jesus Christ in the sense of depending on him alone for salvation. As Alister McGrath has noted, "Luther avoids any suggestion that man is justified *on account of* his faith: justification is *propter Christum*, not *propter fidem*." Faith is thus "*fides apprehensiva*, a faith which 'grasps' Christ and makes him present."[68] For Luther, then, justifying faith involves an absolute dependence on Christ embracing one's entire existence.

When justification by faith alone is understood in this sense, it becomes clear that there is an *intrinsic relation* between faith and salvation as well as between faith and a life of righteousness. Such faith saves precisely because it depends on God alone for salvation and no one but God can save. Furthermore, to place one's life entirely in God's hands by definition involves striving to live as God desires in accordance with God's will. Of course, this does not mean that one will attain perfection; divine forgiveness remains necessary. However, as noted above with regard to Jewish thought, trust in God has both a *passive* and an *active* aspect: when one trusts in God for salvation, one not only resigns oneself passively to God's will but also strives actively to do what God desires. How can one say that one is truly trusting in God if one does not strive to do what God asks and commands of human beings for their own good?

This point has often been overlooked by many Lutheran scholars who have defined faith or *fiducia* almost exclusively in terms of trusting in God's mercy for the forgiveness of sins on account of Christ. This idea was rejected by Trent: "If anyone says that justifying faith is nothing else than confidence in divine mercy, which remits sins for Christ's sake, or that it is this confidence alone that justifies us, let him be anathema."[69] The reason for this rejection seems primarily to be that faith involves confidence not only in God's mercy and forgiveness in Christ but in God's own self. In other words, properly understood, faith involves trusting in God not only for forgiveness in a passive sense but being committed to doing God's will in an active sense, that is, looking to God for the new life God brings about in believers through Christ and the Holy Spirit.

This means that when justification is said to be *by faith alone* (*sola fide*), faith should not be understood as the *basis* upon which believers are justified. Rather, the basis for justification is the new heart and the life of righteousness that result from faith. When believers cling to Christ, Christ brings about that new life of righteousness in them, changing their heart and their will so that they become new persons. Thus, as Luther teaches, they are declared righteous even at present *by virtue of the fact that as long as they continue to cling to Christ, they actually become righteous.* Yet while believers are justified at present because they are beginning to *become* righteous thanks to the work of Christ and the Holy Spirit in them, they are not called to try their best to become righteous or look to themselves for their justification and salvation. Rather, they are merely directed to cling to Christ in faith, trusting in him not only for forgiveness but for the new life of righteousness that God demands.

As noted previously, in Lutheran thought this faith is seen as a gift of God brought about by God's Holy Spirit. In one sense, it is not the result of any human activity. Lutheran theologians have often stressed that before people come to faith, they are not merely passive but are actually actively resisting God.[70] There is thus nothing in them that leads God to create faith in them. Yet because one's faith must be one's own and because believing is an *activity* rather than a passive state, in another sense believers cannot be regarded as entirely passive when they come to faith.

Of course, this does not resolve the problem of why some come to faith and others do not. If people actively resist God's Spirit, then it would appear that God overpowers their will in some sense when bringing them to faith. If so, this raises the question of why God overpowers some and not others. And even if it is said that people remain free to resist the activity of God's Spirit and therefore may refuse to come to faith, this does not resolve the question of why some continue to resist and others do not. As noted above, the question of why some come to faith but not others does not allow for a satisfactory answer, whether it is asked why God chooses to create faith only in some and not others or why some people choose to believe and others do not on the basis of the personal traits with which they were born, the various influences they have had on them from the time they were born, and the diverse contexts in which they have lived.

Faith and the Word of Law and Gospel

Although in Lutheran teaching faith is created by the Holy Spirit, the means that the Spirit uses to create that faith is the proclamation of God's word. This word is comprised of law and gospel. The proclamation of the law leads people to recognize their need for salvation and to despair of attaining that salvation by their own efforts. This prepares them for receiving the gospel, which teaches that God graciously forgives their sins and justifies them for Christ's sake.

According to this understanding of law and gospel, faith and repentance (*poenitentia*) are brought about when the law produces fear of God's wrath and punishment. Driven by this fear, people repent of their sins and flee to Christ in faith so as to find forgiveness and salvation in him. Yet during Luther's own lifetime, such an understanding of the way persons are brought by God to faith and repentance was called into question by his friend and co-worker John Agricola. This led to a controversy between Agricola and Philip Melanchthon that has been documented by Timothy Wengert, among others. Agricola argued that the means by which God creates faith and repentance is the gospel rather than the law. What draws people to God and Christ and leads them to faith and repentance is not the proclamation that God is full of wrath at their sins and threatens them with eternal punishment but the gospel promise that reveals

God's goodness and the gracious forgiveness of sins in Christ; once one becomes aware of this, "one recognizes one's sins and repents."[71] It is the "love of righteousness" that converts a person to God.[72] The law can only force people "to do things through fear of punishment" and reveal to them their sin but it cannot indicate to them where help is to be found.[73] This is the task of the gospel, which creates faith in people and brings about a change of heart in them; as a result of this they become new persons and repent of their sins.[74] "Only from the light of the gospel can Christians learn where they have been (under the rule of darkness), where they are (so that they condemn their previous life), and where they are headed (to God alone who can help)."[75] Thus, for Agricola, "faith preceded knowledge of sin" and "*poenitentia* arises from faith in the gospel."[76]

In contrast, for Melanchthon, "*poenitentia* precedes faith and forgiveness."[77] More in accord with Luther's thought, he argued that "God's wrath, revealed in the law, is a crucial first step in the life of faith," since "[w]here there is no fear, there can be no faith. For faith should comfort the terrified heart, so that it firmly holds that God has forgiven sin for the sake of Christ."[78] According to Melanchthon, "faith cannot be conceived except in a contrite heart."[79] He "asserted that the Christian life moved from law to gospel, or in this case, from *poenitentia* to faith."[80] "Confession occurs when the conscience, terrified before God, acknowledges its sin and admits that it is justly condemned. It does not accuse God's judgment but only asks for grace and mercy and praises the God who justifies sinners"; "it is necessary to convict of sin, which happens through the law, because the remission of sins cannot be understood or received without prior conviction of sins."[81] In short, for Melanchthon the Christian "moves from fear to faith, not the other way around."[82]

Melanchthon's understanding of the role of law and gospel, which is in accordance with that found in Lutheran orthodoxy since his time, clearly reflects not only Luther's own thought on the subject but Luther's personal experience as well. Luther himself had believed that he was under God's wrath due to his inability to keep God's law, which constantly stood accusing him. His terrified conscience found peace only when he came to believe the gospel message that God graciously forgave him his sins and declared him righteous for Christ's sake. This involved a change in the way he viewed God, first as wrathful and then as merciful and forgiving, and was also related to his understanding of Christ's work: in his death, Christ had endured and appeased God's wrath at human sin, in essence transforming the angry Judge into a gracious Father.

When the law's role in justification is defined in terms of accusing sinners, terrifying their consciences and driving them to despair so that they then flee to Christ to find grace, forgiveness, and assurance of salvation in him, then the gospel is inevitably understood in terms of *the proclamation of a God who is distinct from the God proclaimed by the law*. In this case, faith in the gospel involves a *change in one's view of God*: as was the case with Luther, one comes to believe that for Christ's sake God is no longer angry at one's sins but is instead gracious, merciful, and forgiving. The proclamation of the law must then be seen as having the objective of bringing people to adopt a certain view of God that must subsequently be transformed into a *different view* through the preaching of the gospel. This means that they must *already* have a certain belief in God *before* they believe in the gospel. Nevertheless, this belief in God must not be seen as saving faith, since it is not trust in God (*fiducia*) but merely an intellectual belief concerning God's existence and God's wrath against sin.

Yet, in light of Agricola's teaching, the question arises as to whether it is possible for people to come to saving faith and trust in God without having previously believed that they were under God's wrath or having experienced the terrors of conscience and fear of divine condemnation that the law is said to produce by accusing people of sin. Traditionally, because they have understood the gospel and justification in terms of the forgiveness of sins, Lutheran theologians have argued that this is not possible: it makes no sense to proclaim to people that their sins are forgiven if they are not conscious of any need for forgiveness. According to Wengert, this was the argument of Melanchthon himself.

In principle, however, it does seem possible that one might have consciousness of one's sin only *after* hearing that God graciously forgives sins and therefore be led to repentance by the proclamation of God's gracious forgiveness. Yet even in this case, one would still need to recognize that one is a sinner in need of forgiveness; the difference would be that one would come to recognize this *after* hearing God's gracious offer of forgiveness rather than *prior* to that. There would thus be no terrified conscience or fear of divine punishment but rather a sorrow over sins as a result of one's becoming aware of God's grace and mercy. Yet this awareness of the need for forgiveness would still be the result of one's understanding of the *law*. That is, one could first hear the gospel only then to understand the law as well as one's need for the gospel. Thus, in contrast to what Agricola affirmed, repentance would still be brought about by the law together with the gospel, rather than by the gospel alone; yet in contrast to what Melanchthon and others affirmed, one might come to saving faith in Christ by hearing the gospel first, only then to understand the law, without ever passing through the experience of a terrified conscience. This would be analogous to the way a child from infancy first experiences the unconditional love of his or her parents and comes to trust in them *before* recognizing that that love is gracious and undeserved and that it involves forgiveness, since the child is far from perfect.

All of this means that, while the proclamation of the law need not necessarily precede the proclamation of the gospel and the two must be distinguished from each other, law and gospel must always go hand in hand as the one word of God.[83] As Agricola recognized, to proclaim the law without the gospel does not lead to saving faith or do anything other than create fear, terror, or hatred of God. Thus, strictly speaking, it is not the proclamation of the law alone that leads to repentance or drives one to seek God's grace in Christ. How can one be driven to God's grace if the only concept one has is of an angry God who threatens to condemn one for one's sins? One must also hear of the gracious God who forgives in Christ in order to be drawn to that God in true faith (*fiducia*) and repentance. The law can only bring about faith and repentance when it is proclaimed together with the gospel.

At the same time, true faith and repentance cannot be brought about by the proclamation of the gospel alone. This kind of proclamation would involve merely affirming that God loves, forgives, and accepts all people unconditionally. In principle, such an affirmation might involve denying the existence of sin in some sense or simply claiming that sin does not matter and is thus irrelevant. If that is the case, there is no need to change or repent, because there is nothing to be repentant for. Nor is there any need for faith and trust in God in order to be saved, since one is saved and accepted by God even without such faith and trust.

This does not mean, however, that one must experience the feeling of being terrorized and full of fear before the gospel can provide hope and solace. The law can be seen as demonstrating to human beings their need for salvation simply by making manifest to them that they are in a situation in which they are lacking that salvation and cannot obtain it through their own efforts. Rather than instilling fear at God's judgment, the law may instead move people to experience feelings of sadness, emptiness, frustration, or a lack of meaning or fulfillment in life. In the *Heidelberg Disputation*, Luther himself compared the way in which people are led to recognize their sin to the way an illness leads one to seek a physician.[84] Melanchthon spoke in the same terms: "The law indicates disease, the gospel points out the remedy."[85] In this case, while an illness may produce fear in a person, that fear is not necessarily related to a guilty conscience and fear of divine judgment but may simply be due to the desire to live rather than die. In this case, the person seeks help not because she or he feels accused and condemned but because he or she wishes to be restored to health. Thus, if the proclamation of law and gospel leads sinners to see themselves more in terms of sick people who need to be made well than in terms of people standing under God's wrath and judgment, they will not first be moved to conceive of God as angry and then change their conception so as to see God as merciful and forgiving. The second use of the law will also be defined in terms of showing people that they are ill and in need of healing rather than in terms of constantly accusing them of wrongdoing.

Church, Word, and Sacraments

In Lutheran thought, the role of the church is not merely to proclaim God's word of law and gospel but to administer the sacraments, which are "means of grace." In the Roman Catholic tradition as well as others, the sacraments are also understood as means of grace. Nevertheless, due to the different understandings of grace and the role it plays in justification and salvation, the sacraments as well as the church have been viewed differently in these various traditions.

The Lutheran understanding of the sacraments is in large part a reaction to the Roman Catholic understanding. In Roman Catholicism (and perhaps Eastern Orthodoxy as well), because grace is seen in terms of something infused into believers, the sacraments are regarded as means by which believers continue to receive this grace into themselves. Of course, grace is also understood in terms of divine forgiveness, which is granted to believers along with that which is infused into them. Due to its hierarchical understanding of the church, Roman Catholicism sees the sacraments as something given by Christ initially to the apostles and their successors, that is, the church hierarchy or clergy, who in turn administer them to the faithful. In this way, not only the sacraments but the clergy *mediate* God's grace to the laity.

As noted briefly at the outset of this chapter, Luther protested against this understanding of the sacraments, since it gave the church—that is, the hierarchy or clergy—a position of privelege and power over the laity. The church, in effect, had a monopoly over this grace and could distribute it to whomever it desired, just as it might withhold it from those deemed unworthy of it. Because this grace was necessary for salvation, those who wished to be saved had to submit to the church.

Virtually all of the Protestant criticisms of the Roman Catholic understanding of the sacraments and the church go back to this concern. In Protestant thought, the church is defined as the community of all believers rather than being identified primarily with the hierarchy or clergy; thus to say that the sacraments are given by God to the church for the church to administer is to maintain that they are given to *all* believers rather than only to a select group that is above the rest. Protestants regarded other Roman Catholic teachings as oppressive and tyrannical as well. The Roman Catholic practice of withholding the eucharistic wine from the laity and the doctrine of transubstantiation, according to which the priest in essence had the power to make Christ present and mediate him to the laity, reinforced the clergy's position of power over against the common people. The notion that grace is or contains some type of mysterious divine power made the clergy the dispensers of this power so that access to it was to be had only through them. The same was true of divine forgiveness, which was mediated through the clergy as well; through the sacrament of penance, they determined what the laity had to do to be declared righteous by God. This meant that, from the perspective of the laity, the clergy spoke for God as God's representatives; in effect, this involved equating the clergy with God. The same concern was behind the Protestant criticism of the Roman Catholic teaching that the sacraments worked *ex opere operato*, that is, independently of any faith on the part of the person receiving the sacrament: for Roman Catholics, to affirm that the sacraments are effective only when received in faith would make the sacraments' power and efficacy depend on the laity rather than the priest who administered them. In this case, if people did not have faith, the church would cease to have the power to communicate God and God's grace to them.

For these reasons, Luther rejected much of the Roman Catholic teaching regarding the sacraments and instead argued that what gave them their power and efficacy was the divine promise attached to them.[86] While Luther agreed with Roman Catholics in rejecting the idea that the efficacy of the sacraments depended on the worthiness of the priest or minister who administered them, he did so for an entirely different reason: whereas Roman Catholicism claimed that by virtue of his ordination the priest had the power and authority to mediate God's grace through the sacraments no matter what kind of personal life he lived, Luther argued that the divine promises of forgiveness and salvation attached to the sacraments could not be invalidated by any human unworthiness. Luther's concern was thus to make the power and efficacy of the sacraments depend on God alone and not on human beings, whereas the Roman Catholics sought to make their power and efficacy dependent on the divine authority irrevocably given to the clergy, who could not lose this authority even if they lived in immorality and dissolution. For Luther, the only thing that was irrevocable was God's promise of salvation and forgiveness that was attached to the sacraments.

In contrast to Roman Catholic teaching, Luther and the Protestant theologians who followed him defined the grace communicated through the sacraments simply as God's gracious favor, mercy, and forgiveness offered to sinners. The sacraments were viewed as means by which believers might be assured of God's forgiveness and reminded that Christ died for their sins so as to be strengthened in their faith. The clergy had no mysterious divine power at their disposal that they might mediate to believers.[87] Luther thus subjected the clergy and the church to the word of God and the sacraments, instead of subjecting the word of God and the sacraments to the church's hierarchy, as Roman Catholicism did. In this way, believers were directed to look not to the church or its hierarchy for assurance of salvation but to God's word alone.

Luther differed from many other theologians of the Reformation, however, in maintaining that Christ's body and blood are truly present in the bread and wine of Holy Communion.[88] Other Protestant thinkers wished to avoid the Roman Catholic idea that the clergy had a mysterious power to make Christ present to the laity, in which case the laity were in the disadvantaged position of needing the church or clergy in order to have access to Christ. While Luther agreed with them that the clergy had no such power and on this basis rejected together with them the Roman Catholic doctrine of transubstantiation, he nevertheless believed that to deny the doctrine of Christ's real presence in the sacrament was to deny lay people direct access to Christ himself. He thus affirmed that all believers truly possessed Christ, in contrast to both Roman Catholics and other Protestants whose understanding of the sacraments led to the rejection of such an idea, albeit on different grounds. Clearly, Luther's understanding of faith as *fides apprehensiva*, through which Christ and believers were united as a single person, led him to adopt the position he did.

Nevertheless, Luther's position raises the question of whether Christ himself or, more specifically, his body and blood, might be regarded as some type of divine substance that in itself produces certain effects in believers once introduced into them; if so, this would make the Lutheran understanding of the sacraments essentially the same as the Roman Catholic understanding, according to which they are means by which God infuses grace into the soul. Undoubtedly, Luther rejected the idea that Holy Communion was efficacious *ex opere operato*, insisting instead that the reception of Christ's body and blood benefitted only those who had faith. In a sense, this gave believers some "power" over the sacraments, since in the end it was not the clergy who made Christ present but God through their faith. Yet it was still possible to regard the sacraments as having some type of mysterious, quasi-magical effect on believers. In fact, even in circles where the idea of Christ's real presence in the sacrament was rejected or interpreted much differently, the belief that the sacraments possessed some mysterious, quasi-magical power tended to persist among many lay people.

Jesus and the Justification of Sinners

While the doctrine of justification by grace through faith is associated particularly with Paul, it can only be understood properly when it is recognized that its
origin lies not in Paul but in the teaching and practice of Jesus.[89] According to
the Gospels, Jesus repeatedly reached out in grace and mercy to those who were
considered "sinners" and those who were oppressed by various evils caused by
nature, demonic forces, and other human beings. He made no demands on
those he helped before helping them, except at times that they trust in him.
Even when Jesus forgave sins, as in the case of the paralytic or the woman who
anointed his feet (Matt 9:2-8; Luke 7:36-50), or reached out to sinners like
Zacchaeus (Luke 19:1-10), he did not require that they repent first or do
something to "merit" his acceptance and assistance; rather, he took the initiative
in showing them mercy and grace in concrete ways without considering whether
they might be worthy of his love.

Jesus' love, therefore, was *unconditional*. He not only practiced such love
himself but taught his followers to love unconditionally as well. He tells them to
be merciful just as God is merciful and kind to the ungrateful and the wicked, to
refrain from judging others, to forgive those who do them harm, and to love
their enemies (Matt 5:7, 45; 6:14-15; 7:1-5; 9:13; 12:7; 18:21-35; 19:19; 22:39;
Luke 6:27-37; 10:37; 11:42; John 13:34).

At the same time, Jesus insisted on the need to practice the righteousness of
God (Matt 5:6, 10, 20; 6:33; 23:23; Luke 11:42). Yet, as noted in chapter 2, Jesus
defined the righteousness of God in terms of fulfilling the *spirit* of the law, that
is, its underlying principles aimed at the well-being of all. Thus, while Jesus
agreed with other Jewish teachers in affirming that the law must be obeyed, his
redefinition of what constituted proper obedience to the law often provoked
conflict with those who saw Jesus as one who violated the law and taught others
to do the same.

Jesus also remained in continuity with Judaism in general by insisting that
those who practiced the righteousness of God would be justified and saved by
God, while those who did not would be condemned (Matt 12:32; 13:41-43, 49-
50; 25:31-46; Mark 12:38-40; Luke 14:14). This righteousness, however, did not
consist merely of fulfilling the law but fulfilling *Jesus' interpretation* of that law.
Matthew and Luke also speak of Jesus as the one who will judge all people,
saving or justifying some while condemning others (Matt 7:21-23; 10:32-33;
25:31-46; Acts 10:42; 17:31). While Jesus' words of condemnation against those
who refuse to do God's will as defined by Jesus are often harsh (Matt 23:1-36),
they should not be understood as violating the principle of unconditional love;
his words and actions can be seen as motivated, not only by his love for those

being oppressed by the interpretations of the law of his adversaries, but by his love for those adversaries themselves, since he sought that they change their oppressive, unjust ways not only for the good of others but for their own good.

Corresponding to Jesus' redefinition of righteousness was his redefinition of who the righteous are. If the righteous are those who strive to keep the spirit of the law in seeking the well-being of others, then what makes them righteous is that they are committed to practicing unconditional love for others and showing them the same grace and mercy that they themselves have been shown through Jesus. Undoubtedly, they are far from perfect in this regard and remain in need of divine forgiveness, grace, and mercy (Matt 5:43-47; 6:12, 14-15; 18:21-35; 21:28-32; 25:34-40; Luke 6:27-37). But as long as they remain committed to fulfilling the righteousness of the law as defined by Jesus, they are included among the righteous. Because of this commitment, when they inevitably come to practice injustice and unrighteousness, they repent of this and seek forgiveness from God and others, looking to mend their ways and make reparation if necessary. In a sense, it might be said that they sin against their will, since their will is to serve God and others.

If, however, people turn a blind eye to their sin and seek to justify it or refuse to acknowledge it when it is pointed out to them, then they will invariably practice unrighteousness and injustice. The same problem will arise if they define righteousness and unrighteousness in mistaken terms: if they call the good evil and the evil good, they will do evil and injustice rather than practicing what is right and just. This means that they can only practice the righteousness of God by continuing to see themselves as sinners. If they acknowledge this, then they will be able to recognize their sin and constantly seek to correct it so as live righteously. They will also identify their sin as sin, rather than justifying it or calling it good, and in this way will contribute to justice rather than undermining it. For these reasons, those who claim to be righteous and refuse to acknowledge their sin cannot practice justice and righteousness; only sinners can.

A proper understanding of these things makes it possible to grasp the paradox found in Jesus' teaching and practice: namely, that *the righteous are those who see themselves as sinners, while the unrighteous are those who see themselves as righteous*. This is the key to understanding Jesus' teaching. If one does not recognize that one is a sinner, one cannot be righteous because one will inevitably fall into sin but fail to recognize it, thus practicing injustice and doing harm to others. In contrast, when one is conscious of being a sinner and practicing unrighteousness, then it is possible for one to identify and correct one's sin and unrighteousness and thereby come to practice the righteousness and justice commanded by God in God's law. This is how repentance should be understood in Jesus' teaching: the repentance required consists of the recognition that one is a sinner in need of grace. While in one sense repentance involves changing one's ways, strictly speaking, it involves the *desire* to change one's ways, since one must then look to God and God's Son Jesus for the power and ability to change, rather than looking to one's own powers and abilities.

Many of Jesus' actions, teachings, and parables must be understood against the background of these ideas. When criticized for keeping company with the tax collectors and sinners, he claims that he has come not for the righteous but for sinners, since it is the sinners who have need of a physician (Mark 2:15-17; Luke 5:31-32; Matt 9:13). This should not be taken in the sense that some do not need a physician but rather in the sense that some who are ill and thus *do* need a physician refuse to recognize that need. Similarly, after dining at Zacchaeus' home, he affirms that "the Son of Man came to seek out and to save the lost" (Luke 19:10). He criticizes the Jewish leaders for not seeing themselves as sinners in light of John's call to repent and be baptized (Matt 21:25-26, 32). They are hypocrites, presenting themselves as righteous when in reality they are full of sin and injustice (Matt 23:23-28). Those who are truly acceptable to God are those who recognize their sin and repent rather than those who supposedly have no need of repentance (Luke 15:7). They see the log in their own eye rather than pointing out the speck in the eye of others and condemning them for it (Matt 7:1-5). The parable of the prodigal son contrasts those who recognize their sin with those who claim never to have disobeyed God's command and condemn those who do, rather than rejoicing with those who repent (Luke 15:11-36). Perhaps no parable illustrates all of this more clearly than that of the Pharisee and the publican, told by Jesus "to some who trusted in themselves that they were righteous and regarded others with contempt." Whereas the Pharisee claims to be an obedient, upright man, the publican beats his breast and prays, "God, be merciful to me, a sinner!" Jesus then concludes the parable: "I tell you, this man went down to his home justified rather than the other; for all who exalt themselves will be humbled, but all who humble themselves will be exalted" (Luke 18:9-14).

These passages and others stress that, in order to be justified and accepted by God as righteous, one must recognize that *one is a sinner just like everybody else*, entirely dependent on God's grace and mercy. The righteous are those who see themselves as people who are ill in need of a physician, as those who like stray sheep are lost and need to be found, and as people who are dead in sins and need to be made alive, like the prodigal son (Luke 15:3-7, 32). They also see others in the same terms: as fellow sinners who are in need of help and healing as well. Only in this way can they come to practice the true righteousness of God, since if they condemn and judge others rather than identifying with them in solidarity, it is impossible for them to show love and mercy to them in accordance with God's will. However, if they see others as people who are also ill and lost, in need of God's grace, mercy, love, and forgiveness, then they will treat them in the way God desires, thereby practicing the righteousness commanded by God.

Jesus' teaching in this regard also underscores the fact that what truly changes people is not censorship, judgment, and condemnation but grace and mercy. Jesus reached out to sinners in love rather than condemning them and in this way was able to transform them. While at times he felt it necessary to point out the sin of others with a prophetic voice and pronounce words of judgment, what he really desired was to show them mercy and grace, since only this could truly change their hearts.

While in Jesus' teaching the righteous are those who recognize their sin and turn to God for help, they are also those who look to Jesus in faith and heed his call to follow him. The reason for this is that true faith in God involves believing in the God proclaimed and represented by Jesus. Those who reject Jesus' understanding of grace reject not only Jesus but God, believing in a God distinct from the true God associated with Jesus' teaching and activity. For this reason, they seek to kill Jesus, just as they killed the prophets before him. Their own view of God leads them to practice injustice and oppression in relation to others. If one does not have faith in Jesus, one will not accept his understanding of the gospel, seeing oneself as a sinner, and consequently will continue in sin rather than being transformed by Jesus so as to practice righteousness and God's will as these are now defined by him.

Reconsidering Paul's Teaching on Justification by Grace through Faith

Although Paul taught and worked in a context that was in many ways different from that of Jesus, he understood well all that we have just seen and phrased it in his own terms when speaking of justification by grace through faith. In Paul's case, there were Jews who believed that they were righteous because they observed the Mosaic law; they thus excluded uncircumcised Gentiles as "sinners," refusing to admit them into their community until they submitted to all the precepts of the Mosaic law. Paul insists to his readers that they must also see themselves as sinners who have not kept the law: "all, both Jews and Greeks, are under sin. . . all have sinned and fall short of the glory of God" (Rom 3:9, 23). He rejects the claim that some Jews keep the law and can therefore be justifed on that basis: "For 'no human being will be justifed in his sight' by deeds prescribed by the law. . . ." (Rom 3:20). "It is evident that no one is justified before God by the law" (Gal 3:11).

In maintaining that no one can keep the law, Paul seems to run contrary to much Jewish thought of his day, where observance of the law was regarded as a human possibility. However, Paul does seem to admit the possibility of keeping the commandments in the way that many Jews kept them and even claims to have done so himself, writing that in his former life he was "blameless" with regard to righteousness under the law (Phil 3:6).

In order to make sense of his thought, it is necessary to return to the distinction between a literal and a spiritual fulfillment of the law. As noted in chapters 2 and 3, for Paul true fulfillment of the law involves keeping its spirit in accordance with the teaching of Jesus. Those who live by faith fulfill the law and are truly members of God's chosen people Israel, constituting the true circumcision (Rom 2:26-29; 4:13-25; Gal 3:29; 5:14—6:2; 6:16; Phil 3:3). While in one sense they are free from the law, in another they are under the law of Christ (1 Cor 9:20-21).

As noted previously, Paul also follows Jesus in teaching that all people will be judged on the basis of their works. At the same time, however, he insists that justification is by faith apart from works. While this can be understood in the sense that believers do not need to submit to all of the commandments of the Mosaic law in order to be justified, as those associated with the New Perspective on Paul have stressed, at times Paul undoubtedly does seem to question the idea that *any* type of good work in general can merit salvation from God (Rom 4:4-6; 9:10-12; 11:6; cf. Eph 2:8-9; 2 Tim 1:9; Tit 3:4-5).

The apparent contradiction in Paul's thought can be resolved by looking to his discussion in Romans and Galatians regarding what was written of Abraham in Gen 15:6: "he believed God, and it was reckoned to him as righteousness" (Rom 4:3; Gal 3:6). Paul points out that Abraham was accepted as righteous by God from the moment he simply believed God's promises. The fact that this occurred before he had been given the commandment regarding circumcision (Gen 17:9-14) and long before the Torah had been given to Moses demonstrated that neither circumcision nor obedience to the Torah is necessary for one to be accepted as righteous before God; all that is necessary is faith.

Nevertheless, it is important to interpret correctly what faith involves. In Abraham's case, his faith consisted of not doubting God but continuing to believe in God's promises, "hoping against hope" (Rom 4:18) when it seemed impossible that those promises might be fulfilled. Because he believed in God, *he did what God commanded him*, leaving his homeland, going where God told him to go and doing what God told him to do. Thus, while in a sense he was justified by faith alone, the very nature of this faith implied obedience, since one cannot truly trust in God without obeying God; by definition, to fail to do what God asks is to fail to trust God. For this reason, Paul repeatedly links faith to obedience. He defined his task as "to bring about the obedience of faith among all the Gentiles" (Rom 1:5; cf. 15:18). Those who believed were to become "slaves of righteousness" (Rom 6:18-19), since "obedience . . . leads to righteousness" (Rom 6:16). Thus faith and obedience are inseparable (Rom 10:16; 16:26; 2 Cor 9:13).

In Paul's thought, this faith and obedience are also inseparable from Jesus Christ. To believe in Jesus is to follow the teaching and example he gave regarding loving others and being committed to justice and righteousness (Rom 6:13-19; 8:4; 12:1—15:13; 1 Cor 1:10; 11:1; 2 Cor 5:14-15; 8:8-9; Gal 5:13—6:2, Eph 4:20—5:2; Phil 1:9-11; 2:1-8; Col 3:12-17; 1 Thess 3:12-13). It also involves following his same practice of entering into fellowship with "sinners" and associating and identifying with them as a fellow sinner (Gal 2:11-21). Here again, true faith involves a certain way of life. However, for Paul faith is also intimately tied to Jesus' death. In part, this is once again because of the example of love he laid down (Rom 14:7-8; 15:1-4; 2 Cor 5:14-15; Eph 5:2). Yet because Jesus' crucifixion was the consequence of his work to establish a new community open to "sinners" in which all would live under a new covenant, following his interpretation of God's will, and because God's raising of Jesus communicated God's approval and acceptance of Jesus' work as well as of the community of believers under him, for Paul justification is also inseparable from Jesus' death: believers "have been justified through his blood" (Rom 5:7), that is, his faithfulness to death to his God-given task of founding such a community. Justification no longer must be conceived as coming from obedience to the law of Moses as such but from God's grace in sending Jesus and forming a new people through him: "I do not nullify the grace of God; for if justification comes through the law, then Christ died for nothing" (Gal 2:21). In other words, people are now accepted as righteous by God, not by submitting to the Mosaic law, but by living as members of the community established through Jesus and through his death. He dedicated himself to forming such a community in which those for whom salvation was not accessible according to the Mosaic law might now attain that salvation living as members of the new covenant community over which he is Lord (Rom 15:7-12; 1 Cor 11:17-34; cf. Acts 13:38-39; Tit 2:14; 3:4-7). In this way, through his death he made salvation and justification available for all who have faith; they obtain forgiveness of sins as well as a new life of righteousness through the gift of the Holy Spirit now poured out on them.

For Paul, then, God's grace has to do with *all* that God has done in Jesus Christ. That grace has been manifested in Jesus' becoming "poor" for all (2 Cor 8:9), his life and teaching, the giving up of his life (Gal 1:4; 2:20), which also involved God giving him up "for us all" (Rom 8:32), his resurrection, the establishment of the church, and the pouring out of the Holy Spirit. All that has taken place has made it possible for those who had no access to God or salvation under the Mosaic covenant now to have access to all of the promises and blessings of God (Eph 2:11-22). And God did all of this, not because anyone (Jew or Gentile) deserved or merited it, but out of sheer grace and mercy, while all were still sinners at enmity with God (Rom 5:6-10).

This is what Paul has in mind when he speaks of justification being by grace and through faith. Through Christ, God graciously accepts those who were previously not acceptable and transforms them into new people. All that is necessary is that they believe as Abraham did in God's promises, which are now fulfilled in Jesus. When they have such faith, they are made into persons who practice righteousness in conformity with the law of Christ. This new life is not the result of the Mosaic law but of Christ's faithfulness unto death to the task of establishing a new covenant people, as well as God's raising of Christ and pouring out the Holy Spirit on those who become members of that people through faith.

In all of this, the continuity between Jesus and Paul is evident: justification is all about those who are conscious of the fact that they are "sinners" being received into the community of those who are accepted by God as righteous, not on the basis of anything they have done to merit God's mercy, grace, and love, but simply because they believe and trust in God to grant them both forgiveness and a new life of righteousness and obedience. This new life becomes a reality as they live *ek pisteōs*, that is, "out of faith," as the prophet Habakkuk affirms: "The one who is righteous will live out of faith" (Hab 2:4, my translation; Rom 1:17; Gal 3:11). This can be taken to mean alternatively that all who are declared righteous by virtue of their faith will live, that those who live out of faith are declared righteous by God, and that those who are declared righteous by God will live out of faith. In this sense, "the righteousness of God is revealed through faith for faith" (Rom 1:17): once one knows through the gospel that one's justification depends solely on believing in God and accepting God's promises through Jesus, one will come to such faith and consequently will practice the righteousness of God.

If Paul's teaching on justification is in continuity with that of Jesus, then other elements of his thought should also be viewed as being in essential continuity. *The reason that biblical scholars and theologians have failed to see the unity of thought between Jesus and Paul with regard to their understanding of justification is that they have interpreted Paul's writings on the basis of ontological, mystical, and even magical ideas that are as foreign to Paul as they are to Jesus.* In Jesus' teaching as presented in the Gospels, for example, there is no hint of the idea that justification results from

God communicating some mysterious reality or substance ("grace") to people or infusing some quality or power into them. While Jesus does speak of his followers receiving the Holy Spirit, that Spirit is consistently seen as relating personally to people rather than communicating some power or force to them or infusing something into them so that they are changed (Matt 10:20; Luke 11:13; 24:49; John 14:16-17, 26; 15:26; 16:13; 20:22; cf. Mark 1:8). In fact, nowhere in the Gospels do we find any hint of the idea that some type of ontological change is brought about in the human nature of those who come to faith in Jesus.

This is true as well regarding the way that faith is created. While faith is certainly understood as a divine gift in the Gospels, it is not seen as something infused or created magically in people. Faith is created as one observes Jesus' deeds and listens to his teaching (Matt 9:8; 14:33; 15:31; Mark 1:21-28, 45; 7:37; Luke 5:26; 7:16-17; 18:43; 21:38; John 2:11; 4:39-42, 53; 7:31; 8:30; 11:45-48). Faith in Jesus' resurrection and lordship is created by Jesus in his disciples, both women and men, when they see the empty tomb and then experience his presence in their midst (Matt 28:8-10, 17; Luke 24:8-10, 30-52; John 20:1-29). Jesus created faith in Paul as well by appearing to him on the road to Damascus (Acts 9:1-22; 22:2-16; 26:9-19). The creation of faith in people is therefore not analogous to God or the Holy Spirit waving a magic wand to bring something into existence that was not there before; rather, faith is created as one encounters Christ and the Spirit in one's life, not only in direct fashion but especially through the actions and witness of others. Such faith is from beginning to end a gift of God, since it is God's activity that brings it into being rather than anything human beings do.

Similarly, when Paul affirms that "God's love has been poured into our hearts through the Holy Spirit that has been given to us" (Rom 5:5), this should not be understood in the sense that love is some quality, essence, or substance infused into believers. Rather, the idea is that through their experience of the Holy Spirit's activity among them, they have come to have love in their hearts. Love is one of many "fruits" of the Spirit that believers begin to display when they are "guided by the Spirit" (Gal 5:22-25). Righteousness is a divine gift as well but is brought about in believers through the way that God has related to them through Jesus, the Holy Spirit, and their sisters and brothers in the community of believers. There is no basis in Paul's letters or the rest of the New Testament for seeing righteousness as some type of quality or substance infused into believers so as to inhere in them and mysteriously produce some effect in them. Neither should Paul be interpreted as affirming that sin is some such substance inhering in believers like a cancerous tumor which can be eradicated in the same way that medicines fight cancer—as if by dwelling in them, Christ or the Holy Spirit were to produce an effect analogous to the chemical or biological effects that medicines produce in the body of a person who is ill.

The same point must be made regarding Paul's affirmations that believers are "in Christ" and Christ is "in them."[90] There is no clear basis for taking these affirmations literally so as to claim that Paul believed that Jesus actually inhabited the body or soul of believers in some mysterious or mystical fashion so as to produce some type of ontological change in their human nature, mind, or body. Rather, Paul's thought in this regard should be understood in the same sense as his words to the Corinthians: "You are in our hearts, to live and to die together" (2 Cor 7:3). This is merely an expression of mutual solidarity in which they struggle together for the same cause for which Jesus lived and died but should not be taken literally, just as Paul's affirmations of being in Christ and living and dying with him should not be taken literally. Believers have died with Christ, not in an ontological or mystical sense, but in the sense that they identify with the cross (Rom 6:8; 2 Cor 5:14-15; Gal 2:20; 6:14; Col 2:20). Paul's language regarding suffering and dying with Christ should be understood as reflecting the same basic idea found in Jesus' affirmation that one must take up the cross daily to follow him.[91] Those who have identified with Jesus in this sense can be said to have died with him. There is no need to read other ideas back into Paul's language.

Ontological ideas should similarly not be read back into what Paul and the New Testament say regarding the church, baptism, and the Lord's Supper. The New Testament never conceives of the church as having the power to communicate or mediate some type of divine substances or realities, whether these be understood as grace, the Holy Spirit, or Christ himself. Both Christ and the Holy Spirit are free and sovereign persons and cannot be manipulated or mediated by human beings, as if subject to their control. Nor do baptism and the Lord's Supper contain any power, energy, or divine reality that are mysteriously communicated to believers through the water, bread, or wine so that they must cooperate with "it," however that "it" be understood. Strictly speaking, nothing mysterious, mystical, or magical takes place in people when they are baptized or commune. In New Testament thought, they do not participate in some real or ontological sense in Christ or in the event of his death and resurrection. Rather, they are transformed by the power of the word that is communicated with these acts, both by verbal and symbolic means. The metaphysical thought regarding the sacraments and salvation that has been characteristic of both Eastern and Western thought since patristic times is rooted neither in the teaching of Jesus nor in that of Paul.

Undoubtedly, because faith can be said to affect the very being of believers, in a sense it might be affirmed that an ontological change takes place in them. If so, then the idea that the forensic declaration of righteousness involved in justification is based on an ontological change in believers can be regarded as being in conformity with Paul's thought. In either case, however, it is important to note that the basis upon which believers are justified is the change that takes place *in them* as a result of their coming to faith. For this reason, the idea that justification involves God acquitting sinners or declaring them not guilty cannot be regarded as Pauline; nor can justification be defined merely as the forgiveness of sins. While no doubt forgiveness is involved, for Paul as for ancient Judaism in general justification involves a divine declaration that a person is righteous. To be righteous is not to be perfect or free from all sin but to live "out of faith," trusting fully in God in both a passive and an active sense so as to be transformed into people who live in the way God desires. In Paul's mind, this understanding of justification is the same as that found in the Hebrew Scriptures rather than constituting something new (Gen 15:6; Hab 2:4); the only difference is that, now that God's Son Jesus Christ has come, living out of faith involves believing not only in God but in Jesus as the Savior sent by God to fulfill God's promises.

If the analytic/synthetic distinction is applied to Paul's understanding of justification, then justification must be regarded as involving *both* an analytic *and* a synthetic judgment on God's part. On the one hand, the basis for God's gracious acceptance and forgiveness of believers lies *in* them, as an analytic understanding of justification affirms: they are declared righteous by virtue of the new way of being and thinking that is brought about in them as a result of God's grace and their faith. On the other hand, however, justification also involves a synthetic judgment on God's part, since the ground for their forgiveness lies partly *outside* of them in God's gracious acceptance of them in spite of their sinfulness. It is not entirely clear whether Paul would have agreed with Luther's idea that justification is based on an analytic judgment in which God declares believers righteous at present because, as long as they continue to have faith in Christ, God can be certain that they will *become* perfectly righteous in the end after they are raised to new life. In this case, while justification would involve a synthetic judgment as well, this would be only temporary and provisional until the time when believers are perfected. It is probably doubtful that Paul would have understood justification in this way, primarily because he did not equate righteousness with perfection in the way that later Christian theology has: the righteous are not perfect. Nevertheless, Paul does appear to teach that believers will ultimately be perfected in some sense (Phil 1:6, 3:10-12), so the idea that God declares believers righteous now because in Christ they will *become* perfectly righteous may perhaps be seen as being in harmony with his thought.

Whether or not Luther reflected faithfully Paul's teaching on that point, he certainly was mistaken in attributing to Paul the idea that Christ's righteousness is imputed to believers. Strictly speaking, neither this idea nor the idea that Christ's righteousness is actually imparted to believers is to be found in Paul's letters or the New Testament as a whole. At most, it might be said that Christ's righteousness is imparted to them in the sense that they attain to some extent his same righteous way of relating to God and others. It might also be said that his righteousness is imputed to them in the sense that God looks on them as if they were righteous like Christ because they are being transformed by Christ into persons who practice the same type of righteousness that he did. In either case, however, it is not Christ's *own* righteousness that is imparted or imputed to them but a righteousness that is *the same as* or *similar to* that of Christ. Because in New Testament thought perfection was not required of those to be justified, the notion that believers need the perfect righteousness of Christ to be reckoned to them in order to stand before God's presence cannot be considered biblical.

The idea that grace must be merited, either by Christ or by believers themselves, must also be seen as foreign to the New Testament. When grace is understood as the unconditional love of God manifested in all of the different ways that God has related to human beings in history, including especially through Christ and the Holy Spirit, then there can be no conditions for God's grace to be either granted or withheld. In biblical thought, even when human beings reject that grace, it does not come to an end; rather, as in ancient Jewish belief, God graciously seeks various ways of bringing people back to God's self, which may at times include sending hardships or chastisements upon them rather than abandoning them. Of course, in biblical thought, when God's efforts in this regard fail, God may be left with no alternative but to punish or destroy, yet this does not mean that God's love for those who have not accepted God's grace comes to an end; in fact, several passages from the Hebrew Scriptures reflect the idea that God continues to love those who are punished and even punishes them against God's own will (Lev 26:44-45; Ps 81:11-16; 89:31-34; Isa 48:17-19; Lam 3:31-33).

It is also important to distinguish between *unconditional love* and *unconditional acceptance*. While in biblical thought God loves all people unconditionally, God does not accept unconditionally all that people do, since God cannot be pleased when people practice injustice and evil in relation to one another. For people to be justified, therefore, they must meet certain conditions; yet whether they meet those conditions or not, God's love and grace toward them are not thought to cease.

The New Testament language concerning divine rewards and punishments must be viewed against this background. Both Jesus and Paul, for example, speak of God rewarding some and punishing others (Matt 6:1; 16:27; 25:31-46; Luke 6:23, 35; Rom 2:6-16; Col 3:24). While a reward is undoubtedly merited or deserved, in New Testament thought it is nevertheless an act of grace in that any human behavior remains flawed; thus God is being gracious when God rewards the good that human beings do. Furthermore, reward or punishment must be seen as meriting, not God's grace itself, but the *form* which that grace takes: both rewards *and* punishments in Scripture and in ancient Judaism are seen as manifestations of God's grace, since even punishments are seen as having a gracious purpose, as noted in chapter 1.

The difficulty in this, of course, is to reconcile the New Testament concept of eternal punishment with the idea of God's grace and unconditional love. This problem does not arise when it is said that God sends punishments on people in *this* world in order to correct or discipline them or bring them to repentance (Heb 12:5-7), since in that case God's purpose is considered a loving one. It may be argued that God threatens evildoers with eternal punishment for the loving purpose of bringing them to repentance in this life, yet if they fail to repent and consequently are condemned to eternal punishment, one can hardly see this condemnation as an act of grace or love toward them (though perhaps it may be seen as an act of love and grace toward those who had been oppressed by them and are thereby delivered from that oppression). Perhaps the only solution to this problem is to affirm that the condemnation of evildoers in biblical thought is to be seen, not as owing to any lack of grace, mercy, or love on God's part toward them, but only to their refusal to respond properly to that grace, mercy, and love. This does not entirely resolve the difficulty, however, since in principle it might be argued that God could nevertheless save them if God wished to do so.

Because God's grace in the New Testament is seen as being constant for all people, the distinctions between the various types of grace, such as "prevenient," "common," "operative," "cooperative," and "sanctifying," for example, cannot be regarded as biblical. The grace shown by Jesus in accepting and forgiving sinners as they were was the same grace he continued to show them as they then began to follow him. The grace shown by God to Paul when the risen Jesus appeared to him as he was persecuting the church was the same that God continued to show Paul throughout the rest of his life. While God's grace or unconditional love may be said to take different forms depending on circumstances, to speak of different types or kinds of grace is problematic both for biblical and theological reasons.

The fact that the New Testament affirms that those who come to faith may later fall from faith (Mark 4:16-17; Gal 5:4; Heb 6:4-6) means that the idea of a double justification can perhaps be regarded as biblical. Instead of distinguishing between a first or initial justification and a second or definitive one, however, it may be preferable simply to affirm that, in biblical thought, as long as believers remain in this life, the declaration that they are righteous is conditional and provisional and only becomes definitive at the final judgment. Although God's final judgment is said to be based on one's deeds, in New Testament thought this should not be seen as contradicting the affirmation that justification is by faith rather than works. As Kent Yinger has argued, this merely reflects the Jewish view that "one's outward behavior (one's *works* or *way*) will correspond to, and be a visible manifestation of, inward reality."[92] In other words, in New Testament thought *faith saves because it leads to a life of obedience to God's will*, which will obviously be manifested in concrete deeds (though not in perfection); yet in order to live such a life of obedience, believers are constantly called to look, not to their own strength or abilities, but only to God and God's Son Jesus Christ in faith and trust. In this way, they can be assured that God will both bring about in them the works God desires to see and graciously forgive their sins now and at the final judgment.

This also means that the New Testament gospel must be understood not only in terms of the *forgiveness of sins* but the *transformation of believers*. The good news is not only that in Christ God declares believers righteous but also that, through Christ and the Holy Spirit, God brings about in them a new life of justice and righteousness so that they can experience the blessings that result from such a life (Rom 8:6; 14:17; 2 Cor 9:10-11; Gal 5:22-23; Phil 3:7-8). In this way, they are healed and made whole.

CHAPTER 5

Christian Life in the World

In Lutheran thought, those who have been justified by God's grace and mercy through faith are set free to "to serve, help, and in every way deal with [their] neighbor as [they see] that God through Christ has dealt and still deals with [them]."[1] They do this not in order to earn God's favor or merit their salvation but because they have already received God's favor and salvation as a free gift. Justification, then, is to lead to a new life in which believers fulfill God's law with joy and gladness in both the private and the public spheres of their existence.

The Lutheran understanding of the relationship between justification and Christian life in the world, however, raises a number of questions. Once believers have been justified by faith, is it still necessary for them to be transformed *further* in some way while they live in this world? How can it be said that they are "*under obligation* to do what is for [their] neighbor's good" if their salvation does not ultimately depend on any good works they do but only on their faith?[2] Are they still subject to God's law in some sense or do they now live only under the gospel? And if the "sole purpose of the spiritual life" in this world is to "take us to yonder life" in heaven and "the temporal life will be completely destroyed" so that "nothing of it will remain,"[3] as Luther affirmed, what is the sense of working to transform this world into a place of greater peace, justice, and well-being?

Sanctification and the Christian Life in Lutheran Teaching

Lutheran theologians have generally used the term "sanctification" to refer to the life of righteousness that follows upon justification, even though Luther himself did not use this word in a technical sense to distinguish it from justification.[4] He did, however, repeatedly speak of a growth in righteousness resulting from faith: through faith, believers receive a new heart and spirit and consequently begin to live according to God's will. Luther understood this as a natural process analogous to the way a good tree produces good fruits:

> [T]he righteous man of his own accord does all and more than
> the law demands. . . . A good tree needs no instruction or law to
> bear good fruit; its nature causes it to bear according to its kind
> without any law or instruction. I would take to be quite a fool
> any man who would make a book full of laws and statutes for an
> apple tree telling it how to bear apples and not thorns, when the
> tree is able by its own nature to do this better than the man with
> all his books can describe and demand. Just so, by the Spirit and
> by faith all Christians are so thoroughly disposed and condi-
> tioned in their very nature that they do right and keep the law
> better than one can teach them with all manner of statutes.[5]

In Luther's thought, those who have been justified are transformed so that
they begin to fulfill God's law with joy by loving God and others. Luther often
refers to this in terms of an incipient beginning in righteousness or the beginning of a new creation.[6] Nevertheless, although this process begins in the
present life, it will be completed only in the life to come. For that reason, at
present one's justification does not depend on the righteousness one attains in
this life but only on the righteousness of Christ reckoned to believers by faith:

> In the life to come, when we shall be completely cleansed of all
> our faults and sins and shall be as pure as the sun, we shall love
> perfectly and shall be righteous through our perfect love. But
> in this present life such purity is hindered by our flesh, to
> which sin will cling as long as we live. . . . But meanwhile we
> are sustained by the trust that Christ, "who committed no sin
> and on whose lips no guile was found" (1 Peter 2:22), covers us
> with his righteousness. Shaded and protected by this covering,
> this heaven of the forgiveness of sins and this mercy seat, we
> begin to love and to keep the Law. As long as we live, we are
> not justified or accepted by God on account of this keeping of
> the Law. But "when Christ delivers the kingdom to God the
> Father after destroying every authority" (1 Cor. 15:24), and
> when "God is everything to everyone" (1 Cor. 15:28), then
> faith and hope will pass away, and love will be perfect and
> eternal (1 Cor. 13:8). . . . If we were pure of all sin, and if we
> burned with a perfect love toward God and our neighbor, then
> we would certainly be righteous and holy through love, and
> there would be nothing more that God could require of us.

That does not happen in this present life but must be post-poned until the life to come. . . .[7]

This means that in Luther's thought it would be improper to speak of a gradual growth toward perfection that might attain its goal in this world, since that perfection will not take place until believers are raised from the dead. For this reason, their justification does not depend in any way on the level of righteousness they attain in this world.

According to Luther, throughout their life on earth believers are righteous and sinners at the same time (*simul justus et peccator*). They continue to sin because they remain in the flesh and are constantly subject to the desires of that flesh, or concupiscence, as a result of original or inherited sin. Luther regarded both the actions resulting from this concupiscence as well as that concupiscence itself as sin; as such, it is subject to divine wrath and condemnation. With the aid of the Holy Spirit, believers struggle against the "old person" or "old Adam" that still clings to their flesh, seeking to drown it daily;[8] yet they can never totally overcome this power of sin in them, much less approach perfection in this life. Thus, in spite of their beginning in righteousness, believers can only continue to be accepted as righteous in God's sight by depending solely on the righteous-ness of Christ, which avails for them before God until they reach perfection in the life to come. This involves living by faith, which must constantly be strengthened and nourished by the hearing of the proclamation of God's word and the reception of the sacrament of Holy Communion.

As noted briefly in chapter 2, Lutheran scholars have been divided over the question of the role that the law is to play in the life of believers. While Luther never spoke of a third use of the law, some claim that the idea that believers must continue to look to the law for guidance is indeed present in Luther's thought. The idea of a third use of the law was developed by Philip Melanch-thon, who taught that after the law had driven believers to faith in Christ (the second use), it continued to serve the purpose of directing and instructing them in their daily life.[9] According to this line of thought, to claim that the law no longer has any role in the life of believers would result in antinomianism. Because believers remain subject to the power of sin, they also need the law to help restrain their sinful desires. Other Lutheran theologians, however, have argued that the idea of a third use of the law leads to legalism and places the gospel in a subservient relationship to the law, as if the ultimate purpose of the gospel were to enable believers to obey the law. This seems to give the law priority over the gospel.

Just as believers remain sinners in this life and will not be perfected until the resurrection, so also the present world remains under sin and evil. This means that believers are not to hope that the world will eventually become a place of perfect peace and justice. The best that can be hoped for is to hold sin in check as much as possible through the law (first use). God accomplishes this through those to whom God has given authority to wield the sword. On the basis of Luther's teaching, the doctrine of the two kingdoms became a part of Lutheran theology. According to this doctrine, in the present age, God rules the world through the authorities God has established over it and through God's law; this is the temporal kingdom on God's "left hand." However, God also rules over believers in the spiritual kingdom on God's "right hand" by means of the gospel as they are moved by God's grace in Christ to lead a God-pleasing life.[10]

The Life of Faith and Righteousness in Jewish Teaching

Because in ancient Jewish thought justification depends on one's actually living a righteous life in conformity to the law, the idea that a sanctified life *follows* upon justification must be considered foreign to it. Undoubtedly, it was thought that when a person was included as a member of the community of those whom God graciously accepted as righteous, a holy and righteous life should follow. However, one only continued to be justified or counted among the righteous as long as one continued to be committed to living in obedience to God's commandments and repented of one's sins; and one's ultimate justification before God as judge depended on this as well. Thus, in ancient Judaism, justification was not believed simply to *precede* sanctification or a life of holiness and righteousness and bring about such a life as a result or consequence but instead had to do with one's being accepted by God as righteous throughout one's life on the basis of one's commitment to God's law.

The idea of a growth toward perfection also seems to have been foreign to ancient Judaism. To be sure, the righteous would grow in many ways throughout their life and perhaps even come to live more righteously as they advanced in age. But their commitment to obeying the law as well as their repentance when they sinned was to remain constant over the course of their entire lifetime. The idea of perfection is also not characteristic of ancient Jewish thought, at least as this idea has often been understood in Protestantism. As mentioned in chapter 2, the righteous could be called "perfect" even though they were never without sin. A number of passages from the Hebrew Scriptures and other ancient Jewish writings do speak of God's people coming to obey the law fully and abandoning sin at some point in the future. These may have been understood as pointing to an eschatological perfection of the righteous, which would be accomplished when God's Spirit was poured out on the people.[11] Yet once more it is not clear that this perfection was understood in absolute terms.

In the Hebrew Scriptures, the present reality and the new reality that God promised to bring about by redeeming Israel are seen to be in essential continuity with one another; the same is true with regard to the idea of two ages or worlds in ancient Judaism. Those who believed in the resurrection of the dead generally conceived of this in terms of a return to life on *this* earth, though they may also have believed that those raised would be radically transformed so as no longer to suffer or die.[12] However, the idea of a gradual progression toward some kind of utopian existence seems not to have been characteristic of ancient Judaism. The present world had to be brought to an end, perhaps by violent means, before the world to come might become a reality. Especially in Jewish apocalyptic thought, the present age was regarded as increasingly evil and thus some type of radical transformation of this world by God was deemed to be necessary.[13]

In principle, the concept of *simul justus et peccator* seems not to be in conflict with ancient Jewish thought, since it was always recognized that the righteous continued to sin in this life. Generally, however, the righteous were not referred to as "sinners," since this term was reserved for those who refused to submit to God's commandments. As noted in chapter 2, ancient Judaism also came to speak of two tendencies in human beings: a tendency for good and a tendency for evil. Although in the age to come the tendency toward evil might be overcome by God's Spirit, in this life it was up to the righteous themselves to struggle against the tendency toward evil and seek to subdue it, following instead the tendency toward good. Both the Mosaic law and the community of believers provided assistance to each individual member of God's people so that she or he might follow the path of good rather than evil. In this regard, as observed in chapter 2, the law was seen as a remedy for sin, since it served to guide and instruct God's people as Torah. In reality, it can be said that the Torah fulfilled all three of the uses traditionally attributed to the law in Protestantism, serving to curb sin and check evil (first use), make sinful behavior evident so as to drive people to return to God in repentance, seeking God's grace and mercy (second use), and guide them in their moral decisions and behavior (third use).

Christian Life in the World in the New Testament

Although the New Testament does not use the word "sanctification" in the technical sense that it appears in Protestant theology, there can be no doubt that the idea that persons come to live a holy life as a result of their faith is found there. This idea is stressed particularly with regard to those who previously did *not* live a life in accordance with the law, such as the Jewish and Gentile "sinners" who came to faith in Christ. They become "obedient from the heart" and are "set free from sin" in order to be transformed into "slaves of righteousness" who present their members as "slaves to righteousness for sanctification" (Rom 6:17-20). They put away their "former way of life" and "old self, corrupt and deluded by its lusts" so as to be renewed in the spirit of their minds, clothed in a new self "created according to the likeness of God in true righteousness and holiness" (Eph 4:22-24; cf. Rom 6:4; 12:1-3; 1 Co 6:9-11; Col 3:1-17; 1 Thess 1:9; 4:3-7; Tit 3:1-3).

At times, the New Testament speaks of believers "growing" in faith, knowledge, love, righteousness, and obedience (2 Cor 9:10-12; 10:15; Eph 4:11-16; Col 1:9-10; 1 Thess 3:12-13; 2 Thess 1:3; 1 Pet 2:2; 2 Pet 3:18). This implies some kind of process or progression that takes place over the lifetime of believers. The New Testament can also speak of believers becoming perfect or blameless in some sense in this life (Matt 5:48; 19:21; 1 Cor 1:8; 2 Cor 7:1; 10:6; Eph 4:13; Phil 1:10; 2:15; 3:15; Col 1:22, 28; 4:12; 1 Thess 3:13; 5:23; Heb 10:14; Jms 1:4; 2 Pet 3:14). This should not be understood in terms of absolute sinlessness, however, since it is clear that believers also continue to sin and remain in need of forgiveness from God and from one another (Matt 5:23-25; 6:12-15; 18:21-35; Mark 11:25-26; Luke 17:3-4; 2 Cor 2:7, 10; Eph 4:32; Col 3:13; Jms 3:2; 5:15; 1 John 1:9—2:2). Thus even believers remain "sinners and saints" in this world, to the end of their life.

The New Testament writings, including especially the Pauline letters, affirm that even after they come to faith, believers remain subject to the desires of the flesh, which they are to resist (Rom 6:12; 7:5-25; 13:14; 2 Cor 7:1; Gal 5:16; 6:8; 1 Thess 4:3-5; 1 Pet 2:11; 4:1-2; 1 John 2:15-16). God's gift of the Holy Spirit assists and empowers them in this struggle against their sinful desires (Rom 8:1-14; Gal 5:16-25). The New Testament is not clear on whether these desires in themselves are to be regarded as sin requiring forgiveness or only the sinful behavior that can result from these desires. Paul does speak of sin as a power that continues to reside in believers but does not specifically say that this power is something that needs to be forgiven as sin rather than simply overcome (Rom 3:9; 6:12-22; 7:7-25).

Even though the New Testament obviously does not speak of a "third use" of the law, a number of passages indicate that the first Christians continued to look to the law for guidance (Matt 5:17-37; 1 Cor 9:8-9; Eph 6:1-3). At the same time, it is said that believers are free from the law (Rom 6:14-15; 7:6; 1 Cor 9:20-21; Gal 3:23-24; 4:21; 5:18; Eph 2:15). As noted previously, this can be understood in the sense that they are under obligation to fulfill the spirit of the Mosaic law and the righteousness commanded in it yet are not bound to a literal observance of all of the prescriptions of that law.

Although the New Testament affirms that believers are to dedicate themselves to justice and righteousness, the fact that in the first century Christians were such a small minority meant that they could hardly hope to bring about the transformation of society as a whole and establish a world of peace and justice. Much less could they realistically expect that entire societies or nations might become Christian; at best they might strive to be salt and light in the world (Matt 5:13-16), exercising some influence for good in the world on a relatively small scale. As a minority, they tended to see the world and history in apocalyptic terms: the world was subject to the forces of evil and thus was inevitably full of sin and injustice (John 12:31; 2 Cor 4:4; Eph 2:1-2; 6:12). Believers were to refuse to have anything to do with sin and evil, since the present evil age would soon be brought to an end (Rom 12:2; 1 Cor 7:29-31; 11:32; Gal 1:4; 6:14; Eph 4:17—5:20; Col 3:1-11; Jms 4:4; 2 Pet 1:4; 1 John 2:15-17). A couple of passages, most notably Rom 13:1-7 and 1 Pet 2:13-17, exhort believers to be subject to the human authorities. At the same time, the New Testament speaks repeatedly of Christians and Jesus himself being persecuted by the human authorities, which implies that at least some type of passive resistance to those authorities under certain circumstances was believed to be pleasing to God.

While the first Christians expected sin and injustice to continue to prevail in the world in the present age and believed that things would only change when God intervened from above by sending Jesus again in glory and power, Jesus' struggle against evil and suffering throughout his ministry is evidence that he did not believe that one should passively accept such things. Nevertheless, according to the Gospels, Jesus did not believe that his own efforts or those of his disciples would eradicate suffering and evil in the world and eventually lead to some type of utopian world. Thus, while on the one hand Jesus seems to have taught that his followers should actively struggle against evil, sin, and injustice in the world, on the other he apparently believed that human beings could never resolve these problems entirely; only God could accomplish this.

Justification and Sanctification

All Christian traditions agree that faith is to lead to a life of righteousness and holiness and that believers should grow in these things. Disagreements have centered primarily on the question of whether justification and salvation depend on one's living such a life or achieving that growth. While Protestants have traditionally insisted that sanctification is not a condition for justification, other

Christians, including especially Roman Catholics, have argued that ultimately justification and salvation do indeed depend on one living a life of righteousness and obedience after one comes to faith.

The problem with this second view is that it seems to make it necessary to define a certain degree or level of righteousness that one must attain in order to be justified. Virtually all traditions, of course, recognize that those who sin and then sincerely repent can be justified and saved, no matter how often this happens. Christians would also agree that those who come to faith at the very end of their life and thus never have a chance to lead a new life of righteousness can be saved, as the example of the thief on the cross makes evident (Luke 23:39-43). Yet some would argue that this constitutes the exception and that, in the vast majority of cases, those believers who have the opportunity to live a sanctified life must do so in order to be justified and saved. The difficulty, however, lies in defining precisely *how* holy and righteous a life they must lead in order to continue to be justified.

In contrast, the problem with the Protestant view that justification and salvation are in no way dependent on sanctification is that it seems to make sanctification unnecessary and superfluous. Protestants have generally responded to this problem by claiming as Luther did that true faith inevitably produces a sanctified life as a natural consequence. The reality, however, is that believers continue to sin, at times even flagrantly. When this happens, the doctrine of justification by faith alone seems to provide no basis for insisting that they *must* refrain from sinning; all that can be said is that they *should* or *ought* to do so. At most, it can be argued that if a life of righteousness and good works is lacking or insufficient, this is evidence that a person does not truly have saving faith, since true faith cannot exist separately from righteousness and good works.[14] In reality, however, this makes justification depend on works once more, since it raises the question of how many good works are necessary to demonstrate the presence of true faith. This would seem to undermine any certainty believers might have regarding their justification, forcing them to examine themselves constantly to see if their faith is producing sufficient works.

Even when sanctification is not regarded as a condition for justification, at times Protestant thought has stressed the importance of sanctification to such an extent that believers are made to feel pressured to produce a sanctified life. Often this sanctified life is defined not so much in terms of seeking justice and serving others but abstaining from anything associated with carnal pleasure, focusing on personal spiritual growth, and living a pious and godly life. The objective is to be "holy" in the sense of being separated from whatever is profane and worldly, all of which is condemned as sinful. Even when it is maintained that one's salvation does not depend on living such a life, the implicit message is that those who do not submit to such an understanding of the sanctified life run the risk of losing their salvation and are not living in a God-pleasing way; they are then judged to be less spiritual or holy by those who are more pious and godly, with the result that Christians end up being divided into two or more classes. In reality, then, such an understanding of sanctification can involve affirming implicitly a doctrine of justification by works, even though explicitly such a doctrine is rejected.

The idea that believers must grow and make progress in their sanctification raises the same difficulties as the claim that works are necessary for salvation. If this growth or progress is regarded as necessary in some sense, then it must be quantified in order to determine if it is sufficient or acceptable. Believers are once more under pressure to give evidence of their progress in sanctification.

Some Protestants, most notably of the Methodist tradition, have even claimed that Christians can become perfect in some sense in this life. John Wesley defined sin in terms of a voluntary, overt, and deliberate transgression of God's law as one has come to know it and on the basis of this definition claimed that Christians can reach a point in which they no longer sin.[15] Undoubtedly, "omissions, short-comings, mistakes in general and defects of various kinds" continue to exist in the life of all Christians and for this they require forgiveness and the atoning work of Christ; for Wesley, however, these should be understood more as "infirmities" than as "sins properly so-called."[16] Believers also continue to experience sinful desires, even though, strictly speaking, sin no longer reigns in them.[17]

When this kind of perfection is seen as an attainable goal, even if not all believers are expected to reach that goal, they inevitably are placed under pressure to attempt to do so. To say that one *can* achieve progress in one's sanctification or become perfect is to say that one *should* or perhaps even *must* make every effort to do so. Those who do not attain that goal or who do not at least make an effort do so are then seen as inferior Christians in whom there is something deficient or wrong.

In contrast to these ideas, Lutheran theologians, following Luther, have insisted that each believer remains sinful and righteous at the same time throughout life. For Luther, believers are *fully* or *totally* righteous and *fully* or *totally* sinners at the same time (*totaliter peccatores et iusti totaliter*). As Paul Althaus notes,

> This double character remains through all of life. Both are always true of me at one and the same time. This is the great paradox of Christian existence. Neither reason nor legalistic thinking can

understand the contradiction involved in the fact that one and the same man is at one and the same time both a righteous man and a sinner: and he is both completely; it is not as though he were partially righteous and partially a sinner but rather he is completely a sinner and completely righteous.[18]

The reason Luther insists that all believers are fully righteous and fully sinful at the same time is that, if one were to affirm that one were *not* fully righteous in God's eyes on account of Christ, it would then be necessary for one to become *more* righteous in order to be justified. It would therefore be up to Christians themselves to attain this further righteousness and they could not have assurance of salvation. Of course, in one sense this righteousness is only forensic, in that they are not *actually* righteous in their entirety in this life. However, as noted previously, because in Luther's thought believers will become entirely righteous in the future, God is able to look upon them as fully righteous even now.

The affirmation that believers remain fully and totally sinners responds to the same concern. If it were maintained that they are only *partly* sinners, then the goal would be to become *less* of a sinner or even reach a stage in which one is no longer a sinner by leaving sin behind entirely. This would place the burden of justification back on the shoulders of believers, since they would have to constantly be examining themselves to see if they are progressing sufficiently in the process of their own sanctification. Furthermore, this idea stresses that even though they remain sinners, God loves and accepts them *just as they are*; while God certainly wants sinners to change, they do not need to change in order to be accepted and justified by God in God's grace and mercy. If they did, then it would be necessary to say that God does not accept and justify them until they make a certain amount of progress in their sanctification.

The idea of concupiscence also enters in here. Virtually all Christian traditions recognize that, because believers remain subject to fallen human nature, they continue to experience the desires of the flesh associated with concupiscence. All agree as well on the need to attempt to resist and overcome these desires. The Lutheran view that believers remain sinners in their entirety, however, serves to stress that they continue to experience those fleshly desires throughout their entire life and thus can never rid themselves of them or even make them decrease; in this regard, they cannot make "progress" against those desires.[19] Undoubtedly, they can grow in their ability to resist them and in that sense make progress; nevertheless, while at times they may take steps forward, they may also take steps backward. The fact that one falls back does not make one any more of a sinner, however, just as making progress does not make one less of a sinner, because one remains a sinner in one's entirety. This is because believers remain just as subject to sinful desires or concupiscence as unbelievers since this is characteristic of all who exist in human flesh.

This understanding of the existence of believers is based on Luther's interpretation of Rom 7:7-25, where Paul writes of wanting to do the good but not being able to do so because of the sin that dwells inside of him. Following Augustine, Luther understood this to be the situation of believers, who are constantly struggling with themselves, since they are "at the same time completely flesh and completely spirit."[20] As was the case with Paul, "one and the same man at the same time serves the law of God and the law of sin, at the same time is righteous and sins! For he does not say: 'My mind serves the law of God,' nor does he say: 'My flesh serves the law of sin,' but: 'I, the whole man, the same person, I serve a twofold servitude'." Thus "the saints at the same time as they are righteous are also sinners; righteous because they believe in Christ, whose righteousness covers them and is imputed to them, but sinners because they do not fulfill the Law, are not without concupiscence, and are like sick men under the care of a physician; they are sick in fact but healthy in hope and in the fact that they are beginning to be healthy, that is, they are 'being healed'."[21]

As was noted in chapter 2, Lutheran theology understands sin more in terms of one's *being* than one's *actions*. Luther insisted that the real problem is not what sinners *do* but lies at the core of their being; they must receive a new heart in order to be pleasing to God. One's actions are merely like the symptoms of an illness. Therefore, what is necessary is not simply to attempt to control the symptoms but to get at the root of the disease. For this reason, Lutheran thought regards as sinful the concupiscence that is embedded in the heart of every human being. Lutheran theology also tends to understand regeneration in terms of the creation of a totally new person or "new Adam" that is brought about by the Holy Spirit. The old person or "old Adam" continues to exist in believers throughout this life, "hanging around our necks" and constantly burdening believers with sinful desires.[22] The destruction of this old person takes place only at death.[23] At present, believers continue to be the old and the new simultaneously, even though they seek to put the old person to death daily.

In all of this, the concern in Lutheran thought is that believers constantly be directed to look not to themselves but to Christ and to the Holy Spirit.[24] Thus they are not to look inside themselves to see if they have sufficient faith, as if they had to "believe that they believe" in order to have assurance of their justification; nor are they to look at their own works in order to see if those works provide sufficient evidence of true faith, as if their assurance of salvation depended on demonstrating that their faith is producing all of the fruits that it should. Rather, they are to look only to Christ and the Holy Spirit.

When this is understood, then it is possible to speak in terms of some type of growth or progress in righteousness, as Luther himself does: "Christ daily drives out the old Adam more and more in accordance with the extent to which faith and knowledge of Christ grow. For alien righteousness is not instilled all at once, but it begins, makes progress, and is finally perfected at the end through death."[25] Like good works themselves, this progress or growth is the natural and inevitable consequence of clinging to Christ in faith; yet believers are not under any pressure to produce fruits, just as in Luther's thought a tree will naturally grow and produce greater and larger fruit over the course of time without being commanded or pressured to do so.

This must also be borne in mind when speaking of believers "cooperating" in their sanctification. While Lutheran theologians have rejected the idea that persons can cooperate with God in their justification, they have affirmed that the notion of cooperation can rightly be applied to the life of Christians after they have been justified. "For when the Holy Spirit has effected and accomplished new birth and conversion and has altered and renewed the human will solely through his divine power and activity, then the new human will is an instrument and tool of God the Holy Spirit, in that the will not only accepts grace but also cooperates with the Holy Spirit in the works that proceed from it."[26] This does not mean that believers are under pressure to cooperate sufficiently with the Holy Spirit, however, since their sanctification is not regarded as their own work but that of the Holy Spirit to whom they look and on whom they depend entirely.

In order to stress the importance of a life of sanctification and good works, Lutheran theologians have gone so far as to affirm that good works are "necessary," as Article IV of the Formula of Concord affirms. Those who worked on this article rejected the idea that good works were detrimental to salvation. Some had come to affirm this latter idea in an attempt to buttress the doctrine of justification by faith alone, claiming that when believers strive to do good works they easily fall into the trap of looking to those works in order to be assured that they have faith and are justified rather than looking to Christ alone. At the same time, the Lutheran theologians who composed this article rejected the affirmation that good works are necessary *for salvation* (even though Luther himself used such language),[27] since this would once more put believers under pressure to do good works in order to be saved. Thus they simply affirmed that good works are necessary in the sense that they are the necessary fruit or consequence of justifying faith.

Nevertheless, many Christians have continued to regard as problematic the Lutheran refusal to affirm that sanctification and good works *must* follow upon justification and faith. For them, it is not enough simply to affirm that believers *should* or *will* produce good works. The claim that good works are merely necessary but not necessary *for salvation* raises difficulties when it is considered that something can only be called "necessary" when it is viewed in relation to something else that cannot exist or take place without it. Nothing can rightly be called necessary simply in and of itself. In this case, the question arises: If good works are not necessary for salvation or justification, then for what *are* they necessary? In reality, to reject the affirmation that good works are necessary for salvation is to maintain that good works are *not* necessary for salvation, which implies that they are superfluous. In the end, believers are free *not* to do good works if that is their choice, even though by virtue of their faith they *should* feel moved to do them and actually do them.

This same criticism lies behind the objections that have been raised against a number of the other Lutheran teachings mentioned above, especially by Roman Catholic theologians. Roman Catholics have often interpreted the Lutheran teaching that believers remain simultaneously righteous and sinners against the background of a purely forensic doctrine of justification in which believers are accepted by God as righteous solely on the basis of the righteousness of Christ imputed to them, without any real change having taken place in them. Against such an interpretation, Roman Catholic theologians have insisted that an actual change takes place in the essence of those who come to faith, so that they truly *are* righteous with a righteousness of their own. Avery Dulles, for example, argues that there must be more involved than a mere "nonimputation of sins," as if justification took place in a "purely nominalistic way that leaves us internally untouched"; there must be "a real, internal transformation" in which one "in a true sense ceases to be a sinner."[28] Roman Catholic theologians like Dulles have also expressed the concern that the Lutheran teaching might imply that, as sinners, believers continue to be "slaves of sin."[29] The Lutheran idea that something "damnable" remains in those justified is also problematic for Roman Catholicism.[30] This is related to the Roman Catholic belief that concupiscence itself is not sinful: believers cannot be held responsible for experiencing sinful desires but only for succumbing to those desires and following them. Thus, while Roman Catholics have declared that the Lutheran doctrine of *simul justus et peccator* is acceptable if it is understood properly,[31] in general they have remained concerned that it implies that believers need not struggle to overcome sin and grow in righteousness and holiness but are simply to accept themselves as "sinners in their entirety" who are righteous only in the sense that Christ's righteousness is imputed to them.

Roman Catholics and other Christians have also criticized Lutheran teaching for taking an overly negative and pessimistic view of human nature: no matter how hard we may try, we will always remain sinners, and even the good things we do will always be tainted by sin, since the motivations behind our actions are never pure.[32] On the basis of this view of human nature, Lutherans have argued that the sinful person or "old Adam" cannot be reformed but instead must be condemned and destroyed entirely so that a new person or "new Adam" can take its place. This stands in contrast to the Roman Catholic idea that "grace perfects nature." In this case, sinful human nature is capable of being renewed and reformed, since there is something good or "salvageable" in it. This idea in turn is rejected by Lutheran theologians, who would insist that if there is something good or salvageable in our human nature, then we must look inward to ourselves for the ability to change rather than looking to Christ alone.[33]

Ultimately, this constitutes the Lutheran concern: that believers be constantly directed to look to God, Christ, and the Holy Spirit not only for their justification but for their sanctification as well, rather than being directed to look to themselves or their own faith, works, strength, or abilities. For believers to look to themselves for either justification or sanctification not only undermines any assurance of salvation on their part but also leads to divisions and distinctions between Christians, boasting, and hypocrisy. If in principle it is possible for some works to be entirely good, untainted by sin, then we will be under pressure to perform such works and will even blind ourselves to selfish interests that lie behind those works. This leads to hypocrisy, in which we attempt to give others the impression that we are holy, righteous people whose actions are entirely pure when in reality this is not the case. If it is possible for us to become better people through our own efforts, then we will be under constant pressure to do so, and those who in the eyes of others do *not* become better will be viewed as inferior and deficient. If our nature can be transformed by grace, then we will be directed to look inside ourselves to make sure that this transformation is taking place as it should and depend on our own natural powers and abilities rather than on God's grace. If concupiscence itself is not a sin but only what we do in response to those fleshly desires, then the problem of sin no longer has to do with who we are but only what we do; at our core, we are no longer sinners but people who are essentially good and just, even though we frequently fall into sin. And since in our very being we are no longer sinful but have already been transformed into righteous people, we can and should look to our own strength and abilities to overcome the fleshly desires that assail us rather than looking to God alone as the only one capable of overcoming the power of sin in us. In fact, from a Lutheran perspective, sanctification must be seen as having to do, not so much with growing in individual piety and interior holiness, but in one's trust in Christ and in one's service to one's neighbor. The reason why Luther did not define the Christian life primarily in terms of sanctification was that he saw faith as directing believers *outward away from themselves toward God and their neighbor* rather than directing their attention *inward* to their own personal growth in sanctification.

Thus, although there are clearly points of agreement between the Lutheran and Roman Catholic views on justification and the sanctified life, there do in fact seem to be fundamental differences between them. In essence, it might be stated that the main difference is that, in Roman Catholic thought and at times much Protestant thought as well, God's acceptance of sinful believers is seen as depending on their doing their best to live a righteous, sanctified life after they have originally been declared righteous by God's grace. From this perspective, the Lutheran teaching seems to encourage believers merely to accept sin rather than struggle against it. In contrast, Lutheran teaching stresses that God simply accepts believers as they are in spite of their sin and does not make this acceptance depend on any change in them; and if God accepts sinful believers as they are, they are also to accept themselves as they are as well as accepting others as they are. In other words, whereas Roman Catholicism tends to stress that people must first be transformed in order to be accepted by God, Lutheranism stresses that people must first be accepted by God as they are in order then to be transformed.

The Third Use of the Law

According to Article VI of the Formula of Concord, the third purpose for which God's law was given was that those who have been reborn might have "a sure guide, according to which they can orient and conduct their entire life."[34] This is the primary role of the law or Torah in Judaism: it serves to guide and instruct the members of God's people in all aspects of their daily life. The reason that it is necessary for believers to continue to use the law in this way is that their "rebirth and renewal is not perfect in this world" and they are "engaged with the spirit of their minds in continual battle against the flesh, that is, against the perverted nature and character which clings to us until death. . . ." Thus to avoid believers resolving to "perform service to God on the basis of their pious imagination in an arbitrary way of their own choosing, it is necessary for the law of God constantly to light their way."[35] Of course, believers are not under the law and have been liberated from it in the sense that "the law cannot burden those whom Christ has reconciled with God with its curse and cannot torment the reborn with its coercion because they delight in the law of the Lord according to their inward persons."[36] Yet because of "the perverted nature and character which clings to us until death and which because of the old creature is still lodged in the human understanding, will, and all human powers," they must remain "not under the law but in the law; they live and walk in the law of the Lord and yet do nothing because of the compulsion of the law."[37]

Many of these ideas are found in Reformed thought as well. According to Calvin, believers profit by the law in that it serves as "the best instrument for them to learn more thoroughly each day the nature of the Lord's will to which they aspire, and to confirm them in the understanding of it" and also in that it draws them "back from the slippery path of transgression." The latter is necessary because they are still in the flesh: "The law is to the flesh like a whip to an idle and balky ass, to arouse it to work."[38] By exhorting them, it serves as a power "to shake off their sluggishness, by repeatedly urging them, and to pinch them awake to their imperfection," even though it can no longer condemn their consciences by threatening them.[39] In contrast to Lutheran thought, however, where the second use of the law is regarded as primary, Calvin considered this third use the "principal use, which maintains more closely to the proper purpose of the law."[40]

The idea of a third use of the law has been heavily criticized by many Lutheran theologians past and present on various grounds.[41] First of all, if the law is said to fulfill the task of coercing believers into obedience not only through its "instruction and admonition" but "its warning and threatening" as well, so as to restrain sin and hold the flesh and the old Adam in check,[42] then it would appear that we are actually talking about the *first* use of the law rather than a *third* use. And if it serves to "show and indicate, as if in a mirror, that they are still imperfect and impure in this life" so as to make evident to them their sin and their need for Christ,[43] the law is fulfilling the same purpose as it does according to its second use, where it serves to bring people to a knowledge of their sin and point them to Christ.[44] Undoubtedly, because they believe in the gospel, it no longer oppresses them and drives them to despair; but it still accuses them in the sense of pointing out their sin and leading them to repent of it. For these reasons, some have questioned the propriety of speaking of a third use of the law that is distinct from the first two.

However, the idea that the law instructs believers concerning the "eternal and unchanging will of God" actually seems to be slightly different.[45] Because they remain under sin, God's will may not always be clear to them or they may misinterpret it with the result that they seek to serve God in ways that are not actually in accordance with God's will. Thus the law can serve as a guide to direct those who have now come to love the law so that they can discern correctly God's will and do it.

This must be kept in mind when dealing with another common objection to the idea of a third use of the law, namely, that because believers have received the Holy Spirit, the Spirit instructs them regarding God's will for their lives so that they no longer need the law. Led by the Spirit, they do good works spontaneously, without any need for the law's coercion. While this is true and the idea of the law "coercing" believers into obedience may be regarded as the first use rather than the third, as the Formula of Concord affirms, it is still possible for sinful believers to misinterpret God's will. Thus, even though they are instructed by the Holy Spirit directly, it can still be said that the Spirit "uses the law to instruct the reborn and to show and demonstrate" to them what God's will is and in which good works they should walk.[46] If the law was given by God through the Holy Spirit, then in principle there should be no conflict between the revelation of God's will through the Spirit and the revelation of God's will through the law. Yet because believers can misinterpret the impulses of the Holy Spirit just as they can misinterpret the law, it is good to have both.

When speaking of this third use of the law in the life of believers, however, it is not entirely clear to which law Lutheran theology is referring. Article VI of the Formula of Concord refers to the law "written into the heart," to "the law of Christ and the law of the mind," to God's "written law and Word," apparently referring to the Mosaic law, and to the Decalogue.[47] Which of these represents the "eternal and unchanging will of God"? If the law is defined as the natural law that lies behind the Decalogue, it is difficult to see how it can guide and instruct believers to any great extent given the fact that it is so broad and vague. Luther, for example, uses the Ten Commandments to instruct believers in God's will in his Large and Small Catechisms, but even though he expands on their deeper meaning, his teaching remains so general that it cannot always be helpful in determining God's will in specific situations or addressing difficult and at times complex ethical questions. However, to associate the Mosaic law with God's eternal and unchanging will is also problematic for reasons we have seen in chapter 2. And if the law is identified with the "law of Christ," the problem is not only that this is almost as vague as the natural law but that it seems to go beyond the Mosaic law in New Testament thought and at times even to go against it as regards its letter.

Related to this problem is the fact that, while no doubt the Holy Spirit may use any of these laws to guide and instruct believers, there is a great deal of other biblical material that is to serve the same purpose. Although Christians are not under the Mosaic law, it has much to say that can be helpful in guiding them in discerning God's will. Believers can gain a great deal by studying many of the commandments, such as those concerning the sabbath or the Jubilee which are aimed at promoting human well-being, justice, and equity, even though they do not regard these commandments as literally binding today.[48] The narrative sections of the five books of the Mosaic law can also teach them a great deal about God's will. All of this is true as well with regard to the content of the other books in the Hebrew Scriptures, such as the historical writings, the wisdom literature, and the prophetic books: the Holy Spirit can use these to guide and instruct believers as well. Obviously, the same must be said with regard to the New Testament: both the narratives appearing there and the teaching of Jesus and the apostles such as Paul must play an important role in guiding and instructing believers.[49] Much of this teaching goes well beyond the natural or Mosaic law. The Ten Commandments, for example, say nothing about the importance of forgiving others, being peacemakers, showing mercy, praying for one's enemies and doing good to them, or denying oneself and taking up one's cross to follow Jesus. All of this must be taken into account when Christians seek to discern God's will, led by the Spirit. The Spirit also leads them through prayer as well as through the advice and exhortation of fellow believers and at times even unbelievers. It would be difficult to characterize all of this as "law." Thus, to speak of a third use of the law seems to be very limiting when referring to the many ways in which God's Spirit guides believers in discerning God's will.

The primary concern of those who question the propriety of speaking of a third use of the law, however, is that it can easily lead to a legalistic understanding of the Christian life. Living as a Christian then becomes a matter of obeying the rules, commandments, and prohibitions associated with the law and thus loses its joy and spontaneity. As Luther often stressed and the Formula of Concord recognizes, the primary motivating factor behind the behavior of believers should be not the law but the gospel, which fills their hearts with joy and thanksgiving and moves them to love their neighbor and do God's will cheerfully. The gospel should be at the center of a Christian's life, not the law.[50] The gospel not only moves believers to action but serves as the basis for determining what actions should be done and guides them in discerning God's will: it is as believers look to God's grace, love, mercy, and forgiveness in Christ that they are made new persons and enabled to define how they are to relate to others and not as they look to the law, which makes no explicit mention of things such as grace, mercy, and forgiveness.

Lutheran theologians have often felt that the Reformed understanding of the third use of the law contributes to a legalistic view of the Christian life. When Calvin speaks of believers using the law against the flesh "like a whip to an idle and balky ass, to arouse it to work" and in order to "pinch them awake to their imperfection," many Lutherans would ask whether such a description of the Christian life reflects adequately the joy and spontaneity that is supposed to characterize it. Undoubtedly, Reformed theologians would also question whether this in itself is an adequate description of the Christian life and would insist as well that it is to be characterized by joy and spontaneity in doing God's will with a cheerful heart. At the same time, the Formula of Concord also speaks of the law being used to force the old creature into obedience "like a stubborn, recalcitrant donkey,"[51] though of course those Lutherans who reject the idea of a third use of the law would claim that here the Formula of Concord has been influenced by Reformed thinking. Yet the subtle difference between the Lutheran and Reformed positions becomes evident when it is noted that Calvin speaks of this third use as the principal one, whereas in Lutheran thought the second use of the law is primary. In other words, in Reformed thought the law has the primary purpose of constantly directing believers to examine their actions to see if they are living in conformity to God's will, whereas in Lutheran thought the law's primary purpose is that of accusing believers of their sin so that they despair of their own works and abilities and instead flee to Christ and the gospel to find comfort, joy, and peace there. Some Lutheran scholars have argued that this Reformed view of the law gives it priority over the gospel, so that "the gospel stands in service to the law" rather than the law serving the gospel.[52]

On this basis, some Lutheran theologians have argued that a legalistic understanding of the Christian life is the inevitable consequence of affirming a third use of the law, since to speak of a third use implies that the first two uses are now superseded and therefore obsolete for Christians.[53] Even if the threats and punishments that the law is said to employ in order to subdue the flesh of believers are seen as temporal and not eternal, it would seem that the law is still being used to terrorize and oppress them; their lives thus become virtually the same as those who have not believed in the gospel.

In contrast, the concern of those who insist on the need to preserve the idea of a third use of the law is that antinomianism be avoided. Once the law is set aside, moral relativism can easily creep in, since there is no longer an absolute and clearly-defined norm guiding the life of believers, who may at times be led to justify all kinds of morally questionable actions on the basis of the claim that they are being led by God's Spirit or even the "law of Christ." Even though these theologians admit that the second or theological use of the law must be regarded as primary, they insist that to affirm that the law *always* accuses does not mean that it *only* accuses;[54] it can also instruct believers at the same time that it is accusing them. In other words, it can guide them in discerning the works they are to do at the same time that it is constantly pointing out to them that those works are always imperfect and impure so that they continue to look to Christ alone for assurance that they are acceptable to God, rather than to their own works.

Against this, of course, it may be stressed once more that neither the
Mosaic law, nor the natural law, nor the Decalogue can serve as an absolute
and clearly-defined norm. Both the Mosaic law and the Decalogue are clearly
contextual, responding to a particular time and place, even though they
undoubtedly reflect certain norms and principles that can be considered
universal and associated with the natural law written on the hearts of all
people. Even this, however, is problematic, since the content of such a
natural law is virtually impossible to define clearly: in contrast to the context
in which the Reformers wrote, we now live in a global context in which we
are aware that there are many different understandings of what is "natural"
and "reasonable." Thus the idea that there are certain norms on which all
people without exception agree has become difficult to sustain unless we
speak in the most general of terms, such as the need to love others and do to
them what we would have them do to us. This makes it difficult for the
natural law to fulfill any guiding role.

In light of all of this, it should be evident why it has been so difficult for
Lutheran theologians to reach any consensus regarding the idea of a third use of
the law. However, it seems that all can agree that, although believers are led and
guided by the Holy Spirit, that Spirit uses a number of different means to
accomplish this, including the proclamation of both the law and the gospel as
well as Scripture as a whole, prayer, and the community of believers together.
All would also agree that it is necessary to avoid the two extremes of legalism
and antinomianism by seeking to reach agreements among Christians regarding
how God's will for our lives should be understood and yet at the same time not
reducing the Christian life to a servile obedience to rules, regulations, and
prohibitions.

Justification, Justice, and the Two Kingdoms

The Lutheran doctrine of justification has been criticized for leading to ethical
passivity not only on an individual level but on a social level as well. The idea
that believers are to "help their neighbor" seems to direct them to serve isolated
persons in their individual needs rather than seeking to establish peace and
justice on the level of communities, societies, and the world at large; and when
the salvation of those justified is said not to depend on any works that they do,
there seems to be no real motivation for them to be urgently concerned about
social justice. The Mexican Protestant theologian Elsa Tamez, for example, has
argued that "justification when viewed from an abstract, individual, and generic
plane is good news more for the oppressors than for the poor. By beginning
with the event of justification, the former can feel relieved of guilt—pardoned

of their sins—by grace, without confronting the 'wrath of God,' or judgment, or the justice of God, and without the need for any conversion or change of practice."[55] And Ronald Baesler poses the dilemma that has traditionally plagued Lutheran thought in this way: "How can one stimulate human activity in pursuit of justice while at the same time proclaiming human passivity with respect to justification?"[56]

In Lutheran thought, just as believers will always remain sinful in this life, so also the world in general will never be rid of sin and evil until Christ comes again. This seems to represent a pessimistic view of the world and its future similar to the Lutheran understanding of sinful human nature. Luther insisted that "the whole world is evil and that among thousands there is scarcely a single true Christian." He compares those who are not Christians to a "savage wild beast" that needs to be "bound with chains and ropes so that it cannot bite and tear as it would normally do."[57] For this reason, when discussing the first or political use of the law, he defines its purpose primarily in *negative* terms as serving to restrain evil in the world as much as possible so as to avoid chaos rather than in *positive* terms as an instrument for promoting justice, peace, and well-being for people in general. Luther's thought is thus much more in continuity with the apocalyptic thought found in the New Testament, which sees the world as a place in which evil and evildoers hold sway and which must be destroyed by divine intervention from above so that a new world may take its place. Of course, to maintain that the world is subject to evil and evildoers is not the same as affirming that the world itself is bad. For Luther, God's creation is good; however, it has fallen under the influence of evil, including both human and demonic powers who impose their rule and can only be overcome by divine rather than human might.

In contrast, theological positions like those found in the Roman Catholic and Reformed traditions would seem to lend themselves to promoting greater justice in the world. If salvation ultimately depends on how human beings respond to the divine grace given them, as Roman Catholic thought has maintained, then it is up to them to make the world a better place. To claim that human justification ultimately depends on one actually *practicing* righteousness and justice (*iustitia*) would seem to promote a greater activism on the part of believers: this provides a basis for *compelling* them to do the good commanded by God. Or if it is claimed that justification is not an end in itself but has as its purpose that believers come to obey God's law and live a sanctified life, as the Reformed stress on the third use of the law implies, then God's objective can be seen not merely in terms of forgiving people or granting them eternal life, as the Lutheran view might be understood, but establishing communities and societies in which God's law is obeyed on earth. Both of these traditions as well as others have at times seen the church as a divine means to bring about a Christian society where God's law is enforced so that justice and righteousness may prevail and sin and evil may be banished to the extent that this is possible. This is reflected, for example, in Roman Catholic liberation theology, where social justice is the goal, as well as in the history of the Reformed tradition, where there were attempts to establish a Christian social order in places like Geneva and the Puritan communities of the New World.

From the time of Luther, however, Lutheran theologians have consistently rejected the criticism that the Lutheran understanding of justification promotes ethical passivity and quietism. Instead, they have followed Luther in insisting that true fulfillment of the law is not the result of compelling people under threat of punishment to obey it but of faith alone: "faith alone makes a person righteous and fulfils the law," since to fulfill the law is to "do its works with pleasure and love, to live a godly and good life of one's own accord, without the compulsion of the law."[58] In contrast, to fulfill the law "only out of fear of punishment or out of love of reward" is "to practice pure hypocrisy."[59] As a consequence of their faith, therefore, believers are constantly seeking the well-being of their neighbor:

> O it is a living, busy, active, mighty thing, this faith. It is impossi-
> ble for it not to be doing good works incessantly. It does not ask
> whether good works are to be done, but before the question is
> asked, it has already done them, and is constantly doing them. . . .
> Because of it, without compulsion, a person is ready and glad to
> do good to everyone, to serve everyone, to suffer everything, out
> of love and praise to God who has shown him this grace. Thus it
> is impossible to separate works from faith, quite as impossible as
> to separate heat and light from fire.[60]

All of this provides the background necessary for understanding Luther's teaching regarding the two kingdoms.[61] In his treatise *Temporal Authority: To What Extent it Should be Obeyed*, Luther distinguishes between the "kingdom of the world" to which all human beings belong and the "kingdom of God" composed of "all the true believers who are in Christ and under Christ."[62] According to Luther, "God has ordained two governments: the spiritual, by which the Holy Spirit produces Christians and righteous people under Christ; and the temporal, which restrains the un-Christian and wicked so that—no thanks to them—they are obliged to keep still and to maintain an outward peace." Because the wicked predominate in the world, the temporal realm cannot be ruled by the gospel, since this would be like "loosing the ropes and chains of the savage wild beasts and letting them bite and mangle everyone."[63] For this reason, the law and the sword are necessary, which are to be administered by the government to keep peace and order.

True believers, of course, belong to the kingdom of God and to the extent that they live in this kingdom are not in need of the temporal government; they are led by the Holy Spirit, who "both teaches and makes them to do injustice to no one, to love everyone, and to suffer injustice and even death willingly and cheerfully at the hands of anyone. Where there is nothing but the unadulterated doing of right and bearing of wrong, there is no need for any suit, litigation, court, judge, penalty, law, or sword."[64] Nevertheless, because Christians live not for themselves but for their neighbor, they do what is useful to others; and since "the sword is most beneficial and necessary for the whole world in order to preserve peace, punish sin, and restrain the wicked," Christians submit willingly to the governing authorities, supporting them and paying taxes.[65]

Luther's doctrine of the two kingdoms has been the subject of much criticism. The most common of these is that it appears to lay the basis for dividing the world into two separate and distinct spheres: the public, political, civil, secular, or temporal on the one hand, and the private, religious, ecclesiastical, or spiritual on the other. Christians and the church are then to be concerned only about the salvation of souls. Robert Benne characterizes this view thus: "The secular world and the world of the church are seen as two separate realities. The secular world becomes autonomous, running according to its own principles and rules, and the Christian must simply submit to them. The church preaches the gospel, which then affects only the inner souls of Christians and perhaps their intimate relationships."[66]

In reality, however, it is difficult to see how a careful reading of Luther could lead to such a conclusion. As Benne insists, Luther's thought on the subject is "highly dialectical and paradoxical" and thus is much more complex than is often recognized.[67] Brent W. Sockness underscores the same point, noting that "Luther's notion of two kingdoms is highly flexible and fluid," since he uses it to denote two classes of human beings, Christians and non-Christians, to refer to two types of persons, to draw a contrast between inner and external aspects of individuals, and "as a way of speaking about the correct relationsip between the activities and responsibilites of the church and state."[68] Furthermore, it is important to understand Luther's thought in his own context, where his objective was "to return to the state its proper competence in administering secular affairs," since the church had established its dominion over this realm by usurping "massive political power."[69]

Far from advising Christians to detach themselves from civil affairs, Luther argues that the faith of Christians must naturally and inevitably lead them to become involved in the temporal realm. This is because faith cannot exist without bearing fruit, which consists of love for the neighbor; and because the neighbor exists in the temporal realm and not merely the spiritual realm, one must serve in the temporal realm so that there may be peace and well-being there. As Walter Altmann notes, Luther himself was constantly compelled to address the political authorities regarding temporal affairs, such as economic, political, educational, and social reform, and taught that the church must proclaim God's will to the state.[70] Even though Luther often insisted that Christians should be subject to the political authorities on the basis of his interpretation of Romans 13, he regarded this as an act of sacrificial love on their part.[71] While he regarded such subjection as necessary for the sake of social order and to avoid chaos, he saw it as the responsibility of both individual Christians and the church to actively proclaim God's will in the temporal realm;[72] in that sense, he might even be said to have affirmed the need for Christians and the church to raise a prophetic voice as he himself repeatedly did. Thus, subjection was not to be equated with indifference or passivity in the face of sin, evil, and injustice. Luther's ultimate concern, however, was for the gospel: whenever the actions of either secular or ecclesiastical authorities presented a threat to the gospel or the Christian faith, it was necessary to disobey those authorities. On this basis, he could even call the secular princes to become involved in church affairs on the basis of their baptism, since all Christians are called to defend the gospel when it is at risk.[73] This involves exercising one's divinely-given vocation, and since the vocation of the princes was to exercise secular power, their involvement in church affairs was justified and necessary.

While many of the criticisms of Luther's teaching regarding the two kingdoms may not be entirely justified, his affirmation that the faith by which believers are justified will inevitably impel them to serve their neighbor in the temporal realm does raise the question of whether their justification is a goal in itself or instead has another goal, namely, their service of the neighbor in the temporal realm. Often Luther's thought is summarized by affirming that through the gospel of divine forgiveness believers are "set free from bondage to sin and for genuine interest in the welfare of the neighbor."[74] The question that arises in this regard is the same one that arises with regard to the Lutheran and Reformed teaching concerning sanctification and the third use of the law: In justifying sinners, is God's ultimate goal that of providing for their salvation in an other-worldly realm and in the meantime granting them peace of mind in the present on that basis? Or is it that of bringing about in them a new, sanctified life so that they fulfill God's law and serve their neighbor? To maintain the latter would imply that God's ultimate concern is for *this* world: God forgives and renews people so that they may be at work in the world helping their neighbors in various ways. Here the problem may be phrased in terms of Luther's own analogy: Does not one plant a tree to obtain its fruits, so that the tree is not an end in itself? If so, is not God's real objective in justifying believers that of enabling them to produce good fruits?

In essence, this is the same problem that was first noted in chapter 1. If salvation has to do with a future world and that world can only be brought about by an act of God, it is not clear why believers should be concerned with human wholeness and social justice in the present world except perhaps to make it a place of greater well-being and less suffering in the meantime, while they await the salvation to come. This problem is evident in Luther's thought: at times he expresses his expectation of the world's imminent end, perhaps during his own lifetime.[75] Given Luther's belief that this world will not get better but remain subject to sin and evil until it comes to an end, it is not difficult to understand why the Lutheran tradition has been characterized as "defeatist" with "quietistic tendencies in it," as Reinhold Niebuhr did.[76] The affirmation that in Luther's thought "God is not ultimately interested in the law" leads to the same problem:[77] God no longer cares if people fulfill the law in this world so as to make it a better place, since God's ultimate concern is that people be brought to believe in the gospel so as to obtain eternal life.

Of course, it would be entirely unfair to Luther to affirm that his concern was only with the salvation of souls in the life to come, given his deep involvement in the political and social affairs of his day. However, it is important to note the unresolved tension in his thought, the same unresolved tension that has existed in most Christian thinkers: even though the world to come is to be established by God alone and not by human effort, and even though the present world is "passing away" (1 Cor 7:31; 1 John 2:17), God still desires that people work for a better world in the present, as Jesus himself did.

Lutheran Teaching on the Christian Life in Light of the New Testament

While the New Testament undoubtedly speaks of the need for Christians to become sanctified or holy (Rom 6:19; 1 Co 7:34; 2 Co 7:1; 1 Thess 4:3, 7; Heb 12:14; 1 Pet 1:15-16), it is just as common to see the sanctification of believers as something that has already been accomplished (Acts 20:32; 26:18; 1 Co 1:2; 3:17; 6:11; Eph 4:24; Heb 2:11; 10:10, 14). The notion that believers have already been sanctified is reflected as well in the fact that by far the most common designation to refer to believers in the New Testament is "saints" or "holy ones"; this designation occurs some fifty times there. Whether regarded as something already accomplished or something that must still take place, their sanctification is usually seen as something that God or Christ accomplishes rather than being the result of their own efforts (John 17:17, 19; 1 Thess 3:13; 5:23; Heb 2:11).

At times, holiness or sanctification is undoubtedly associated with being separated from the sin and evil that are in the world and practicing abstinence, though not necessarily withdrawing from the world itself (John 17:15-17; 1 Cor 7:34; 2 Cor 6:14—7:1; 1 Thess 4:3; 2 Tim 2:21-22; Heb 7:26). It is also common, however, for holiness and sanctification to be associated with loving others, being at peace with them, and especially practicing righteousness, which should also be understood in terms of seeking justice (*dikaiosunē; iustitia*), as was observed in chapter 2 (Luke 1:75; Rom 6:19-22; 1 Cor 1:30; Eph 4:24; 1 Thess 3:12-13; 1 Tim 2:15; Heb 12:14; Rev 22:11). Holiness therefore must be seen not merely in terms of individual piety or avoiding sinful behavior but doing God's will in relation to others. This idea is easily lost when holiness is defined primarily as being set apart from the "profane," in which case believers would be called to isolate themselves from unbelievers and the world in general rather than going out to engage the world and serve others. This would run contrary to the practice of Jesus himself, who consciously sought out the company of sinners and the unrighteous.

In fact, Jesus himself generally defined the life he sought to bring about in others not in terms of holiness or sanctification but in terms of following him in serving others and reaching out to them in love as his disciples. His ethical teaching centered on how his followers should relate to others, forgiving them, making peace with them, refraining from judging them or making them stumble, seeking justice for all, and practicing love, mercy, and kindness to everyone, including one's enemies. For Jesus, the life of believers is best summarized not only in the commandment to love God and to love one's neighbor as oneself but also in his call to deny oneself, take up one's cross, and follow him in giving up one's life for others. Even when Jesus talks about being perfect or pure, he has in mind loving one's enemies, being merciful, and refraining from actions that do harm to others (Matt 5:7-9, 43-48; 15:19-20). For Jesus, it is these things that define the Christian life rather than some type of personal piety in relation to God.

Similarly, while the idea of doing "good works" is found repeatedly throughout the New Testament, it can also be a somewhat limiting concept, at least in the way it has commonly been understood. Good works are generally associated with concrete acts of assistance for those in need. While this is undoubtedly of great importance in New Testament thought (Matt 25:31-46; Acts 9:36; 2 Cor 9:8; 1 Tim 5:10; 6:18), believers are called to a life that involves much more than that. Life in Christ also has to do with struggling against evil and injustice wherever they are present, treating others (including those *not* in any dire need) in ways that build them up and contribute to their well-being, using kind words while refraining from hurtful ones, being humble, patient, and fair in one's dealings with others, actively promoting peace and harmony, speaking the truth in love, raising a prophetic voice, and advocating on behalf of the oppressed. A righteous and God-pleasing life also has to do with avoiding words and actions that contribute to injustice and oppression. Many of these things do not immediately come to mind when one speaks of "good works," yet must be understood as an integral part of the Christian life in New Testament thought.

All of this goes well beyond what is explicitly commanded in the law of Moses or the Decalogue as well as whatever the law written by God on human hearts is understood as prescribing. This makes it questionable whether the idea of a third use of the law should be regarded as being in harmony with New Testament teaching. Undoubtedly, believers are still to look to the Mosaic law for guidance and direction but even then it must be interpreted on the basis of the "law of Christ." It is this law of Christ that is especially to guide the life of believers but, like the concept of a natural law written on human hearts, it remains so general and broad that in itself its only real value may be that of reminding believers that they are to follow Christ's teaching and example so as to love in the way that he did. For this reason, in New Testament thought, as believers follow the law of Christ they may actually find it necessary to depart at times from what is prescribed explicitly in Scripture.

The traditional Protestant understanding of sanctification also seems to be much more *individualistic* than the New Testament view of Christian life. Even though much of the ethical teaching in the New Testament has to do with individual behavior, it is almost always addressed to communities as a whole, rather than particular individuals, and therefore must be seen as outlining the way in which believers are called to live together in community with others and in society in general. Believers are called not merely to carry out "good works" on an individual basis but to work together as a community in working for what is just and right. Paul's image of the church as a body in which all the members have special gifts and functions underscores this point (1 Cor 12:4-31; cf. Eph 4:11-16). Believers are called not merely to grow in their own personal holiness and righteousness but to organize themselves and form alliances with one another to carry out ministry, pooling their resources and gifts to seek the well-being of all (Acts 2:44-47; 4:32-35).

With regard to the idea that believers must be active in serving others without expecting that their efforts will eventually lead to a world of perfect peace and justice, Lutheran teaching must be regarded as being in essential harmony with the teaching of both Jesus and the New Testament in general. Just as Jesus himself simply sought to do God's will in bringing justice, life, peace, healing, and wholeness into the lives of others on both a spiritual and a material level, leaving in God's hands the question of how and when God would establish God's reign, so also he taught his followers to do the same, rather than being preoccupied with "times or periods" established by God regarding the coming of that reign (Acts 1:6-8; cf. Mark 13:32).

As has been the case in Lutheran thought, the New Testament does not prescribe a single model of interaction and relationships with the authorities of this world. At times, believers cooperated with those authorities and used those relationships to their advantage in carrying out God's mission, while at other times they refused to obey them submissively and instead suffered the consequences of this refusal. Here the same understanding of fulfilling the spirit of the law in seeking justice appears to have guided their behavior: the way in which believers related to the world and to those who had power and financial resources was to depend on what would best serve God's will for human well-being. Rather than establishing clear-cut, well-defined rules for those relationships, believers were free to establish different types of relationships with those in power and authority as well as among themselves, yet were bound to the law of Christ in the sense of being required to seek justice and the good of all in love.

CHAPTER 6

Redeeming the Gospel

"How can I find a gracious God?" Whether consciously or not, in framing the problem of human salvation in this way, Protestant theology has taken as its starting point and center the idea that by nature God is perfect in holiness and righteousness. This provides the basis for defining salvation in terms of human beings also needing to be perfectly holy and righteous in order to be received into communion with God in eternity. Yet because human nature is deemed imperfect and fallen, it is affirmed that human beings cannot attain this level of perfect holiness and righteousness. God's law in turn is viewed as having the purpose of defining for human beings the moral perfection required of them in order for them to be in harmony with God's nature and consequently making evident to them their own sin and imperfection so that they know that they stand under God's judgment as sinners. Although God in mercy wants to forgive their sins and save them, God's perfect righteousness and justice are inflexible and must be satisfied, making it impossible for God to freely forgive sins. For this reason, the only way in which human beings can be saved is for God's Son to become human and satisfy fully the demands of God's law on their behalf and in their stead through his life, passion, and death. Once Christ has done this, it then becomes possible for God to accept and justify sinful human beings without compromising God's perfection, since God is enabled to view sinners as if they were perfect by reckoning Christ's righteousness to them. In this way, they find the gracious God they needed. Everything thus revolves around a particular understanding of God's nature.

Such an understanding of salvation is problematic, not only because it is rooted in philosophical ideas that are for the most part foreign to biblical thought, but because it results in a gospel that in today's world seems irrelevant and incapable of impacting and transforming human lives in the way that the gospel proclaimed by Jesus Christ and the apostles originally did. If the Christian proclamation is to recover its transforming power, we must move to an understanding of the gospel that revolves around the concepts of salvation as wholeness for all, the community of believers, and of course Jesus Christ and the cross.

God and Salvation

A return to a more biblical understanding of salvation requires that we define it in a more holistic fashion, employing as synonyms terms such as wholeness, well-being, *shalom*, and justice. In this case, to be *saved* is to be *healed and made whole*. As noted in chapter 2, the Hebrew word *shalom* can be understood in terms of a total well-being embracing body, mind, and soul not only on an individual level but on the level of communities of different types. In Greek and Latin as well, the concept of salvation originally had to do with wholeness and well-being: the Greek adjective *sōs* from which the noun *sōtēria* is derived means "sound, whole, complete, healthy," while the Latin *salus* from which our word "salvation" comes embraces most of the same ideas. In biblical thought, this *shalom* is something that can be experienced to some extent in the present, yet it is also an eschatological concept; both the Hebrew Scriptures and the New Testament look forward to a new age when God's people will attain a life of wholeness and well-being together with the created order in general, free from suffering, death, and all other evils. This *shalom* goes hand-in-hand with *justice*, which can be defined in terms of *wholeness and well-being for all without exception*: justice exists when equity and harmony reign and no one is oppressed, marginalized, or excluded from God's blessings.

When salvation is understood in this way, it becomes evident that there is an *intrinsic* relation between human behavior and well-being. By nature and by definition, there can only be wholeness when human beings behave in ways that contribute to human well-being while at the same time avoiding behavior that undermines and destroys it. The behavior necessary for salvation to become a reality is above all *love*, understood as *a commitment to seeking wholeness for all*. According to this understanding, salvation is not brought about simply by an act of divine omnipotence, nor is the central idea that of taking human beings out of the present world in order to introduce them into a heavenly, other-worldly existence. Instead, salvation as wholeness and *shalom* for all is to a great extent the natural, intrinsic consequence of human behavior.

At the same time, however, salvation cannot be regarded as resulting solely from human efforts. As human beings, we are not capable of transforming our world into a place of perfect peace, justice, and well-being for all. We cannot create utopias. In part, this is due to the limits imposed on us by nature: it lies beyond our powers to eradicate all evil in the world, raise the dead, and do away with every cause of pain and suffering. The inability of human beings to save ourselves can also be attributed to some type of pernicious tendency or power to which all are subject in our present condition. The doctrine of original sin has generally been understood in this fashion: we are constantly under the influence of sinful desires ("concupiscence") that lead us to do things that harm ourselves and one another and are unable to overcome this power or tendency completely.

All of this means that alongside the *intrinsic* relation between human activity and salvation we must continue to maintain an *extrinsic* relation as well. In other words, if we are to be saved, our salvation must come not only from our own efforts and activity but from the activity of God. To posit only an intrinsic relation would destroy any real hope for the future, since our salvation would then depend solely on us. For there to be hope for us to live in a world where *shalom* and justice truly reign in fullness, there must be a God who, unlike us, is capable of bringing about such a world.

To speak of an extrinsic relation between human activity and salvation, of course, requires that we accept the idea of a personal God whose actions play a role in determining what takes place in human history. As was noted in chapter 1, many today find this idea problematic, especially in light of our increased appreciation of the vastness and complexity of our universe. Yet to deny the existence of a personal God is just as problematic, if not more so. It is not clear how human persons who are capable of loving and caring deeply for others could have their origin in some type of impersonal force or power that in itself is incapable of such love. It also seems impossible to speak of this world having any type of inherent meaning or purpose unless there is a personal creator God who has given it meaning and purpose. This is true even if it is argued that over time human beings can eventually create a world that, if not perfect, is close to it, perhaps by overcoming illness and death and transforming human nature and nature as a whole so that all may experience well-being and fullness of life unlike anything we know at present. In that case, it would still seem necessary to posit a personal God who has established in human beings the capacity to evolve and develop toward a certain goal and has also directed history toward that goal. As a personal being, this God must have a will as well as the ability to influence human history in some way to bring that will to pass.

The idea of an intrinsic relation between human activity and salvation or wholeness, however, raises difficulties of a different kind. As Protestant theology has always insisted, once our salvation is said to depend at least in part on what *we* do, it would appear that we can have no assurance of salvation, since, as sinful and imperfect beings, we may not do what is necessary on our end to make that salvation come to pass. Only if our salvation depends on God alone can we be certain that some day we will achieve the wholeness God originally intended for us.

In reality, however, in order to have certainty regarding salvation we must believe that God will bring it about; and since believing is something that *we* do, it is not correct to say that our certainty of salvation does not depend in any way *on us.* Ultimately it is our faith that constitutes the grounds for our certainty rather than some type of certainty constituting the grounds for our faith. Furthermore, strictly speaking, it is not belief in the doctrine that salvation depends on God alone that provides certainty but trusting in God as one who is all-powerful and has promised to grant us salvation rather than trusting in our own capacities. That, of course, is an act of faith.

While traditional Protestant teaching has rightly directed believers to look to God alone rather than to ourselves for assurance of salvation, it has generally limited this to include looking only to what God in Christ has done *for us* and not to what God in Christ has done, is doing, and will do *in and among us*. Because of this, it has regarded the idea that our salvation depends on God alone and the idea that it also depends on us as mutually exclusive. Yet once it is recognized that, even though our salvation and wholeness depend on what *we* do, we can do that which is necessary for us to be made whole *only by looking to God alone in faith and trust rather than to ourselves or our own capacities*, it becomes evident that there is no contradiction in affirming that our salvation depends on God alone and nevertheless depends on us as well, since it depends on *what God does in and among us as we look to God*. In other words, our assurance of salvation comes not from believing that God does it all and we do nothing but from trusting in God alone to do all that is necessary for us to be made whole and saved. This is true even with regard to our faith itself: we do not look to ourselves to see if we have sufficient trust and faith in God in order to be assured of salvation, much less to our works to see if they give sufficient evidence of saving faith, but instead look to God alone even for the faith and trust we need to be saved and made whole. Thus we are constantly directed to God rather than to ourselves, even though our salvation does indeed depend on what we do as well as what God does for us and in us.

A more serious difficulty with regard to the idea of an intrinsic relation between human activity and salvation arises when we affirm that salvation involves God introducing human beings into another world that is in some way distinct from the present one. If the new world will be brought about by an act of divine omnipotence, how can we affirm any type of intrinsic relation between what we do in this world and our being made whole in that new world? This problem does not arise when salvation is regarded as something that takes place in the present world, since then it is possible to speak of both an intrinsic and extrinsic relation between our actions and our wholeness: our actions have natural consequences, yet God can also be said to intervene actively in history, responding in various ways to our actions in order to bring about our well-being and that of others. In contrast, it would seem that the only relation there can be between our actions in this world and a salvation that takes place in a life to come is an extrinsic one, since a new world established by an act of divine omnipotence can hardly be seen as a natural consequence of what human beings do in the present world.

Yet once we recognize that human well-being in this world is inseparable from the experience of loving and being loved and depends more than anything else on this experience, then it can be argued that in order to be made whole in a world to come we must acquire in the present world the capacity to love God and others. In that case, those who refuse to love and give of themselves to others are unable to experience wholeness not only in this world but the next, because by definition only those who are able to live in love can be made whole. This idea would be similar to that noted in chapter 1, according to which God does not impose salvation by force on those who do not wish to live in communion with God. In contrast to this latter idea, however, God might still be said to judge human beings on the basis of what they do rather than letting human beings judge for themselves whether they wish to be saved, since their actions would determine whether or not they are capable of living in love and thus of being made whole by God.

If such a view is adopted, then salvation must be seen as depending not only on God or the individual but on the communities of which people form part. The reason for this is that *only those who have first been loved can come to practice love toward others*. We cannot love until we have come to experience the love of others; and because such an experience of love requires more than one person, it can only take place where there is some type of community. This means that human wholeness and well-being require that one belong to communities in which one acquires the capacity to love by being nurtured in love through one's relations with others. In this case, then, if there is to be human wholeness and well-being in the life to come, that life must be seen as one that is also to be lived in a community characterized by love; and in the present life, the task of bringing people into that type of community is also an urgent one, since both their present and future wholeness depend on it. *We are all responsible for the salvation of one another.*

The fact that the experience of love in community is necessary for human wholeness also means that individual human beings can only be whole when they are committed to loving others, since by definition one who is not committed to loving others cannot form part of a community characterized by the love of all toward one another. To love others, of course, is to seek their well-being and wholeness. Therefore *one can only be whole to the extent that one seeks the wholeness of others together with one's own.* One seeks this not only through one's direct relationships with others but by entreating God and others to act on behalf of their wholeness as well. That is, one's efforts must be aimed, not only at doing what is necessary for others to experience one's own love, but enabling and encouraging others to be active sharing their own love with others as well. Of course, because God is the source of all love, when we share our love we are also sharing God's love; and when we experience the love of others in community, we are experiencing not only their love but that of God. For this reason, looking to God alone for salvation must also involve looking to others who are God's instruments for sharing God's love with us and other people, just as each of us must be God's instruments through whom others experience God's love and salvation.

Although the idea that we must be loved and learn to love others in order to be made whole both in this world and the next makes it possible to establish some intrinsic relation between what we do in this life and our salvation in the life to come, it nevertheless remains problematic in that it implies that those who do not experience love or learn to love in this life will never be able to attain wholeness. This brings us back to the question posed by traditional Protestant theology as to why some are saved and not others. If people can only be made whole in this life and the life to come if they acquire the capacity to love by experiencing genuine love in the context of a community based on such love, how can those who never experience such love be blamed for never acquiring that capacity? If God is all-powerful and loving, why does God not simply enable *all* people to acquire the capacity to love so that they may be made whole both in this life and the life to come? Cannot God ultimately introduce those who never knew genuine love in the context of a community in this world into a community where they may come to know, experience, and practice such love in the world to come so as to be saved?

In reality, there appears to be no satisfactory answer to this problem, which is ultimately the problem of evil: Why does God allow evil to continue to exist? Why does God not just simply save all people and make all people whole? These questions cannot be answered satisfactorily by limiting God to what is by nature possible, since this involves subjecting God to nature, whether it be the nature of the world, human nature, or God's own nature. In fact, even if it is affirmed that in the end God will save all people and make them whole, the fact that salvation has to do with wholeness in *this* world as well means that the question of why a God who is both loving and just allows some in this world to experience much greater pain and suffering than others remains problematic.

While there may be no satisfactory answer to the traditional question of why only some might be saved and not others, as the Lutheran Confessions themselves attest,[1] the affirmation that in order to be made whole in this life and the next we must experience the love of others and also learn to practice love ourselves does enable us to stress that the salvation of each person does not depend solely on God or that person individually but on *all of us*. When individuals are not able to experience wholeness because they have never experienced genuine, unconditional love in the context of a human community, the problem must be seen to lie not simply in those individuals themselves, as if every person were responsible for his or her own salvation, but *in all of us together*, who must be responsible for each other. The lack of salvation and wholeness of some must then be regarded, not only as the result of their own individual decisions, but also as the consequence of many others failing to reach out to them in order to embrace them in love to the degree that they should.

In the end, of course, we are called, not to speculate on the question of why some might be saved and not others or to blame God, others, or ourselves for the lack of salvation and wholeness for some, but to follow Jesus in dedicating ourselves to seeking *shalom* and justice for all. As we do so, we simply entrust ourselves and others to God as he did in life and death, imploring God that *all* may come to experience wholeness and salvation in this life and the life to come while ultimately leaving it up to God to respond to questions for which we have no satisfactory answers. Just as God's response to Jesus' own unanswered question on the cross eventually came on Easter Sunday, so also we trust that God's response to our petition and efforts for the salvation of others and ourselves will eventually come, even seeing anticipated in God's response to Jesus God's response to us as well.

The Law and Sin

When God's holy and perfect nature is taken as the starting point for defining God's law and that law is seen as having the primary purpose of pointing out to fallen human beings that they stand under God's judgment for falling far short of the perfection God demands from them, the law will inevitably be viewed in the way that Luther viewed it: as an oppressive tyrant that constantly stands accusing and condemning sinners. While God's law can also be said to restrain sin in the world to some extent (according to its first use) and guide believers in the ethical decisions they make (according to its third use), once salvation is defined in other-worldly terms, these functions of the law do not actually contribute to human salvation, since they affect only life in this world. The intrinsic relation between obedience to the law and human salvation is also lost: God gives the law for God's own sake rather than for the sake of human beings, whose motivation to attempt to obey the law is no longer that of attaining the well-being that results as a natural consequence from such obedience but that of seeking to obtain God's favor so that God might grant them salvation in eternity. Once it is affirmed that, because of their fallen condition, it is impossible for them to obtain God's favor in this way, any attempt to fulfill the law is seen to be futile and it is no longer clear what purpose there may be in still seeking to observe it, other than attempting to make conditions in this world somewhat more bearable.

In the same way, when God's perfect and holy nature is taken as the starting point for defining sin, sin is understood primarily as an offense against God's holiness. The intrinsic relation between sin and human suffering is lost: God prohibits sin for God's own sake, to safeguard God's holiness, rather than out of love and concern for the welfare of human beings, who harm themselves and others whom God loves when they sin.

Once salvation is defined in terms of *shalom* and wholeness for all, however, then the purpose of God's law must be seen as that of prescribing and mandating the behavior that leads to that *shalom* and wholeness *for the good of human beings themselves*. God's law is thus an expression of God's love. In this case, the extrinsic relation between human behavior and human well-being is dependent on the intrinsic relation: God rewards obedience to the law and chastises disobedience for the purpose of bringing human beings into greater conformity with the law for their own good, due to the well-being that is brought about naturally by their observance of the law. The law can only be understood in this way, of course, when an intrinsic relation between human behavior and human salvation is maintained with regard to life, not only in this world, but in the world to come as well. If we affirm that what we do in this life has consequences both for this life and the life to come, then the law can be seen as defining the way of life necessary to attain that wholeness for ourselves and others both in the present and in the future.

The understanding of salvation as *shalom* for all also leads to a definition of sin as human activity that opposes, diminishes, undermines, or destroys that *shalom*. In most cases, of course, sin affects negatively those who practice it, yet often the harm it does to the well-being of others is even greater; and because God loves *all* people, God insists that human beings refrain from sin in all its forms so that *shalom* and justice may prevail for all. In other words, God prohibits sinful behavior because it is bad for human beings due to its intrinsic consequences. Traditional Western theology has generally affirmed the opposite, defining certain behavior as bad or sinful because it is prohibited by God. The question of *why* God deems certain behavior sinful tends to be overlooked when the primary concern is for God's nature rather than human well-being, since God is thought to prohibit sin for God's own sake rather than for the sake of human beings.

From a Christian perspective, the full meaning and content of God's law can be defined only by looking to the teaching, life, and death of Jesus Christ.

Undoubtedly, both the law written on human hearts and the Mosaic law can also be identified with God's law and have at their heart the commandment to love God and one another, as Jesus taught. In this regard, what we learn from Jesus regarding God's will is no different from what we learn in those laws. For Christians, however, as God's Son Jesus embodies a much deeper understanding of God's will and defines what constitutes love of God and others in a way that goes well beyond the natural or Mosaic law. In him we learn that God's will is that we deny ourselves and take up our cross daily to follow him, that we practice forgiveness and actively seek peace and reconciliation with and among others, and that we dedicate our lives to seeking the wholeness of all people, including ourselves; none of this is prescribed in so many words in the Mosaic law or any type of natural law. The same must be said with regard to Jesus' teaching concerning things such as not insulting or judging others or seeing them as objects for our pleasure, turning the other cheek, loving one's enemies, and not pursuing wealth (Matt 5:21-30, 38-48; 6:19-34). Obedience to God's law involves being committed to helping to bring healing and justice into the lives of all in the way that Jesus did, rather than merely observing certain legal prescriptions or abstaining from that which God's law expressly prohibits; as his own teaching and practice make clear, human wholeness requires much more than the literal application of biblical precepts

To understand God's law in terms of what we see in Jesus involves not only fleshing out the content of the natural law written on human hearts but relativizing the Mosaic law, which must then be seen as an expression of God's will that is not binding on people of all times and places but was instead limited to a specific group of people in a particular time and place.[2] This means understanding the Mosaic law in terms that are different from the way it has been understood in Judaism, since it involves affirming that many of the prescriptions of the Mosaic law are no longer an expression of God's will for us today as we have come to understand it in Jesus. This is not the same as rejecting the Mosaic law outright, since as an expression of God's will in another time and place it can undoubtedly help us as we seek to discern God's will in our own present-day contexts. However, from a Christian perspective, it must be read and interpreted on the basis of what we see in Jesus, who goes far beyond what we encounter in the Mosaic law. Undoubtedly, the task of defining God's will for us today in the various contexts in which we live is extremely complex. But through Jesus and the Holy Spirit, we believe we are given both the ability and the freedom to interpret God's will for our lives and our world and also believe that this will cannot simply be identified with any written code, be it the Mosaic law or any other law. As Christians, we affirm that Jesus is the criterion by which all is to be judged, just as he is the one whom God has established to be the judge of all people and things.

Protestant theology has traditionally maintained that God must demand perfect obedience to God's law due to God's holy nature, which prevents God from accepting anything imperfect into God's presence. As has been noted repeatedly in this study, however, the idea that human beings must be absolutely perfect in their obedience in order to be declared righteous by God runs contrary to biblical thought, where the righteous inevitably sin but also repent of their sin.

Rather than rejecting the idea that anything less than perfect obedience to God's law is unacceptable to God, however, we must uphold this idea but understand it against the background of God's concern for the wholeness and well-being of all. In a sense, God does indeed demand perfection and deem all forms of sin intolerable, because it is *never* acceptable to God for us to do harm to ourselves and others. God's love for us also leads God to hate sin in all its forms because of what it does to us. In fact, as human beings, we should hate every manifestation of sin as well because of the harm it does to us and others, all of whom are the objects of God's love and must be the object of ours as well. We must regard not only the sin of others but our own sin as something that is never acceptable and which should even arouse our own wrath as much as it may be said to arouse that of God.

This means that we also can and should see the law as establishing an ideal that is unattainable for us, as Protestant teaching has traditionally affirmed. We can never love God with all our heart, soul, mind, and strength, or truly love our neighbor as ourselves; in fact, we are even incapable of loving ourselves as we ought and as God loves us. For that same reason, we can never be completely whole in this life.

Because the law establishes an ideal that we can never attain, it shows us that we are sinners and directs us to seek mercy from God, as the Lutheran teaching regarding the second use of the law affirms. As noted in chapter 4, however, there are at least two images used in Scripture and the Lutheran tradition to speak of our condition under the law: that of being under God's wrath and condemnation for our sin and that of being persons who are ill and in need of a physician. It is this latter image that Jesus initially employs in his ministry to speak of sinners (Matt 9:12; Mark 2:17; Luke 5:31) and there are good reasons to give this image priority today as well. The law shows us that we are ailing, broken, ill, even diseased, and thus need to turn to God and God's Son Jesus for help. In this case, just as a person who is ill sees the physician as someone who wants to help, rather than as someone who condemns that person for being ill, so we must see God and Christ. This, in fact, is how Jesus wanted sinners to see him: as someone who wanted to heal them and make them whole. When we recognize our sin and come to see how it harms us and makes it impossible for us to be whole, we see God and Christ, not as *judging* or *condemning* us, but as *wanting to help us* out of love; God and God's Son and Spirit are our friends and allies who want the same thing that we want, namely, that we be healed from our sinful ways for our own good and that of others. In this case, contrary to much traditional Lutheran teaching, the goal of the proclamation that we have not observed God's law is not initially that of instilling fear of divine punishment in us but that of making us conscious of our illness and brokenness, as well as our need for a divine physician to heal us. The idea, then, is not first to proclaim a God of wrath who must subsequently be transformed into a gracious God, as Lutheran teaching has generally done, but a God of unconditional love who from beginning to end is on our side. Precisely because of that unconditional love that seeks our well-being, God wants us to stop sinning for our own sake and that of others and also wants us to recognize our need for help and healing, in order that we may receive that help and healing through Christ.

Repentance should be understood against the background of these same ideas. As God's law is proclaimed to us as an unattainable ideal, we recognize that we have sinned and lament the fact that we have harmed ourselves and others through our actions, thereby undermining our wholeness together with that of others, which is inseparable from our own. Seeing ourselves as sinners, we then turn to God and to Christ asking not only for forgiveness but for help in overcoming our sin, knowing that because of God's love in Christ that help will not be denied us.

Nevertheless, the biblical idea that sinners are under God's wrath and condemnation on account of their disobedience to God's law must not simply be discarded. Rather, this image must be employed in a different context, namely, that of those who persistently refuse to recognize and condemn their own sin and to repent of it. It is common for human beings either to see themselves as persons who have no sin or to see themselves as less sinful than others. This leads them to place themselves above others and to claim the right to define God's will for them. Identifying themselves with God, they judge and condemn others as if they were God, seeing themselves as superior to those who are not as good as them. This was what the Pharisees condemned by Jesus did. They refused to acknowledge themselves as sinners in need of repentance and thus rejected baptism at the hands of John (Matt 3:7-10; 21:32), in contrast to Jesus, who identified with sinners by undergoing John's baptism of repentance. Instead, they oppressed others and justified it in the name of God and God's law, calling evil good and good evil and claiming to be serving God (Matt 23:4, 13, 23).

When people refuse to see themselves as sinners, this refusal not only makes it impossible for *them* to be healed but harms others, especially those who do recognize their sin and admit to being sinners. This latter group is made to feel obligated to submit to those who are supposedly superior because they are *not* sinners and therefore stand in God's place. The superior group then uses its position of dominance over those who acknowledge their sin in order to subject and oppress them in God's name. When those who do not belong to the superior group see and experience this oppression and rebel against it, they are accused of rebelling against God because those against whom they are rebelling are identified with God. If those who rebel have accepted the identification of God with the oppressive superior group, they may even reject belief in God altogether, because they see God as an oppressive figure; in this way, the superior group has even robbed them of any faith they might have in a God who actually loves and cares for them. They may even refuse to acknowledge their sin, since in that context to admit that they are sinners would be used against them and would make them feel obligated to submit to the group claiming to be superior and to represent God. And because those who are labeled "sinners" end up rejecting God and refusing to acknowledge their sin out of fear that this will be used against them, they cannot be healed by God. All of this must be seen to arouse God's wrath in intense fashion because of the tremendous harm done to the oppressed group by those who as God's supposed representatives end up neither entering into God's kingdom themselves nor letting others enter (Matt 23:13).

Luther also strongly objected to the idea that some groups or persons were holier or less sinful than others and thus stood in the place of God as God's representatives in relation to the rest, who had to submit to them in order to be saved. In fact, the rejection of this idea was a central tenet of the Reformation. In Luther's day, it was the pope, the church hierarchy, and the clergy who supposedly stood above all other Christians and thus had the right to dictate God's will to them. For this reason, Luther and the other Reformers rejected doctrines and practices that maintained the hierarchy and clergy in a position of superiority in relation to the laity; instead, they affirmed the equality of all the members of the community on the basis of the claim that all are equally sinners. In order to stress this point, in his translation of the New Testament into German, Luther consistently translated the Greek word *ekklēsia* as *Gemeinde*, "congregation" or "community," rather than *Kirche*, "church," since this latter term was generally understood as referring to the church hierarchy and clergy.[3] For Luther, what Christ had come to establish was not a hierarchical or organizational structure but a community of equals; God's gifts of grace, wholeness, and salvation come from participation in a community of believers rather than being channeled through a hierarchy. The stress on the equality of all believers in the community also led the Reformers to reject the practice of canonizing certain Christians as saints, as if they had been holier than others and were therefore closer to God.

In both biblical and Protestant thought, therefore, *all Christians* are equally sinners and in need of healing from God. For this reason, the proclamation of the law should lead all to confess not only that *they* are sinners but that *everyone else is as well*, including especially those who deny that they are sinners and instead sit in judgment on others. Recognition of one's sin must not put one in a position of disadvantage or subjection in relation to others who claim to be less sinful or without sin, since this claim is false; and no one has the right to label others as sinners without recognizing that one is just as sinful as they are. All must recognize and condemn their own sin just as readily as they recognize and condemn that of others.

Grace, Faith, and the Gospel of Justification

Perhaps the most problematic aspect of the traditional Protestant and Roman Catholic understandings of grace is the idea that God's grace must be earned or merited, either by Christ or by human beings as well. This idea is based once more on the claim that God's perfectly righteous nature will not allow God to be gracious and merciful to sinners until God's justice is satisfied. Some of the conceptions of grace that are found in the various Christian traditions must also be seen as problematic, particularly when grace is viewed as some type of divine power, substance, or quality infused into believers by God.

Grace in biblical thought is best understood as God's *unmerited favor and unconditional love for all people*. This unconditional love must be defined in turn as an unconditional commitment to seeking the well-being and wholeness of all; it is not merely some sentiment or favorable attitude toward human beings, nor is it to be equated with divine forgiveness. Undoubtedly, as Robert W. Jenson has noted, in biblical thought the term "grace" embraces more than simply God's favor, often referring to the gifts God gives;[4] yet even these gifts must be seen as expressions of God's unmerited and unconditional love. God's unconditional love for all of humanity is a constant from the beginning to the end of human history. It is not something that had to be merited by Christ, nor has God at any point in time ever ceased to love humanity as a whole unconditionally. While at times human beings have forgotten or denied God's unconditional love, it has never ceased to exist. This is embodied particularly in Jesus' ministry: while Jesus did not reveal a different God than that found in the Hebrew Scriptures and Jewish tradition, he did find it necessary to insist through his words and actions that the God of the Hebrew Scriptures is a God of unconditional love over against those who rejected such an idea and instead claimed that God's love was conditional.

As noted above, in order for people to be made whole, they must experience genuine love in their lives, a love that is unconditional. In his ministry, Jesus' first task was to share that love with all those around him but especially with those who were outcast, marginalized, and labeled as "sinners." The reason he reached out particularly to them was not only their openness to recognizing their need for healing, in contrast to the religious authorities, but also his desire that they come to see God as one who loved them unconditionally and wished to heal them rather than as one who simply condemned them; this latter view of God had been imposed on them by oppressive religious authorities who claimed to represent God.

In order for people in our world to be healed and made whole, the same thing that took place in Jesus' ministry must happen today: people must come to experience the unconditional love of God. This takes place in the context of communities where God's unconditional love is lived and shared with the same passion, conviction, and total dedication that we can observe in Jesus. Jesus' objective in life and death was that communities of this type be established throughout the world. His ministry was oriented fully toward that goal and he consequently gave up his life so that it might become a reality. By means of baptism, people are brought into communities by pure grace so that they may be loved unconditionally and nurtured there as they also learn to love others unconditionally and help nurture them.

Faithful to Jesus' teaching and practice, the Lutheran tradition along with many other Christian traditions has always held as a central tenet the idea that *the only thing that can truly change people and transform their lives is God's grace or unconditional love.* As Luther constantly stressed, the law cannot change human hearts; only the gospel can do this.[5] People who live in ways that do themselves and others harm and destroy *shalom* cannot be truly transformed by legal prescriptions and commandments and threats of punishment or even promises of reward for obedience; these things can change their outward behavior but not their heart. Instead, what changes people is *grace*, that is, the unconditional love of God that we see in Christ and that is to be reflected in the community established through him. The remedy for sin is not the law but the gospel, which must be understood as the proclamation in word and deed of God's unconditional love for all people in Christ. And since all are sinners, the gospel proclaims God's unconditional love for sinners, a love that never ceases no matter what people do and never gives up on them.

While it is necessary to experience this unconditional love in order to be made whole, however, such wholeness also requires that people learn to love God and others unconditionally in the context of a community characterized by this kind of love. As noted above, this is due in part to the fact that one can hardly live as part of a community of unconditional love if one is not committed to such love oneself. In addition, however, people can only be whole when they learn to love and give of themselves to others unconditionally, since by nature wholeness requires giving just as much as receiving. At the same time, of course, they must also avoid actions that destroy the wholeness of others and themselves. In other words, they must fulfill God's law.

This, of course, is impossible for us as sinners. And because nothing less than perfection is acceptable to God and to us as well, since love requires that we never deem it acceptable to do anything that harms ourselves and others who are together with us the objects of God's unconditional love, we must see ourselves as unacceptable in our sinful condition. In this sense, because of God's love for us, God will not and cannot accept us as we are; *and neither can we.*

Here it is important to return to the distinction between *unconditional love* and *unconditional acceptance* mentioned in chapter 4. While Jesus *loved* all people unconditionally and taught his disciples to do the same, he did not *accept* all people unconditionally and did not teach his disciples to do so either, just as he insisted that God did not accept all people unconditionally.

This, then, is the problem. It is not a problem rooted in God's nature, namely, how God can mercifully save the sinners God loves without compromising God's absolute justice and righteousness, as traditional Protestant theology has affirmed. Rather, the problem is how God can make those who are unacceptable acceptable while at the same time refusing to accept them in the sinful condition in which they find themselves. In other words, how can God accept us in order to heal us without also accepting the sin which is part of us because of the tremendous harm it does to ourselves and to all whom God loves unconditionally? Obviously, in order for God to accept us and draw near to us, we must be acceptable to God, living as God wants; yet we cannot become acceptable to God unless we are first able to experience God's unconditional love, since it is this alone that transforms people. God can only heal us by accepting us while we are still unacceptable, but as long as we remain unacceptable it is not clear how God can accept us. It is not a problem of reconciling God to God's own self or to us, as traditional Protestant theology has taught, but of reconciling us to God and to one another by making us acceptable.

This is what God accomplishes in Jesus: in him, God draws near to sinners, those who are unacceptable to God, so that they may become acceptable. Yet Jesus makes them acceptable, not by constituting in himself some perfect righteousness that can then be imputed to them so that God can regard them as righteous without compromising God's justice, but by doing what is necessary to bring them into conformity with God's will. The objective of the coming of God's Son was not to make it possible for God to forgive sinners for their sins or to merit such forgiveness for them but to transform human beings into people who might live according to God's will. *This was the only thing that could ever satisfy God.*

The way Jesus did this was not only to draw near to sinners in unconditional love so that they might see their need for a divine physician and seek help but to offer them that help. Yet just as those who are ill need to have trust in the physician who is treating them and follow that physician's instructions, so also the way that sinners are made whole is by trusting in Jesus and following him. In other words, they are *made whole by faith*. Faith must be understood not merely as trusting in God or Christ for forgiveness but *following Christ*, placing one's life in God's hands and being committed to living according to God's will as defined by Christ. It is this faith that enables one to be transformed. This transformation is not the work of believers themselves, however, but is accomplished by God through Christ and the Holy Spirit in the context of the community of believers. As observed previously, believers do not look to themselves for their salvation but solely to Christ and God's Spirit, who proceeds from him. Yet they look to Christ with regard, not only to what Christ has done *for* them, but to what Christ does *in* them as well; in that sense, it can be said that they look inward, yet this still involves looking to Christ who is active in them and not to themselves or their own strength or efforts.

Once faith is understood in this way, it becomes clear that salvation must be said to be *by faith alone* and that *there is an intrinsic relation between salvation and faith*. Faith does not save simply because, for some unknown reason, God has decided that faith will be the condition upon which God will save human beings. In that case, there would be only an extrinsic relation between faith and salvation. Instead, there is an intrinsic relation in that faith leads one to live in a way that enables one to be made whole both by the natural consequences of one's actions and by the activity of God through Jesus, the Holy Spirit, and the community of Jesus' followers.

In this regard, it must be stressed that God's grace, understood as unconditional love, is not in itself enough to make people whole. The same must be said regarding forgiveness. In Scriptural thought, God can forgive sins freely and often does so, simply overlooking sins without punishing them; it is never implied that there is something in God's nature that makes it impossible for God to do this. The problem, however, is that simply forgiving people or not holding their sins against them does not necessarily transform them or lead to a change in their way of life. In fact, it can instead make things worse, leading people to practice sin more freely without any concern for the consequences. To love others is not always to forgive them but also to hold them accountable for their behavior when they do harm to themselves and others, as well as insisting that they alter that behavior for their own good and that of others. Once again, then, the problem is not that of making it possible for God to forgive but of God's forgiveness accomplishing its objective, namely, the transformation of sinners.

For this reason, while God's love is unconditional, in biblical thought God's forgiveness is not unconditional but conditional. The condition upon which people are forgiven is that they repent, that is, admit that they are sinners in need of God's transforming love and help, and that they have faith, that is, trust in God *not only for forgiveness but for their transformation*; and, by definition, this faith and trust will involve being committed to living in accordance with God's will because believers know that, due to the intrinsic relation between obedience and wholeness, the only way they can attain the wholeness God wants for them and that they want for themselves is to commit themselves to living as God wills. Of course, believers will be far from perfect in this regard and thus will always be in need of divine forgiveness. To be committed to living in conformity with God's will is not the same as actually attaining such conformity, though of course this commitment will inevitably be manifested in concrete ways in their life.

Does this mean, however, that they must *earn* or *merit* God's forgiveness by their repentance and faith? In this case, the burden for obtaining divine forgiveness would be placed on their shoulders. But when this is seen in the context of God's unconditional love, it becomes clear that simply recognizing that they are sinners in need of help and turning to God in Christ for that help ensures that they will both receive God's forgiveness and be transformed by God's grace. In this context, therefore, the notion of merit is inappropriate, unless it be said that repentance and faith merit, not God's unconditional love or grace in itself, but the form that that grace takes, namely, that of forgiveness.

The fact that salvation cannot be equated with forgiveness means that *the gospel must not be understood merely as the proclamation of the forgiveness of sins*, as it has been in traditional Lutheran thought. It must also include the proclamation that in Christ God transforms and heals sinners. In other words, the gospel must be understood as the proclamation that out of pure grace, through no merit of our own, God reaches out to us who are ill and broken to make us whole by forgiving *and transforming* us in Christ. This takes place through faith alone, as we look solely to Christ for both the forgiveness and the transformation that will give us healing and wholeness.

Just as the Lutheran tradition has equated the proclamation of divine forgiveness with the gospel, so also has it equated the forgiveness of sins with justification and seen this as the goal of God's work in Christ. This has once again involved taking as starting point and center the idea that God is perfectly holy and righteous by nature. In this case, the problem is defined, not in terms of how sinners may be transformed so as to be restored to wholeness, but how God may forgive sinners without compromising God's holy nature. Forgiveness itself is then said to constitute the objective, rather than the transformation of sinners: once God has been enabled to forgive sinners, there is no further obstacle to their salvation. The intrinsic relation between faith and salvation is thereby lost once again: faith becomes the condition God has established to forgive people for no necessary reason, rather than being seen as necessary because by definition one can be made whole only by clinging to Christ and following him. In contrast, if salvation has to do with the transformation of sinners and not just their forgiveness, then it is not enough for believers merely to be forgiven or pronounced righteous by God; they must also be transformed. Forgiveness thus cannot be an end in itself but can only be a means to that end.

For this reason, the traditional Lutheran teaching that justification is nothing but the forgiveness of sins must be rejected. As noted previously, in biblical thought justification is understood not simply in terms of being forgiven but of being *declared righteous*; that is, it involves a recognition that one *really is righteous*. Yet what makes one truly righteous is simply that one admits to being a broken sinner in dire need of healing and that one looks to Christ in faith to receive from him the help and healing that God offers to all through him. Because there is not only an *intrinsic* relation between salvation and faith but an *extrinsic* one as well, however, justification must be defined as *God declaring those who recognize their sin and turn to God in faith to be acceptable to God, because their repentance and faith make it possible for God to carry out the task of transforming them into the persons God wants them to be through Christ and the Holy Spirit.* Because their recognition of their brokenness and their turning to Christ in faith make it possible for Christ to begin to help, heal, and transform them, God accepts them even now, in spite of the fact that through their sin they continue to do harm to themselves and others whom God loves, and in that sense are still unacceptable. Justification is therefore not unconditional, as some Lutheran theologians have affirmed, but conditional on one's recognizing one's sin and looking in faith to Christ in order to be forgiven and transformed through him.

Yet all of this takes place *in the context of the Christian community*. The doctrine of justification has often been conceived of primarily in individual terms.

In the New Testament, however, the discussions over justification had to do with the question of who was to be included in the church or community of believers: to be justified was to be accepted as a member of the community of those declared righteous by God. It is in the context of this community that people come to experience God's unconditional love in Christ, are brought to faith, acknowledge their sin, receive God's forgiveness, and begin to be transformed and renewed; all of this is brought about *through other members of the community as God's instruments*. People who have not yet been incorporated into the community are first *made to belong* by being showered with God's unconditional love so as to come to *believe*. Through baptism they are graciously received into the community so that they may there continue to experience God's love and receive the gifts of God's Spirit at the same time that they share their own love with others, together with the gifts they have received. As they are loved unconditionally, they also learn to love others unconditionally; this makes it possible for them to experience in part the wholeness that comes from God together with those with whom they share their love. As they participate in worship, the Lord's Supper, and other activities in the community, they not only continue to experience God's transforming grace in Christ through the other members but also become the means by which God communicates that same grace to others both inside and outside of the community. This in turn also serves as a means by which they experience grace, since they are transformed, not just by *receiving*, but by *giving* and enabling others to give of themselves as well.

As noted in chapter 3, in New Testament thought, all of this is what Jesus sought in life and death. He gave up his life so that there might now be throughout the world a community in which people might experience God's grace, receive forgiveness, and be transformed into new persons who live according to God's will. In other words, Jesus died so that people who were not acceptable to God and did not have access to God's blessings of forgiveness and wholeness might *become* acceptable and attain those blessings by being incorporated into the community over which he is Lord. This is not simply the Jewish community or Israel but a *new* community that lives under a new covenant and a new law, the "law of Christ." They understand God's will differently and their faith and trust in God leads them to be committed to that will, even though they inevitably fail to live according to that will in the way they would like and the way God would like. In spite of this, however, they are accepted by God and one another as righteous as they cling to Christ as their Lord, trusting solely in him for salvation, which by definition involves following him in faith as his disciple.

Jesus' death leads to the existence of this community in several ways. It is the consequence and culmination of a life dedicated to bringing others into a community where they might experience God's unconditional love and be made whole. Jesus died because he would not back down from his commitment to that task; and when faced with death, he did not run or hide but offered up his life to God, imploring that what he had lived and was dying for might not come to an end but instead might become a reality for people everywhere by spreading throughout the world. In this sense, he "died for us" (Rom 5:8). His death was also a petition to God that God accept all of those sinful people whose wholeness he sought, in spite of their sin; he "died for our sins" (1 Cor 15:3). God's response was to raise Jesus so that he might complete the task of giving them that wholeness in accordance with God's will. Jesus' resurrection is God's Yes to what Jesus sought in life and death and thus God's Yes to the definitive forgiveness and transformation of all the members of Jesus' community of followers of every time and place (Rom 4:25).

The love shown by Jesus in giving up his life so that others might experience life and wholeness, as well as God's own love in giving God's beloved Son up to death, also made it possible for this community to exist in the sense that this act of unconditional love, unlike any other, defines forever the community as one where this same love lies at its heart and core. Jesus' death is like a seed of grain planted in the earth so that it might sprout into communities throughout the world where the same unconditional love that knows no limits is lived and shared (John 12:24). If his death is said to have been "necessary," this should be understood in the sense that the communities he sought to establish could only be characterized by that kind of love if such an act of love were to constitute the sole foundation upon which they were to be edified; any other foundation would not have achieved God's purposes. The love of God and Christ of which the cross is the fullest expression and the supreme symbol is the criterion, norm, and measure by which all is judged in this community; and for this reason nothing but the cross must stand at the center of the faith and life of those who call themselves Jesus' followers.

This understanding of Jesus' death stands in contrast to the traditional interpretations of the cross, which take as their starting point and center the idea that by nature God must be perfectly righteous and just. In this case, Jesus' work is defined in terms of meeting a divine need to save human beings without compromising God's justice, rather than in terms of God reaching out to meet *our* needs and make us whole. Similarly, the *Christus Victor* idea is ultimately based on the idea that it would not have been just on God's part simply to overthrow Satan by force. According to these ideas, the obstacle to be overcome is located *outside* of human beings, rather than *in* them, and a transformation of human beings themselves is not the condition that must be addressed in order for them to be saved. Such interpretations of the cross must be rejected because *they obscure the gospel* and are incompatible with it.

In contrast, a proper understanding of the gospel locates the real problem *in us*, that is, in the sin that is in us and has us enslaved, thus preventing us from being healed. *This is just as much a cause of consternation to us as it is to God*; and until we can have assurance that this sin is being overcome now and will be overcome fully in the future, *there can be no gospel because there can be no wholeness*. The gospel proclaims our transformation just as much as our forgiveness, because to be told only that God forgives us without also being told that God transforms us so that we are able to stop hurting ourselves and others is not in itself good news. Our transformation is the real goal, rather than constituting an "after-effect" of our being justified. While "to be justified" means to be *declared* righteous, the basis for this divine declaration must be, not only what Christ has done *for* us, but what Christ is doing and ultimately will do *in and among us* as we live in the context of the community founded through his death, looking to him in faith together with others who do the same alongside of us. Undoubtedly, as the one mediator between God and humanity, his work has a Godward aspect "for us" in that he implores a God who demands that we be perfect *for our own sake* to graciously accept us who are imperfect and thus unacceptable; but the basis for this petition and for God's granting it is that which Christ is graciously doing and will do *in and among us* as we cling to him alone in faith, living as his disciples and as members of the community over which he is Lord by virtue of his death and resurrection.

The Transformation of Christians and the World

Because of the priority it has given to the concept of God's nature, traditional Protestant theology has generally failed to regard human history and the Christian life as having any type of clear goal or purpose other than that of glorifying God by reflecting the same qualities associated with God's nature. If the sole condition for salvation is that God be able to forgive and justify believing sinners without compromising God's perfect righteousness and Christ's coming and death have already accomplished this, then the only thing that still truly matters in human history is that a greater number of people be brought to faith so that they may be included among those to be saved. According to this way of thinking, in the "secular" sphere, the only real concern of Christians is that peace and order prevail so that the gospel can be preached and more people can be brought to saving faith. Furthermore, the way in which the doctrine of justification by faith alone has often been understood makes the goal of faith the *forgiveness* of believers rather than their *transformation*. This is reflected in the traditional Lutheran understanding of sanctification: because sanctification does not contribute in any way to one's justification and salvation, the sanctified life has no real purpose or goal other than perhaps reflecting attributes associated with God's holy and righteous nature for God's glory so that others may be brought to faith.

Once salvation is defined as something that has to do with this world as well as the next, however, and an *intrinsic* relation between human activity and that salvation is posited, then human history and the Christian life are understood in very different terms. The objective is no longer that God be enabled by Christ to justly declare sinners righteous; nor is it that believers come to actually practice righteousness and holiness in the sense of living pious and godly lives on an individual level, separated from all that is worldly. Rather than *righteousness*, the objective becomes *justice*, that is, *shalom* and wholeness for all people and creation itself. This depends not only on God's activity but that of human beings, who can only be made whole as they seek that wholeness for themselves and others. This in turn can happen only as they look to God in faith rather than to themselves, depending entirely on God for what is necessary for that wholeness to become a reality. Yet because by definition faith involves trusting in God and only those who strive to do what God wills can be said to be truly trusting God, a life of commitment to obedience to God's will is not merely something that *ought* to happen as a result of one's faith but is inseparable from that faith. If the term *sanctification* is used to denote this new life, therefore, sanctification must be said to be essential to salvation, since *people cannot be made whole if they are not striving to live in accordance with God's will*, trusting entirely in God and not in themselves for the power and ability to do so.

Yet the very notion of sanctification or becoming holy seems so closely associated with the traditional stress on God's perfect and holy nature that it would be preferable either to redefine what is meant by "holiness," both divine and human, or to look for some other term to characterize the life of those who have been justified by faith. If the former option is preferred, holiness must be understood as a commitment to justice and an opposition to all forms of injustice and oppression, rather than in terms of separation from whatever is considered impure or profane. While it involves abstaining from sin, it must be remembered that sin involves any action that harms others and destroys wholeness. Sanctification will then be understood in terms of growing in one's firm commitment to doing what is necessary to promote greater *shalom* and justice in human communities and societies and the world at large. In this case, sanctification has a clear objective and has to do, not so much with individual behavior in relation to God, but with seeking greater well-being for all in this world. The focus is on the transformation of a world that is sinful and unjust, rather than on some type of pious, ascetic withdrawal from a world that is simply condemned as evil. Unfortunately, sanctification has generally been associated with the latter idea. For this reason, it may instead be preferable to opt for the other alternative, abandoning this use of the word *sanctification* so as to refer instead to the Christian life in terms of something such as discipleship, following Christ, or transformation: what characterizes Christians must be their commitment to well-being and wholeness for all as followers of Jesus.

Because wholeness can only be experienced in community and one can only seek the wholeness of all by working together with others in the context of a community, the Christian life cannot be defined primarily in terms of individual behavior. By definition, it must involve sharing in community. In this sense, it can perhaps be said that "outside of the church there is no salvation" when this is understood as meaning that, outside of a life in the community of others who are equally committed to seeking justice and *shalom* for all in the way Jesus taught, there can be no true wholeness.

Similarly, the work of the Holy Spirit must be understood not merely in relation to individual believers but to believers insofar as they relate to one another in community. They experience God's grace through one another. Baptism and Holy Communion are means of grace, not because through them some mysterious power, energy, quality, or substance is imparted to believers, but because they are celebrated in the context of a community in which all are committed to the same unconditional love manifested by Christ in his life and death; in this sense, believers share in his death in baptism and make his death present in Holy Communion. This involves, not some mystical or ontological participation in Christ as a person or in his death on the cross, but an appropriation of the unconditional love of God in Christ that transforms us and makes us one with God and one another. According to the Augsburg Confession, the church exists wherever "the gospel is purely preached and the holy sacraments are administered according to the gospel" in the assembly of believers;[6] today we might say that wherever the unconditional love of God in Christ is shared in word and action, there is Christ's community.

If the idea of a third use of the law is to be maintained, it must be understood in the sense of the lives of believers being determined and oriented by the unconditional and unbounded love of God manifested in Christ and the cross. As noted above, it is Christ who defines for Christians the true meaning and content of God's law, giving them a much deeper and broader understanding of God's will than can be found in the prescriptions of either the Mosaic law or any law based on natural principles. While these laws can be of help in considering ethical questions, what must really guide believers is the love of God in Christ, which goes far beyond those laws. The Christian life must not be primarily about rules, regulations, prohibitions, and commandments, but about sharing God's unconditional love with others in ways that no legal code could ever articulate or prescribe. Led by God's Holy Spirit of spontaneity, creativity, joy, compassion, and grace, Christians reach out to others with the goal of bringing forgiveness, reconciliation, edification, healing, and wholeness into the lives of all, rejoicing with those who rejoice and suffering with those who suffer. Because the life of following Christ as his disciple is characterized by freedom and a commitment to the well-being of others that is always looking for new and resourceful ways to respond to the ever-changing needs and problems of our world, if the idea of a third use of the law is maintained, great care must be taken not to fall into a legalistic understanding of the Christian life.

To affirm this, however, is not to fall into the opposite extreme of antinomianism. Christians are indeed under a law, the law of Christ, and are led by the Spirit. Their commitment to wholeness for all drives them to constantly be discerning between right and wrong, just and unjust, that which contributes to wholeness and that which undermines and destroys it. Together they seek to define right and wrong in clear terms and avoid falling into a moral relativism that confuses what is just with what is unjust and oppressive. Undoubtedly, the fact that believers remain sinners whose understanding of God's will can often be clouded or mistaken means that they must examine their efforts to share God's love with others on the basis of some objective, external criteria; otherwise they can easily fall into calling what is right wrong and what is wrong right and may end up justifying sinful behavior in the name of love. They may also define wholeness in ways that are actually contrary to true wholeness. The letter of God's law is therefore indispensable in helping to orient them and, in many contexts, clearly-defined rules and regulations are necessary. However, it is not merely the law given by God to Moses or that written on human hearts that enables them to examine their behavior to see if it conforms to God's will; rather, this is something they do together as a community, in dialogue with God's word and with one another, including not only other members of the community but those outside the community as well. As they do this, they look to Christ and are led by God's Spirit so as to be able to discern God's will; in this way, they are able to remain faithful to Scripture while at the same time going beyond it to address new realities and situations not contemplated there and to respond to the changing needs of people in our modern world.

Furthermore, because all believers remain sinful, we must reject the idea that certain individuals in the community have greater access to God and thus have divine authority to unilaterally define God's will for others, who must merely submit to them as to God. According to a Lutheran understanding of the church, God's word and the sacraments are given *to the community as a whole*, which then calls someone to administer them. No matter if they are pastor, bishop, or pope, those who are placed in leadership roles by God through the call of the community are *just as much sinners as everyone else* and are therefore just as prone to falling into sinful actions as the rest of the community. For this reason, all of the members of the community are called to judge one another's behavior as well as to have their own behavior judged by others; this includes its leaders as well. The Lutheran teaching that all are saints and sinners in their entirety helps avoid the establishment of oppressive relationships in the community, since if believers are said to be only *partly* saints and sinners, then it can be argued that some are less sinners and more saints than others and therefore have the right to represent God in relation to others. This would put them in a place that corresponds to God alone.

Just as all believers remain sinful in this life even as God accepts them as righteous by virtue of what they are becoming in Christ through faith, so also the world as a whole must be seen as inevitably subject to sin while it awaits its ultimate transformation by God into a place of justice (Rom 8:19-23). The traditional understanding of salvation as a phenomenon having to do almost exclusively with the world to come as well as the doctrine of justification by faith alone apart from works raise together the question of why believers should be concerned about making the present world a place of greater justice, equity, and well-being for all: If all that is necessary to be saved is to have faith and if that salvation involves the destruction of this world by God so as to introduce us into another world, what sense can there be in striving to improve the quality of human life in this world? This is the difficulty raised by an apocalyptic worldview. At the other extreme, however, is the idea that human beings can eventually create for themselves a utopian existence on earth. By definition, this would have to involve the eradication of sin and evil, something which most people would consider impossible. Yet if that is the case, what should be our goal as Christians?

When salvation is understood in terms of wholeness, however, then by definition our own wholeness requires that we reach out to seek the wholeness of others. This is not only because the wholeness of each depends on the wholeness of others but also because, by its very nature, wholeness can only exist when one gives of oneself to others and seeks their wholeness together with one's own. This commitment to the wholeness of all is the *consequence and expression of one's faith*, since truly trusting in God and clinging to Christ involves being committed to God's will; and God's will is precisely that there be wholeness for all, not only in a future world, but in the present.

This means that the concern of Christians for justice in the world is not to be seen as a direct consequence of their justification. Lutheran theology has often attempted to establish some connection between "justification and justice," claiming that as a result of their having been justified, believers will or should be concerned about seeking justice in the world and serving their neighbor. Instead, the concern for justice and for one's neighbor must be seen as following *from faith* rather than from justification itself. It is not because one has been forgiven or declared righteous that one seeks the well-being of others but because truly trusting in God and Christ alone by definition means being committed to doing what God desires; and what God desires is that one seek the well-being of all. Thus it is living by faith that leads both to justification and to a commitment to justice, rather than justification itself leading to that commitment. In fact, as noted previously, it is this commitment to God's will for justice that constitutes the basis for one's justification; yet this commitment is not something that believers bring about in themselves but something that God brings about in them as they cling to Christ in faith.

By definition, to seek justice is to oppose all forms of sin and evil. Just as believers cannot passively accept the existence of sin and evil in themselves, neither can they accept it in the world around them. Yet because sin and evil are an inevitable part of this world, it is not realistic to expect that human efforts can ever rid the world of them. On the contrary, believers are aware that sin and evil pervade all of reality and are present in every human structure and system, including the Christian community, just as they are present in all human beings, including believers themselves. This means that, from a Christian perspective, no human structure or system, be it political, social, religious, economic, or of any other type, can be considered free of sin and evil. God therefore cannot be identified with any particular people, country, nation, political party, church body, or any other human organization or group, and Christians must reject any attempt to do so.

Christians, therefore, are not called to attempt to establish some type of utopian existence on earth, not only because this is an impossibility, but also because it inevitably involves identifying some kind of human construction or system with God. When this happens, the result is oppression and injustice, since the sin and evil inherent in such a construction or system are denied or overlooked and people are therefore hurt. Neither, however, are Christians called to flee from the world as something evil in itself or given over to destruction. Instead, just as God graciously accepts sinners in God's unconditional love but rejects their sin precisely because of that love, so also are Christians called to love the world unconditionally, while rejecting the sin and evil that are in it.

This is precisely what we see in Jesus. Jesus neither sought to establish some type of utopian kingdom on earth nor taught his followers to flee from the world. Instead, he dedicated himself to seeking the wholeness of others in all that he said and did, loving all people unconditionally while at the same time rejecting sin and evil in every form. In this sinful world, however, such dedication and unconditional love lead to conflict and a cross. Jesus' response to this was not to stop loving the world by seeking the wholeness of all, nor to stop struggling against sin and evil, but to continue in his path, entrusting himself and the salvation that he sought for others to God, who subsequently raised him from the dead.

This, then, is the way that the world is to be saved: not by the establishment of human systems and structures that are identified with God or God's kingdom, nor by fleeing from the world and giving it up to destruction, but by *dying to the world as Jesus did* (cf. Gal 6:15). To die to the world is to love it unconditionally but to oppose and reject the sin and evil in it. It is not to look for salvation in this world as if it were something that human beings might bring about by themselves, since this world will always remain subject to sin and evil; neither, however, is it to abandon this world so as to look to God for salvation solely in a world to come. Rather, it is to follow Jesus in loving this world without limits, seeking its wholeness and transformation by struggling against sin, evil, injustice, and oppression, knowing full well that in this sinful world this will lead, not to utopias, prosperity, and success, but to rejection, frustration, and the cross; that is, to a life in which one "dies every day" as Paul did (1 Cor 15:31). This is what it means to take up one's cross daily and follow Jesus (Luke 9:23). Yet, as they take up the cross and the dying that comes with it, believers offer up to God with Jesus their life and that of others, trusting that God will ultimately complete the transformation and salvation of all to which they have dedicated themselves. This is how the world will be saved and made whole: by people dying to the world by living for others and placing the lives of others in God's hands together with their own, so that together they may be transformed as Jesus was when God raised him.

This is what the church is: the community of those who die with Christ to the world in the sense of loving the world by seeking the wholeness of all and consequently opposing the sin, evil, and injustice found in the world. In baptism, they die with Christ by renouncing sin in all its forms and manifestations and instead clinging to Christ and his cross in faith. As they partake of Christ's body and blood in Holy Communion, they identify themselves as members of the new covenant community founded through Christ's death, recalling Christ's love for them at the same time that they commit themselves to living in that same love by taking up their own cross.

The fact that the majority of people throughout the world are not Christian means that, as Christians seek wholeness for all, they must join efforts not only with other Christians but with those who are not Christian as well. When salvation is defined in terms of healing and wholeness, then mission must be seen as involving working together toward the wholeness that God desires for all, including both Christians and non-Christians. *All* need to be made whole as individuals and communities but can only attain wholeness for themselves as they seek it for others.

Although they must join with non-Christians who are committed to the same goals of justice and well-being for all in order to carry out their mission, Christians will be motivated and guided by their understanding of the gospel of Christ and his cross. This cannot be expected, of course, of those who have not embraced the gospel as their own. Nevertheless, as the Lutheran doctrine of the two kingdoms affirms, God is active to bring justice and wholeness into the world not only through the gospel and those who live under it but also through God's law among *all* people. The idea of a natural law written on the hearts of all people provides a basis for working together with those who do not consider themselves Jesus' disciples, even though it might be said that all who are committed to practicing justice and seeking wholeness for all are following Christ in a sense. Rather than limiting God's revelation to God's past act of writing a natural law on the hearts of all people, we may also see God as acting through the Holy Spirit throughout history among human beings everywhere to reveal God's will to them to some degree.

Because from a Christian perspective wholeness is intimately tied to faith in Christ, as Christians seek wholeness for others, they will also give witness to their conviction that wholeness is found in Christ and often invite others to experience this as well. This does not involve trying to convert others to faith in Christ. According to Lutheran teaching, that is the work of God's Spirit alone, who creates faith wherever and whenever it pleases God.[7] Because that same Spirit has been active among people who do not share the Christian faith, Christians must not only share their faith with others but encourage others to share their faith as well and listen to them, since God speaks to Christians through non-Christians just as God speaks to non-Christians through Christians.

This means that justice and wholeness are also to be found outside of the Christian faith. As Lutheran theology affirms, there is a civil righteousness, or rather, a civil justice (*iustitia*) that God gives in the world through the law as God rules in the "kingdom of the left hand." The problem with this civil justice is not that it is of no value before God but that it lacks fullness and is not yet perfect as God wishes it to be. Of course, this is true of the wholeness that Christians experience in this world as well, since in this world it is impossible to be made fully whole, and Christians also live in the kingdom on the left and not just the kingdom on the right. However, from a Christian perspective, the gospel gives wholeness in a way that the law alone cannot. For this reason, Christians seek to share God's unconditional love in Christ with others in word and deed and consider this an urgent task in a suffering world. In this regard, of course, they will differ from many other people, since there are many principles of the Christian faith that others may not agree with, such as the notion that love must be unconditional. It is this, however, to which Christians seek to give witness in accordance with their faith in Christ.

Does this mean that in order to attain salvation in the world to come, people must follow Jesus in faith? If those who are committed to justice and well-being for all can be regarded as following Jesus in a sense even though they do not consider themselves Christian, can it not be said that they too may attain that salvation? And since all people including believers are sinners who oppose God's will for wholeness and can only be healed by an act of God, cannot God ultimately make non-believers whole just as God promises to grant wholeness to believers? Even if it is argued that there are certain conditions that must be present in a person in order for that person to be justified and made whole in the end, cannot God still act to bring about those conditions? Ultimately, as noted above, it is not human beings who must answer these questions but God alone. All that we can do is continue to seek God's will that all people be made whole both by striving toward that end ourselves together with others and by imploring God that this become a reality, as Jesus himself did in his life and death.

The Lutheran Confessional Tradition

In light of what we have seen throughout the present study, it should be clear that many of the doctrines found in the Lutheran tradition can no longer be considered grounded in Scripture nor theologically sound. Among these are the interpretations of Christ's death that are based on the concepts of penal substitution and vicarious satisfaction, the idea of a "joyous exchange" between Christ and believers in which Christ's righteousness is imputed or imparted to believers and their sin is imputed or imparted to Christ, the notion that God's law is a "tyrant" rather than an expression of God's grace, and above all the idea that Christ needed to merit God's grace for us. This means that we cannot continue to adhere to such doctrines while at the same time affirming the principle of *sola Scriptura*; we must choose one or the other. In addition, the starting point and center of Christian theology must be God's desire for wholeness for all rather than a certain understanding of God's nature.

A number of other doctrines require significant modification. Salvation, for example, must be defined in a way that embraces not only existence in a blessed life to come following death but human wholeness and well-being in this world as well. Faith is best understood in terms of trusting in God by following Jesus, so that it is inseparable from a commitment to doing God's will as defined by Jesus; faith trusts in God, not only for forgiveness, but for the new life necessary to be made whole, and thus seeks to do what Christ the physician prescribes. Justification must be seen as involving, not only divine forgiveness, but God's declaration that sinful believers are acceptable to God because the faith in Christ that God has graciously brought about in them allows God to transform them and others through them in the way God desires. The gospel is thus God's promise, not only of forgiveness, but of wholeness and transformation as well. The proclamation of the law should bring people to repent in the sense of recognizing that they are sinners in need of healing and point them to God as one who lovingly wishes to accomplish that healing through Christ; only when people have persistently refused to acknowledge their sin and instead willfully insist on behaving in ways that oppress and harm others should the proclamation of the law speak of God's wrath and judgment upon their sin. Even in that case, however, it must be stressed that God's wrath is rooted in God's unconditional love for them and for others, since God wants them to change their ways not only for the good of others but for their own good. Those who oppress others cannot experience wholeness. Of course, most of these ideas that are problematic are found not only in the Lutheran tradition but in others as well; to that extent, they must also be rejected or modified there.

Nevertheless, there are of course a number of key Lutheran teachings that must be seen as being in essential harmony with Scripture. Among these are the Lutheran understanding of grace as God's undeserved love, mercy, and favor rather than some type of power, energy, substance, or quality infused by God into a person's soul, the idea that believers are wholly righteous and wholly sinful at the same time, and the understanding of the church as a community of believers rather than a hierarchical organization.

Of much greater importance, however, is the observation that the concept that Lutheran theology maintains at its heart and core must also be regarded as lying at the heart and core of the New Testament. This is the gospel: that in Christ God freely and graciously accepts sinners on no other condition than that they recognize themselves as sinners and receive through faith what God offers them so that they may be healed. Undoubtedly, the Lutheran tradition has generally failed to define salvation primarily in terms of wholeness and healing. Instead, it has limited faith to trusting in Christ for forgiveness of sins, rather than understanding it in terms of following Christ so as to receive through him, not only forgiveness, but a new way of life that enables one to be made whole together with others. The Lutheran tradition has also rightly stressed that human beings themselves can never merit God's grace, mercy, and unconditional love through their own works or efforts, yet nevertheless has also misunderstood this: rather than affirming that it is impossible to merit God's grace because by definition unconditional love cannot be merited or deserved, it has maintained that in principle it would have been possible to merit God's grace if human beings had been perfect, but since they have fallen into sin, this is no longer a possibility and Christ must merit that grace for them.

The idea that God loves sinners unconditionally and lays down no condition for accepting them other than that they admit their need for help and receive the healing God offers them in Jesus must be seen as the central concept of the teaching and ministry not only of Jesus but of Paul as well. When Paul speaks of justification by grace through faith, this is what he has in mind. The Lutheran tradition has generally looked to Paul as the one who articulated the doctrine of justification most clearly and placed it in the center of his theology. In reality, however, Paul's teaching must be regarded as entirely dependent on the teaching and practice of Jesus himself, whose ministry from beginning to end was focused on reaching out to sinners with God's unconditional love to bring God's healing and wholeness into their life. In Paul's thought, *this is what Jesus lived and died for. This is what his ministry was all about and this is what his death on the cross was all about.* And the gospel proclaims nothing but this: that God's love for all people is so great that God was willing to give up God's only Son so that we might be made whole through him as we live under him in faith alongside others in the community he established through his death, depending on him alone and not on our own strength, merits, or abilities. This is Paul's gospel and it must be ours as well.

Many Lutherans, of course, will no doubt find it problematic to assert that Luther and the Lutheran theologians who followed him had such a clear understanding and firm grasp of the essence of the New Testament gospel, while nevertheless holding to so many ideas that do not reflect faithfully or adequately biblical teaching. In particular, the fact that many of these ideas are found in the Lutheran confessional writings that Lutherans regard as normative raises the question of how those writings may continue to be considered normative if such ideas are rejected. Of course, this problem is not new; many attempts have been made to propose how Lutherans may continue to subscribe to the Confessional writings as normative, while at the same time rejecting some of the teachings and ideas that they contain.[8]

Perhaps the most satisfactory solution to this problem is simply to see the Lutheran Confessional writings for what they are: the testimony and confession of faith of those who, like us today, strove to apprehend and communicate the gospel to the best of their abilities in the context in which they lived.[9] As is true of people in every time and place, including our own, their context limited them in many ways. They worked within certain theological and philosophical frameworks and made many assumptions that are fundamentally distinct from those of our day and age. Furthermore, they did not have access to many of the theological, biblical, and historical resources at our disposal today. It is hardly surprising, therefore, that in framing their understanding of the gospel, they made use of many ideas and concepts that five centuries of biblical scholarship and theological reflection have shown to be no longer tenable.

To be Lutheran today, therefore, should not be defined in terms of assenting literally to everything contained in the Confessions to which Lutherans subscribe but affirming that, in spite of the limitations they faced, Luther and the other Lutheran theologians involved in the composition of the Confessional writings captured with accuracy and power the essence of the gospel of Jesus Christ for their own context. Naturally, there are other related aspects of Luther's writings and the Confessions that those of us who are Lutheran continue to regard as valid and normative today, even though we may understand them slightly differently than they did. As we hold to the basic truths that we believe are expressed in our theological tradition, we see ourselves standing in historical continuity with all of those who originally affixed their signature to the Lutheran Confessional writings and those who have continued to subscribe to them over the centuries, while at the same time viewing these writings from a critical perspective. To do so involves standing, not *contrary* to them, but *in fidelity* to them, as well as to the principle of *ecclesia reformata semper reformanda*: the reformed church always being reformed.

To admit that there are certain teachings found in the Lutheran tradition that are neither biblically-grounded nor theologically sound, of course, is not easy for those of us who are Lutheran. It is one thing to reject Luther's inflammatory statements about the Jews; it is another to reject some of the central doctrines of his thought, such as the penal substitution understanding of Christ's work and the idea of a joyous exchange, and to insist that others require serious modification. Many of these ideas are deeply engrained not only in Lutheran theological writings but in Lutheran hymnody and devotional life. Yet once we recognize that many of these ideas are not in fact grounded in Scripture and are not theologically sound, we must assume a critical attitude toward them so as to be conscious of how they may communicate images of God and salvation that can undermine human wholeness instead of contributing to it. This is not the same as simply discarding and eliminating from our confessional and devotional tradition everything that we now consider theologically problematic in iconoclastic fashion. Rather, as Luther did with regard to the Roman Catholic tradition, we seek to retain as much as possible of our tradition, seeing it as a source of tremendous wealth, while nevertheless reworking and reformulating it so as to make sure the gospel is not compromised but remains clear and pure.

To recognize that certain doctrines that have traditionally formed part of Lutheran teaching are no longer tenable in the form in which they appear in Luther's writings and the Lutheran Confessional documents has several benefits. First, it allows those of us who are Lutheran to maintain our integrity. Rather than feeling obliged to give the impression that we are in agreement with doctrines that deep down we find troublesome or problematic, such as the penal substitution interpretation of Christ's death, for example, we can openly affirm what we sincerely believe to be true in our hearts, giving witness of our faith in the saving power of the gospel of Jesus Christ as we have come to grasp it today in our own contexts. We can subscribe to our Confessional writings without feeling that we are being dishonest with ourselves because we are not fully in agreement with everything they affirm literally, while at the same time proclaiming firmly and enthusiastically our conviction that those writings capture and convey the essence of the gospel beautifully in the language and thought-world of their own time and place; and on that basis we proudly yet humbly declare ourselves to be in continuity with those who had the boldness and courage to compose them and subscribe to them over the centuries. The importance of being able to witness to our faith with such integrity without feeling that we are betraying our heritage must not be overlooked or underestimated. In large part, the crisis in the proclamation of the gospel today is the result of many in the church feeling obliged to share a message about which they have a number of serious reservations, due to many of the theological problems associated with the traditional Protestant understanding of the gospel that we have seen in this study.

A second benefit of recognizing the problematic nature of certain aspects of our traditional Lutheran teaching is that it can contribute to greater unity among Christians. Once we are willing to admit openly that some of the things we have taught are not completely in accordance with Scripture and are not entirely sound theologically, we not only make it possible to enter more fully and deeply into dialogue with those who have differed from us but also establish a precedent for them to question many of their own traditional teachings on the same basis. By taking a critical attitude toward our own tradition with integrity and encouraging others to do so together with us, we can then join others in taking a critical attitude toward their own traditions as well, without anyone feeling threatened or offended. This opens the way for all together to come to a fuller understanding of the gospel that incorporates the valuable insights and contributions of each tradition, yet lays aside the problematic elements that are found in all of them, as we recognize that our traditions, like all of us, are righteous and sinful at the same time.

Third and most important, however, by admitting that many of the teachings in our tradition are no longer tenable for biblical and theological reasons, we can proclaim with boldness and enthusiasm a gospel that is truly relevant for our world today and that is capable of transforming people's lives in dramatic and radical fashion in the way that the gospel proclaimed by Jesus' first followers did. Rather than seeing others as persons who, in distinction from believers, are under divine judgment and need to be delivered from God's wrath by coming to accept our own belief system as true, we can see them as people who are sick and broken just like we are and who thus need to be healed and made whole together with us; and we can then share our testimony and conviction that this healing and wholeness are found in Jesus Christ and in the community of sinners over which he is Lord. Rather than proclaiming a God whose love and grace must first be earned, either by us or by God's own Son on a cross, we can proclaim a God who loves all people unconditionally and unreservedly and was willing to send God's only Son into our sinful and violent world to reach out to those who are unacceptable so that they might be made whole. Like the gospel proclaimed boldly by Paul, this is a gospel of which we have no reason to be ashamed in the least (Rom 1:16), a message that we can enthusiastically share as good news, in contrast to the message that begins by condemning people in God's name and then demands that they become like us if they wish to be "saved."

In the end, this is the urgent question facing us as Christians today: whether we will proclaim an irrelevant and at times unhealthy gospel that has lost its power to transform and impact people's lives and to draw them to experience wholeness through faith in Christ, because we are concerned primarily about preserving our tradition intact and inviolate; or whether we will take the step of radically revising our proclamation of the gospel, not only so that it is more in accord with biblical teaching, but also so that it can have the redemptive power that it once did. A radical transformation of our churches must begin with a radical transformation of our teaching, as in Reformation times. As both Jesus and Luther taught, tradition is valuable and important and is not simply to be discarded lightly; but if it is not continually revised and reformulated, it becomes oppressive rather than liberating, destroying human wholeness rather than contributing to it. The question to which the gospel responds is not "How can I find a gracious God?" but "How can we all together find healing and wholeness?" Until we stop offering answers to the wrong question and start offering answers to the right one, the gospel we proclaim will be neither redeemed nor redeeming.

ABBREVIATIONS

AGAJU	Arbeiten zur Geschichte des antiken Judentums und des Urchristentums
AUS	American University Studies
CH	*Church History*
ConBOT	Coniectanea Biblica Old Testament Series
CTJ	*Calvin Theological Journal*
CTQ	*Concordia Theological Quarterly*
CurTM	*Currents in Theology and Mission*
EvQ	*Evangelical Quarterly*
ExpT	*Expository Times*
GOTR	*Greek Orthodox Theological Review*
HBM	Hebrew Bible Monographs
ICC	International Critical Commentary
JAAR	*Journal of the American Academy of Religion*
JES	*Journal of Ecumenical Studies*
JRE	*Journal of Religious Ethics*
JSNT	*Journal for the Study of the New Testament*
JSNTS	*Journal for the Study of the New Testament* Supplement Series
JSOTS	*Journal for the Study of the Old Testament* Supplement Series
JTS	*Journal of Theological Studies*
LCC	Library of Christian Classics
LCD	Lutherans and Catholics in Dialogue
LF	*Lutheran Forum*
LQ	*Lutheran Quarterly*
LRPT	Library of Religious and Philosophical Thought
LV	Lutheran Voices
MLN	*Modern Language Notes*
ModTh	*Modern Theology*
NovT	*Novum Testamentum*
NovTSup	Supplement to *Novum Testamentum*
NRSV	New Revised Standard Version of the Bible
NTG	New Testament Guides
ProEccl	*Pro Ecclesia*
RelSt	*Religious Studies*
SJT	*Scottish Journal of Theology*
SNTSMS	Society for New Testament Studies Monograph Series
SVTQ	*St. Vladimir Theological Quarterly*
T&R	Theology and Religion
ThStud	*Theological Studies*
ThT	*Theology Today*
W&W	*Word and World*
WTJ	*Westminster Theological Journal*
WUNT	Wissenschaftliche Untersuchungen zum Neuen Testament

NOTES

Introduction

[1] See Document 98, "Message of the Assembly," in *Proceedings of the Fourth Assembly of the Lutheran World Federation*, July 30 – August 11, 1963, Helsinki, Finland (Berlin and Hamburg: Lutherisches Verlagshaus, 1965), 426.

[2] See especially Rudolf Bultmann, *Jesus Christ and Mythology* (New York: Charles Scribner's Sons, 1958).

[3] For a summary of this discussion, see especially Stephen Westerholm, *Perspectives Old and New on Paul: The "Lutheran" Paul and His Critics* (Grand Rapids: Eerdmans, 2004), 249-58.

[4] For a summary of these criticisms, see J. Denny Weaver, *The Nonviolent Atonement* (Grand Rapids: Eerdmans, 2001), 122-78.

[5] David A. Brondos, *Paul on the Cross: Reconstructing the Apostle's Story of Redemption* (Minneapolis: Fortress Press, 2006).

[6] David A. Brondos, *Fortress Introduction to Salvation and the Cross* (Minneapolis: Fortress Press, 2007).

Chapter One: God and Salvation

[1] American edition of *Luther's Works* (hereafter *LW*), ed. Jaroslav J. Pelikan and Helmut T. Lehmann (Philadelphia: Fortress Press and St. Louis: Concordia, 1955-1986), 34:336.

[2] On this point and what follows, see especially Walther Eichrodt, *Theology of the Old Testament*, trans. J. A. Baker (Philadelphia: Westminster, 1961, 1967), 2:152-62.

[3] See Eichrodt, *Theology*, 2:434-43; E. P. Sanders, *Judaism: Practice and Belief, 63 BCE–66 CE* (Philadelphia: Trinity Press International, 1992), 270-75.

[4] On the ancient Jewish views regarding human suffering and its purposes, see N. Clayton Croy, *Endurance in Suffering: Hebrews 12.1-13 in its Rhetorical, Religious, and Philosophical Context*, SNTSMS 98 (Cambridge: Cambridge University Press, 1998), 77-133.

[5] See Sanders, *Judaism*, 298-303; Ed Condra, *Salvation for the Righteous Revealed: Jesus Amid Covenantal and Messianic Expectations in Second Temple Judaism*, AGAJU 51 (Leiden: Brill, 2002), 63-65, 83-84.

[6] Philip Melanchthon, in *Melanchthon on Christian Doctrine*, trans. and ed. Clyde L. Manschreck (Oxford: Oxford University Press, 1965), 95.

[7] On this question, see especially Staffan Olofsson, *God is My Rock: A Study of Translation Technique and Theological Exegesis in the Septuagint*, ConBOT 31 (Stockholm: Almqvist & Wiksell International, 1990), 5-11.

[8] See, for example, Siegfried Reinhart, "The Mortality of God and the Immortality of Man in Gregory of Nyssa," in Philip J. Hefner, ed., *The Scope of Grace: Essays on Nature and Grace in*

Honor of Joseph Sittler (Philadelphia: Fortress Press, 1964), 88-92; Jaroslav Pelikan, *Christianity and Classical Culture: The Metamorphosis of Natural Theology in the Christian Encounter with Hellenism* (New Haven, Conn.: Yale University Press, 1993), 273-76.

[9] Paul Tillich, *Systematic Theology* (Chicago: University of Chicago Press, 1951-1963), 1:245.

[10] Rosemary Radford Ruether, *Introducing Redemption in Christian Feminism* (Sheffield: Sheffield Academic Press, 1998), 119.

[11] Rosemary Radford Ruether, *Sexism and God Talk: Toward a Feminist Theology*, 10th anniversary ed. (Boston: Beacon, 1993), 70.

[12] Ibid., 257.

[13] Ruether, *Introducing Redemption*, 106.

[14] Gordon D. Kaufman, "On Thinking of God as Serendipitous Creativity," *JAAR* 69, no. 2 (2001): 410-11.

[15] Valerie A. Karras, "Beyond Justification: An Orthodox Perspective," in William G. Rusch, ed., *Justification and the Future of the Ecumenical Movement: The Joint Declaration on the Doctrine of Justification* (Collegeville, Minn.: Liturgical Press, 2003), 99.

[16] Ibid., 104, 110.

[17] Nonna Verna Harrison, "Theosis as Salvation: An Orthodox Perspective," *ProEccl* 6, no. 4 (1997): 438.

[18] Bishop Maximos Aghiorgoussis, "Orthodox Soteriology," in John Meyendorff and Robert Tobias, eds., *Salvation in Christ: A Lutheran-Orthodox Dialogue* (Minneapolis: Augsburg Fortress Press, 1992), 56.

[19] See John Breck, "Divine Initiative: Salvation in Orthodox Theology," in Meyendorff and Tobias, eds., *Salvation in Christ*, 111-12.

[20] See, for example, Aghiorgoussis, "Orthodox Soteriology," 55-56.

[21] Karras, "Beyond Justification," 116-17.

[22] Harrison, "Theosis," 438; cf. Karras, "Beyond Justification," 111-15; Aghiorgoussis, "Orthodox Soteriology," 46.

[23] Albrecht Ritschl, *The Christian Doctrine of Justification and Reconciliation: The Positive Development of the Doctrine*, ed. and trans. H. R. Mackintosh and A. B. Macaulay, 3rd ed., LRPT (Clifton, N.J.: Reference Book Publishers, 1966), 42.

[24] Ibid., 90.

[25] Ibid., 323, 351.

[26] Ibid., 320-21.

[27] Wolfhart Pannenberg, *Jesus, God and Man*, trans. Lewis L. Wilkins and Duane A. Priebe, 2nd ed. (Philadelphia: Westminster, 1977), 265. Cf. Kent L. Yinger, *Paul, Judaism, and Judgment according to Deeds*, SNTSMS 105 (Cambridge: Cambridge University Press, 1999), 26-28.

[28] Pannenberg, *Jesus*, 265.

[29] Eberhard Jüngel, *Justification: The Heart of the Christian Faith: A Theological Study with an Ecumenical Purpose*, trans. Jeffrey F. Cayzer (New York: T & T Clark, 2001), 133.

[30] Ibid., 134.

[31] Douglas John Hall, *The Cross in our Context: Jesus and the Suffering World* (Minneapolis: Fortress Press, 2003), 218.

[32] David Scaer, "The Third Use of the Law: Resolving the Tension," *CTQ* 69, no. 3/4 (2005): 256-57.

33 On the origin and history of the doctrine of purgatory, see especially Jacques Le Goff, *The Birth of Purgatory*, trans. Arthur Goldhammer (Chicago: University of Chicago Press, 1984).

34 See James Jorgenson, "The Debate over the Patristic Texts on Purgatory at the Council of Ferrara-Florence, 1438," *SVTQ* 30, no. 4 (1986): 309-34.

35 See John R. Sachs, "Apocatastasis in Patristic Theology," *ThStud* 54 (1993): 617-40.

36 Hall, *Cross*, 219-24.

37 Rosemary Radford Ruether, *Gaia & God: An Ecofeminist Theology of Earth Healing* (San Francisco: HarperSanFrancisco, 1992), 227.

38 See, for example, Jürgen Moltmann, "The End of Everything is God: Has Belief in Hell had its Day?," *ExpT* 108, no. 9 (1997): 263-64.

Chapter Two: Justice, Righteousness, and the Law

1 On this discussion, see Stephen Westerholm, *Perspectives Old and New on Paul: The "Lutheran" Paul and His Critics* (Grand Rapids: Eerdmans, 2004), especially 101-258.

2 See William H. Lazareth, in Lazareth and Péri Rasolondraibe, *Lutheran Identity and Mission: Evangelical and Evangelistic?* (Minneapolis: Fortress Press, 1994), 46-49.

3 See the American edition of *Luther's Works* (hereafter *LW*), ed. Jaroslav J. Pelikan and Helmut T. Lehmann (Philadelphia: Fortress Press and St. Louis: Concordia, 1955-1986), 35:367-69. See also Paul Althaus, *The Ethics of Martin Luther*, trans. Robert C. Schultz (Philadelphia: Fortress Press, 1972), 15.

4 See Eberhard Jüngel, *Justification: The Heart of the Christian Faith: A Theological Study with an Ecumenical Purpose*, trans. Jeffrey F. Cayzer (New York: T & T Clark, 2001), 99; William H. Lazareth, *Christians in Society: Luther, the Bible, and Social Ethics* (Minneapolis: Fortress Press, 2001), 229-30. Both of these works contain references to Luther's writings on this subject.

5 Werner Elert, *Law and Gospel*, trans. Edward H. Schroeder (Philadelphia: Fortress Press, 1967), 8.

6 *LW* 31:54.

7 *LW* 26:309.

8 Thomas M. McDonough, *The Law and the Gospel in Luther: A Study of Martin Luther's Confessional Writings* (Oxford: Oxford University Press, 1963), 68. See *LW* 12:316; 22:144; 26:309-12; 39:188; Formula of Concord 1, VI, 1; 2, VI, 1.

9 *LW* 26:308. In Reformed theology, following Calvin, what Lutherans regard as the second or theological use of the law is considered the first use, and the first or political use of the law is spoken of as the second use; see John Calvin, *Institutes of the Christian Religion* 2.7.6-11.

10 See Lazareth, *Christians in Society*, 167-73.

11 See Timothy J. Wengert, *Law and Gospel: Philip Melanchthon's Debate with John Agricola of Eisleben over Poenitentia* (Grand Rapids: Baker Academic, 1997), 91, 199.

12 See ibid., 121.

13 See ibid., 190.

14 E. P. Sanders, *Paul and Palestinian Judaism* (Philadelphia: Fortress Press, 1977), 110.

15 See ibid., 110, 137-43, 147, 157-68, 203-5.

16 Ibid., 75.

[17] See especially Simon Gathercole, *Where is Boasting? Early Jewish Soteriology and Paul's Response in Romans 1-5* (Grand Rapids: Eerdmans, 2002), 151-56.

[18] See Sanders, *Paul*, 85, 92-97, 146-47, 293, 382-83, 419-22.

[19] See Bruce D. Chilton and Jacob Neusner, *Classical Christianity and Rabbinic Judaism: Comparing Theologies* (Grand Rapids: Baker Academic, 2004), 118-21.

[20] On the Noahic commandments, see Irving J. Mandelbaum, "The Purpose of Laws of Diverse Kinds," in Alan J. Avery-Peck, ed., *The Literature of Early Rabbinic Judaism: Issues in Talmudic Redaction and Interpretation* (Lanham, Md.: University Press of America, 1989), 111-20.

[21] See George W. E. Nickelsburg, *Ancient Judaism and Christian Origins: Diversity, Continuity, and Transformation* (Minneapolis: Fortress Press, 2003), 54-57; William R. G. Loader, *Jesus' Attitude toward the Law: A Study of the Gospels*, WUNT 2, 97 (Tübingen: Mohr Siebeck, 1997), 509-18.

[22] See, for example, Philip Melanchthon, in *Melanchthon and Bucer*, ed. Wilhelm Pauck, LCC 19 (Philadelphia: Westminster, 1969), 53, 61-62, 121; Calvin, *Institutes* 2.7.16.

[23] See *LW* 1:277-78; 25:19-20, 187, 377; 35:168, 173; 40:92, 98; Lazareth, *Christians in Society*, 153-58; Althaus, *Ethics*, 25-35.

[24] See Randall C. Zachman, "What do Theologians Mean by Law?," *W&W* 21, no. 3 (2001): 235-42; Otto A. Piper, "What is Natural Law?," *ThT* 2, no. 4 (1946): 459-71.

[25] George A. F. Knight, *A Christian Theology of the Old Testament* (Richmond, Va.: John Knox, 1959), 250, 253.

[26] See Yairah Amit, "The Jubilee Law: An Attempt at Instituting Social Justice," in Henning Graf Reventlow and Yair Hoffman, eds., *Justice and Righteousness: Biblical Themes and Their Influence*, JSOTS 137 (Sheffield: JSOT Press, 1992), 51.

[27] On this idea in Jewish thought, see Sanders, *Paul*, 125-47.

[28] See, for example, Ps 82:3-4; 112:4; 116:5; 143:11-12; 145:17; Isa 11:4; 30:18. See also Leroy H. Pelton, "Biblical Justice," *JAAR* 71, no. 4 (2003): 737-65; Jason J. Ripley, "Covenantal Concepts of Justice and Righteousness, and Catholic-Protestant Reconciliation: Theological Implications and Explorations," *JES* 38, no. 1 (2000): 95-103.

[29] Robert W. Jenson, "Justification as a Triune Event," *ModTh* 11, no. 4 (1995): 422.

[30] Jüngel, *Justification*, 78.

[31] Paul Althaus, *The Divine Command: A New Perspective on Law and Gospel*, ed. Franklin Sherman (Philadelphia: Fortress Press, 1966), 23; cf. Calvin *Institutes*, 2.1.8.

[32] Martin Chemnitz, *Examination of the Council of Trent*, trans. Fred Kramer (St. Louis: Concordia, 1971-1986), 1:488.

[33] See Sanders, *Paul*, 128-47.

[34] See ibid., 107-9.

[35] See ibid., 92-96, 134-35.

[36] See Gerhard Ebeling, *Luther: An Introduction to His Thought*, trans. R. A. Wilson (Philadelphia: Fortress Press, 1970), 138.

[37] Chilton and Neusner, *Classical Christianity*, 94, 105-7.

[38] See ibid., 190-91.

[39] This idea was found in many of the church fathers as well as Anselm; see Tatha Wiley, *Original Sin: Origins, Development, Contemporary Meaning* (New York: Paulist Press, 2002), 82. See also Calvin, *Institutes* 2.1.5-6, 8.

[40] *LW* 26:370.

41 Gerhard O. Forde, *The Law-Gospel Debate: An Interpretation of its Historical Development* (Minneapolis: Augsburg, 1969), 177; cf. Joseph A. Burgess and Marc Kolden, "Introduction: Gerhard O. Forde and the Doctrine of Justification," in Burgess and Kolden, eds., *By Faith Alone: Essays on Justification in Honor of Gerhard O. Forde* (Grand Rapids: Eerdmans, 2004), 17.

42 See Jacob Neusner, *Torah: From Scroll to Symbol in Formative Judaism* (Philadelphia: Fortress Press, 1985), 118-19.

43 See Jonathan Klawans, *Purity, Sacrifice, and the Temple: Symbolism and Supersessionism in the Study of Ancient Judaism* (Oxford: Oxford University Press, 2006), 217-21, 244.

44 See Sanders, *Paul*, 112-14.

45 See David Wenham, *Paul, Follower of Jesus or Founder of Christianity?* (Grand Rapids: Eerdmans, 1995), 229-30.

46 On Paul's understanding of this phrase, see John M. G. Barclay, *Obeying the Truth: A Study of Paul's Ethics in Galatians* (Minneapolis: Fortress Press, 1991), 125-45.

Chapter Three: Justification and the Work of Christ

1 Most of the discussion concerning Anselm's understanding of Christ's death in the present chapter is based on what I have presented in *Fortress Introduction to Salvation and the Cross* (Minneapolis: Fortress Press, 2007), 76-87.

2 Anselm of Canterbury, *Cur Deus Homo* 2.16. Quotations are taken from volume 3 of *Anselm of Canterbury*, ed. and trans. Jasper Hopkins and Herbert Richardson (Toronto: Edwin Mellen, 1976).

3 See the American edition of *Luther's Works* (hereafter *LW*), ed. Jaroslav J. Pelikan and Helmut T. Lehmann (Philadelphia: Fortress Press and St. Louis: Concordia, 1955-1986), 13:326.

4 *LW* 52:252-53.

5 Anselm, *Cur Deus Homo* 1.15.

6 *LW* 51:92. Cf. *LW* 3:215; 22:147, 392-93; 25:67-68, 284; 26:32-33, 277-78, 325; 27:288; 41:139-40; 51:92-93, 317; 52:280.

7 *LW* 25:31-33.

8 On Luther's understanding of the saving significance of Christ's death on the cross, see my *Fortress Introduction to Salvation and the Cross*, 92-98.

9 *LW* 26:168; see also *LW* 26:166-67, 278, 284; 31:298, 351-52; 51:316.

10 Apology to the Augsburg Confession 1, III, 179, 252. Quotations are from Robert Kolb and Timothy J. Wengert, eds., *The Book of Concord: The Confessions of the Evangelical Lutheran Church* (Minneapolis: Fortress Press, 2000).

11 See Robert S. Paul, *The Atonement and the Sacraments: The Relation of the Atonement to the Sacraments of Baptism and the Lord's Supper* (New York: Abingdon, 1960), 168-93.

12 On this understanding of Christ's work, as well as the points that follow, see my *Paul on the Cross: Reconstructing the Apostle's Story of Redemption* (Minneapolis: Fortress Press, 2006), 151-66.

13 See W. D. Davies, *Paul and Rabbinic Judaism: Some Rabbinic Elements in Pauline Theology*, 2nd ed. (London: SPCK, 1955), 100-109.

14 On much of what follows in this section, see my *Paul on the Cross*, 11-31.

15 See E. P. Sanders, *Paul and Palestinian Judaism* (Philadelphia: Fortress Press, 1977), 157-82.

16 See, for example, Stephen Finlan, *Problems with Atonement: The Origins Of, And Controversy About, The Atonement Doctrine* (Collegeville, Minn.: Liturgical Press, 2005), 13, 34-35; Jay Sklar, *Sin, Impurity, Sacrifice, and Atonement: The Priestly Conceptions*, HBM 2 (Sheffield: Sheffield Phoenix, 2005), 163, 173, 186-87.

17 See James D. G. Dunn, *Romans* (Dallas: Word Books, 1988), 1:172, 181; Dunn, "Paul's Understanding of the Death of Jesus," in S. W. Sykes, ed., *Sacrifice and Redemption: Durham Essays in Theology* (Cambridge: Cambridge University Press, 1991), 44-46; Jacob Milgrom, *Studies in Cultic Theology and Terminology* (Leiden: Brill, 1983), 89; Milgrom, "Atonement in the OT," "Day of Atonement," and "Sacrifices and offerings, OT," in *Interpreter's Dictionary of the Bible* (Nashville, TN: Abingdon, 1976), Supplementary Volume, 78-80, 83, 766-68.

18 See my *Paul on the Cross*, 23-26.

19 On the diversity of Jewish thought regarding the salvation of Gentiles, see T. L. Donaldson, *Paul and the Gentiles: Remapping the Apostle's Convictional World* (Minneapolis: Fortress Press, 1997), 65-74; George W. E. Nickelsburg, *Ancient Judaism and Christian Origins: Diversity, Continuity, and Transformation* (Minneapolis: Fortress Press, 2003), 75-79.

20 Anselm, *Cur Deus Homo* 1.24.

21 Anselm, *Cur Deus Homo* 1.15.

22 *LW* 30:36; cf. *LW* 22:459; 26:132, 176.

23 See Joanne Carlson Brown and Rebecca Parker, "For God so Loved the World?," in Brown and Carole R. Bohn, eds., *Christianity, Patriarchy, and Abuse: A Feminist Critique* (Cleveland: Pilgrim Press, 1989), 7-11.

24 See Anselm, *Cur Deus Homo* 1.9.

25 These ideas are already present in Luther; see *LW* 26:325; 52:280. See also the Formula of Concord 2, III, 12; J. Denny Weaver, *The Nonviolent Atonement* (Grand Rapids: Eerdmans, 2001), 197-98.

26 On this distinction in Protestant thought, see Alister E. McGrath, *Iustitia Dei: A History of the Christian Doctrine of Justification* (Cambridge: Cambridge University Press, 1986), 2:45-48; Alan C. Clifford, *Atonement and Justification: English Evangelical Theology, 1640-1790: An Evaluation* (Oxford: Clarendon, 1990), 171, 180-81n24, 190-91.

27 See Kazoh Kitamori, *Theology of the Pain of God* (Richmond: John Knox, 1965), 21.

28 Carl E. Braaten, *Justification: The Article by which the Church Stands or Falls* (Minneapolis: Fortress Press, 1990), 105.

29 See, for example, James Denney, *The Death of Christ* (London: Tyndale, 1951), 188-89.

30 See Paul Fiddes, *Past Event and Present Salvation: The Christian Idea of Atonement* (Louisville, Ky.: Westminster John Knox, 1989), 101-2.

31 See, for example, Leon Morris, *The Apostolic Preaching of the Cross* (Grand Rapids: Eerdmans, 1965), 293; H. D. McDonald, *The Atonement of the Death of Christ: In Faith, Revelation, and History* (Grand Rapids: Baker, 1985), 29.

32 Anselm, *Cur Deus Homo* 2.18. The idea that the satisfaction rendered by Christ was of infinite proportions was later taken up by Protestant theologians; see Martin Chemnitz, *Examination of the Council of Trent*, trans. Fred Kramer (St. Louis: Concordia, 1971-1986), 1:499.

33 For attempts to establish this type of equivalency in the thought of Lutheran Orthodoxy, see Heinrich Schmid, *The Doctrinal Theology of the Evangelical Lutheran Church*, trans. Charles A. Hay and Henry E. Jacobs, 3rd ed. (Minneapolis: Augsburg, reprint, 1899), 359-60.

34 On this concept, see McGrath, *Iustitia Dei*, 2:31, 44-45.

35 See, for example, *LW* 26:277-80; 51:317.

36 See, for example, Margaret E. Thrall, *A Critical and Exegetical Commentary on the Second Epistle to the Corinthians*, ICC (Edinburgh: T & T Clark, 1994), 1:337; Ernest Best, *Ephesians*, NTG (Edinburgh: T & T Clark, 1998), 215; Rudolf Schnackenburg, *Ephesians: A Commentary*, trans. Helen Heron (Edinburgh: T & T Clark 1991), 249.

37 See McGrath, *Iustitia Dei*, 2:48.

38 On the debate over the use of this phrase between John Wesley and the Moravians, see Herbert Boyd McGonigle, *Sufficient Saving Grace: John Wesley's Evangelical Arminianism* (Carlisle: Paternoster, 2001), 169-70.

39 Whether or not Calvin himself actually taught the doctrine of limited atonement has been debated by many scholars. On this discussion, as well as the doctrine itself, see especially Hans Boersma, "Calvin and the Extent of the Atonement," *EvQ* 64, no. 4 (1992): 333-55; Roger Nicole, "John Calvin's View of the Extent of the Atonement," *WTJ* 47 (1985): 197-225.

40 See Gerhard O. Forde, *The Law-Gospel Debate: An Interpretation of its Historical Development* (Minneapolis: Augsburg, 1969), 69-70; Peter Stuhlmacher, *Reconciliation, Law, and Righteousness: Essays in Biblical Theology* (Philadelphia: Fortress Press, 1986), 55.

41 Council of Trent, Fourteenth Session, Decree on the Sacrament of Penance, Ch. 8; cf. Ch. 1.

42 See especially *LW* 31:297-99; Paul Althaus, *The Theology of Martin Luther*, trans. Robert C. Schultz (Philadelphia: Fortress Press, 1966), 227-33.

43 See, for example, Formula of Concord 2, III, 55-57.

44 See, for example, Braaten, *Justification*, 98.

45 See Althaus, *Theology*, 234-42; *LW* 32:24, 28; 27:21-22, 227; 34:153.

46 *LW* 26:277.

47 *LW* 31:351.

48 *LW* 31:299.

49 *LW* 12:239; 26:38, 167.

50 Tuomo Mannermaa, *Christ Present in Faith: Luther's View of Justification* (Minneapolis: Fortress Press, 2005), 18.

51 Ibid., 40, 37.

52 Tuomo Mannermaa, "Justification and *Theosis* in Lutheran-Orthodox Perspective," in Carl E. Braaten and Robert W. Jenson, eds., *Union with Christ: The New Finnish Interpretation of Luther* (Grand Rapids: Eerdmans, 1998), 29.

53 Mannermaa, *Christ Present in Faith*, 19.

54 Ibid., 37.

55 Simo Peura, "Christ as Favor and Gift," in Braaten and Jenson, eds., *Union with Christ*, 53.

56 Mannermaa rejects such an idea; see "Why is Luther so Fascinating? Modern Finnish Luther Research," in Braaten and Jenson, eds., *Union with Christ*, 4-9.

57 On the background to Luther's teaching in this regard, see Werner Elert, *The Structure of Lutheranism*, trans. Walter A. Hansen (St. Louis: Concordia, 1962), 154-76.

58 Mannermaa, *Christ Present in Faith*, 13.

59 See Mannermaa, "Justification and *Theosis*," 29-31.

[60] See *LW* 25:68: "He was not 'sinful flesh,' but yet He was like us in all respects except for sin." Luther's thought on this question seems to have been similar to that of Calvin, who taught that the fallen flesh Christ assumed from Mary was sanctified and cleansed from sin either by his divinity or the work of the Holy Spirit, so that it ceased to be sinful and fallen flesh; see Bruce L. McCormack, "For Us and Our Salvation: Incarnation and Atonement in the Reformed Tradition," *GOTR* 43 (1998): 295-96; George Yule, "Luther's Understanding of Justification by Faith Alone in Terms of Catholic Christology," in George Yule, ed., *Luther: Theologian for Catholics and Protestants* (Edinburgh: T & T Clark, 1985), 100-101.

[61] Mannermaa, "Justification and *Theosis*," 31.

[62] Peura, "Christ as Favor," 54.

[63] Nonna Verna Harrison, "Theosis as Salvation: An Orthodox Perspective," *ProEccl* 6, no. 4 (1997): 436. Cf. Mannermaa, *Christ Present in Faith*, 59, 66.

[64] Peura, "Christ as Favor," 42-69; Mannermaa, *Christ Present in Faith*, 19-21.

[65] Albrecht Ritschl, *The Christian Doctrine of Justification and Reconciliation: The Positive Development of the Doctrine*, ed. and trans. H. R. Mackintosh and A. B. Macaulay, 3rd ed., LRPT (Clifton, N.J.: Reference Book Publishers, 1966), 40, 264, 478. On Ritschl's understanding of Christ's work, see my *Fortress Introduction to Salvation and the Cross* (Minneapolis: Fortress Press, 2007), 116-29.

[66] Ritschl, *Christian Doctrine*, 537.

[67] Ibid., 108; cf. 540.

[68] Ibid., 100.

[69] Ibid., 537.

[70] Ibid., 591-92, 551.

[71] Ibid., 581; cf. 582-83.

[72] Gerhard O. Forde, "The Work of Christ," in Carl E. Braaten and Robert W. Jenson, eds., *Christian Dogmatics* (Philadelphia: Fortress Press, 1984), 2:15, 81, 92-93.

[73] Ibid., 2:93, 81, 11.

[74] Ibid., 2:66.

[75] Ibid., 2:50, 72.

[76] Ibid., 2:67, 74.

[77] Ibid., 2:50-51.

[78] Ibid., 2:50, 52.

[79] Ibid., 2:58.

[80] Ibid., 2:11.

[81] Ibid., 2:80, 92.

[82] Ibid., 2:72.

[83] Ibid., 2:80.

[84] Ibid., 2:65, 74.

[85] Ibid., 2:92.

[86] Ibid., 2:92.

[87] Ibid., 2:72.

[88] Ibid., 2:74.

[89] Ibid., 2:92.

[90] Ibid., 2:65.

[91] Ibid., 2:50-51.

[92] Colin Gunton, *The Actuality of Atonement* (Grand Rapids: Eerdmans, 1988), 77; David McNaughton, "Reparation and Atonement," *RelSt* 28 (1992): 144; Weaver, *Nonviolent Atonement*, 49, 36.

[93] So, for example, McDonald, *Atonement*, 38-39.

[94] See Brown and Parker, "For God so Loved the World?," 11-23.

[95] Gustav Aulén, *Christus Victor: An Historical Study of the Three Main Types of the Idea of Atonement*, trans. A. G. Hebert (New York: MacMillan, 1969), 4.

[96] See ibid., 42-55.

[97] *LW* 26:370.

[98] *LW* 52:156.

[99] On this idea in Luther's thought, see Althaus, *Theology*, 220.

[100] *LW* 7:227; cf. *LW* 2:280; 12:27, 127; 22:392-93; 26:278-89, 325; 41:140; 52:278-80.

[101] *LW* 26:282, 287.

[102] See *LW* 22:24; 26:267. On this idea in the church fathers, see Aulén, *Christus Victor*, 51-53.

[103] Weaver, *Nonviolent Atonement*, 45.

[104] David Seeley, *The Noble Death: Graeco-Roman Martyrology and Paul's Concept of Salvation*, JSNTS 28 (Sheffield: Sheffield Academic Press, 1990), 104.

[105] See, for example, John Calvin, *Institutes of the Christian Religion* 2.16.14; 3.1.1; Dennis J. Tamburello, *Union with Christ: John Calvin and the Mysticism of St. Bernard* (Louisville, Ky.: Westminster John Knox, 1994), 84-101.

[106] For references, as well as much of what follows, see my *Paul on the Cross*, 4-7, 151-89.

[107] Sanders, *Paul*, 467.

[108] Ibid., 507.

[109] C. E. B. Cranfield, *A Critical and Exegetical Commentary on the Epistle to the Romans*, ICC (Edinburgh: T & T Clark, 1975), 1:309.

[110] Sanders, *Paul*, 522-23.

[111] Mannermaa, *Christ Present in Faith*, 37.

[112] Karl Barth, *Church Dogmatics*, trans. and ed. G. W. Bromiley and T. F. Torrance (Edinburgh: T & T Clark, 1936-1969), 4.1:295.

[113] Ibid., 4.1:222, 253, 555.

[114] Sanders, *Paul*, 507.

[115] See my *Paul on the Cross*, 154-89.

[116] On all that follows in this section, see my *Paul on the Cross*, 33-149; *Fortress Introduction to Salvation and the Cross*, 19-48.

[117] For the background to the idea that what had previously been offered at the temple was now offered through Jesus, see James D. G. Dunn, *Jesus Remembered* (Grand Rapids: Eerdmans, 2003), 785-90.

[118] On the following, see Elisabeth Schüssler Fiorenza, *In Memory of Her: A Feminist Reconstruction of Christian Origins* (New York: Crossroad, 1983), 122-30.

[119] As David E. Aune notes, biblical scholars are now recognizing that the idea of an imputation of Christ's righteousness to believers is not found in the New Testament ("Recent Readings of Paul Relating to Justification by Faith," in Aune, ed., *Rereading Paul Together: Protestant and Catholic Perspectives on Justification* [Grand Rapids: Baker Academic, 2006], 231-33).

[120] On this and what follows, see my *Paul on the Cross*, 166-89.

Chapter Four: Grace, Faith, and the Gospel

[1] Apology to the Augsburg Confession 1, II, 42; Formula of Concord 2, V, 1.

[2] American edition of *Luther's Works* (hereafter *LW*), ed. Jaroslav J. Pelikan and Helmut T. Lehmann (Philadelphia: Fortress Press and St. Louis: Concordia, 1955-1986), 44:126-39, 165, 168.

[3] On these points, see especially Luther's *Treatise on Christian Liberty*, *LW* 31:351-58.

[4] See especially *LW* 36:64-69; 35:369.

[5] See the Council of Trent, Fourteenth Session, Decree on the Sacrament of Penance, Ch. 8; Sixth Session, Decree on Justification, Ch. 5-7, 10, 16; Canon 32.

[6] See, for example, *LW* 12:331; 22:147-48; 23:87; 30:3, 29; 32:227-28; 33:150, 280; 36:298; 52:241; 53:82. Cf. Augsburg Confession 2, V, 3.

[7] E. P. Sanders, *Paul and Palestinian Judaism* (Philadelphia: Fortress Press, 1977), 38, 291-98, 419-22.

[8] On the ancient Hebrew and Jewish understanding of divine grace, see especially Stephen Duffy, *The Dynamics of Grace: Perspectives in Theological Anthropology* (Collegeville, Minn.: Liturgical Press, 1993), 17-26.

[9] On the ancient Jewish distinction between righteous and sinners, see especially Severino Pancaro, *The Law in the Fourth Gospel: The Torah and the Gospel, Moses and Jesus, Judaism and Christianity according to John*, NovTSup 42 (Leiden: Brill, 1977), 30-44.

[10] See, for example, Ps 7:1-5, 8-10; 17:1-4; 26:1-12.

[11] On this understanding of faith in ancient Judaism, see George W. E. Nickelsburg, *Ancient Judaism and Christian Origins* (Minneapolis: Fortress Press, 2003), 38-39.

[12] See, for example, Deut 7:7-8; 9:4-6; Neh 9:16-37; Ps 25:6-7; 51:1-9; 89:31-34; 106:6-8, 43-47; 146:3-7; 147:10-11; Isa 54:7-8; Jer 17:5-8; Lam 3:32-33; Ez 39:25-29; Hos 14:4; Zech 4:6.

[13] Matt 13:41-43, 49; 25:37-40; Luke 1:5-6; 2:25; 23:50; Acts 10:22; Rom 2:13; 1 John 3:7; Rev 22:11.

[14] See, for example, James D. G. Dunn, *Romans* (Dallas: Word Books, 1988), 1:296, 298, 421; J. A. Ziesler, *The Meaning of Righteousness in Paul: A Linguistic and Theological Inquiry*, SNTSMS 20 (Cambridge: Cambridge University Press, 1972), 22.

[15] See Gerhard O. Forde, "Forensic Justification and Law in Lutheran Theology," in H. George Anderson, T. Austin Murphy, and Joseph A. Burgess, eds., *Justification by Faith*, LCD 7 (Minneapolis: Augsburg, 1985), 278-79; Christopher J. Malloy, *Engrafted into Christ: A Critique of the Joint Declaration*, AUS VII, T&R 233 (New York: Peter Lang, 2005), 44; Eberhard Jüngel, *Justification: The Heart of the Christian Faith: A Theological Study with an Ecumenical Purpose*, trans. Jeffrey F. Cayzer (New York: T & T Clark, 2001), 208-10.

[16] See, for example, Carl E. Braaten, *Justification: The Article by which the Church Stands or Falls* (Minneapolis: Fortress Press, 1990), 14.

[17] Gerhard O. Forde, *The Law-Gospel Debate: An Interpretation of its Historical Development* (Minneapolis: Augsburg, 1969), 23-24; cf. 35, 51, 85.

[18] Ibid., 29-31; cf. 34-35.

[19] Ibid., 36.

[20] Alister E. McGrath, *Iustitia Dei: A History of the Christian Doctrine of Justification* (Cambridge: Cambridge University Press, 1986), 2:48-49

[21] Braaten, *Justification*, 24, 26.

[22] See Karl Barth, *Church Dogmatics*, trans. and ed. G. W. Bromiley and T. F. Torrance (Edinburgh: T & T Clark, 1936-1969), 4.1: 317, 558-61; 4.2:511; 4.3: 269, 279-80.

[23] Council of Trent, Sixth Session, Decree on Justification, Ch. 10.

[24] Council of Trent, Sixth Session, Decree on Justification, Ch. 14. On the Council of Trent's doctrine of double justification, see McGrath, *Iustitia Dei*, 2:84-85; Malloy, *Engrafted*, 31-33.

[25] Richard Baxter, quoted in Herbert Boyd McGonigle, *Sufficient Saving Grace: John Wesley's Evangelical Arminianism* (Carlisle: Paternoster, 2001), 165-66.

[26] See McGonigle, *Sufficient Saving Grace*, 232; Alan C. Clifford, *Atonement and Justification: English Evangelical Theology 1640-1790. An Evaluation* (Oxford: Clarendon, 1990), 205.

[27] George H. Tavard has argued, for example, that Wesley restored the idea of doing what is within oneself (*facere quod in se est*) as a condition for faith and therefore justification (*Justification: An Ecumenical Study* [New York: Paulist Press, 1983], 89).

[28] See Sanders, *Paul*, 17, 424-25.

[29] See the *Joint Declaration on the Doctrine of Justification* of the Lutheran World Federation and the Roman Catholic Church; Hans Küng, *Justification: The Doctrine of Karl Barth and a Catholic Reflection*, trans. Thomas Collins, Edmund E. Tolk, and David Granskou (New York: Thomas Nelson & Sons, 1964). On the differences between Barth and Küng on the doctrine of justification, see Alister E. McGrath, "Justification: Barth, Trent, and Küng," *SJT* 34 (1981): 517-29.

[30] Avery Dulles, "Justification in Contemporary Catholic Theology," in George H. Anderson *et al.*, eds., *Justification by Faith*, 273. See also Malloy, *Engrafted*, 48, 293-307.

[31] On the Roman Catholic distinction between created and uncreated grace, see McGrath, *Iustitia Dei*, 1:78-79; Dulles, "Justification," 258-60.

[32] See Vladimir Lossky, "The Procession of the Holy Spirit in Orthodox Trinitarian Theology," in Daniel B. Clendenin, ed., *Eastern Orthodox Theology: A Contemporary Reader* (Grand Rapids: Baker, 1995), 176-78; John Breck, "Divine Initiative: Salvation in Orthodox Theology," in John Meyendorff and Robert Tobias, eds., *Salvation in Christ: A Lutheran-Orthodox Dialogue* (Minneapolis: Augsburg Fortress Press, 1992), 108.

[33] See Malloy, *Engrafted*, 15n50; McGrath, *Iustitia Dei*, 1:100.

[34] See, for example, Jüngel, *Justification*, 189-96.

[35] Philip Melanchthon, in *Melanchthon and Bucer*, ed. Wilhelm Pauck, LCC 19 (Philadelphia: Westminster, 1969), 88.

[36] Tuomo Mannermaa, "Justification and *Theosis* in Lutheran-Orthodox Perspective," in Carl E. Braaten and Robert W. Jenson, eds., *Union with Christ: The New Finnish Interpretation of Luther* (Grand Rapids: Eerdmans, 1998), 10, 15-16.

[37] Tuomo Mannermaa, *Christ Present in Faith: Luther's View of Justification* (Minneapolis: Fortress Press, 2005), 9.

[38] Mannermaa, "Justification and *Theosis*," 32.

[39] Mannermaa, *Christ Present in Faith*, 24-25.

[40] Ibid., 37.

[41] Ibid., 52.

[42] Ibid., 66.

[43] John Calvin, *Institutes of the Christian Religion* 3.1.1.

[44] On these ideas concerning grace in the writings of Calvin and Wesley, see especially Robert K. Johnston, "Rethinking Common Grace: Toward a Theology of Co-Relation," in Robert K. Johnston, L. Gregory Jones, and Jonathan R. Wilson, eds., *Grace Upon Grace: Essays in Honor of Thomas A. Langford* (Nashville: Abingdon, 1999), 56-60. On Wesley's view in particular, see McGonigle, *Sufficient Saving Grace*, 177.

[45] *LW* 22:147-48; 30:29; 32:228; 33:150; 52:241, 252-53; 53:82. Cf. Calvin, *Institutes* 2.15.6; 2.17.3, 5; Philip Melanchthon, in *Melanchthon on Christian Doctrine*, trans. and ed. Clyde L. Manschreck (Oxford: Oxford University Press, 1965), 153.

[46] *LW* 25:349. Cf. Council of Trent, Sixth Session, Decree on Justification, Ch. 3, 7; Calvin, *Institutes* 3.1.2.

[47] Council of Trent, Sixth Session, Decree on Justification, Ch. 10.

[48] See McGrath, *Iustitia Dei*, 1:84-88, 101-5.

[49] Council of Trent, Sixth Session, Decree on Justification, Ch. 5; cf. Ch. 6.

[50] Council of Trent, Sixth Session, Decree on Justification, Ch. 10.

[51] Council of Trent, Sixth Session, Decree on Justification, Ch. 14.

[52] Council of Trent, Sixth Session, Decree on Justification, Canon 24.

[53] McGrath traces this distinction back to Augustine (*Iustitia Dei*, 1:27; cf. 1:104-9).

[54] On the background and history of this distinction, see Thomas M. McDonough, *The Law and Gospel in Luther* (Oxford: Oxford University Press, 1963), 156-62.

[55] Formula of Concord 1, XI, 20; 2, XI, 88.

[56] See M. Charles Bell, "Calvin and the Extent of the Atonement," *EvQ* 55 (1983): 115-23; Stephen Westerholm notes that this interpretation goes back to Augustine (*Perspectives Old and New on Paul: The "Lutheran" Paul and His Critics* [Grand Rapids: Eerdmans, 2004], 19).

[57] See Formula of Concord 1, XI, 2; 2, XI, 4; cf. Calvin, *Institutes* 3.22.1-3; 3.24.3.

[58] Braaten notes that this was the view of almost all of the "orthodox Lutheran divines" of the seventeenth century (Braaten, *Justification*, 37-38).

[59] This doctrine has been associated with the "Five Points of Calvinism," and apparently grew out of Calvin's view that humanity is "corrupt and perverted in every part" (*Institutes* 2.3.1)

[60] See, for example, Calvin, *Institutes* 3.23.3.

[61] On these discussions, see Gerhard O. Forde, "Christian Life," in Carl E. Braaten and Robert W. Jenson, eds., *Christian Dogmatics* (Philadelphia: Fortress Press, 1984), 2:428-29.

[62] See Braaten, *Justification*, 27.

[63] Gerhard O. Forde, *Justification by Faith: A Matter of Death and Life* (Philadelphia: Fortress Press, 1982), 27-28; Braaten, *Justification*, 25.

[64] Athanasian Creed. Quotation taken from *The Book of Concord: The Confessions of the Evangelical Lutheran Church*, ed. Robert Kolb and Timothy Wengert (Minneapolis: Fortress Press, 2000).

[65] William Hordern, *Living by Grace* (Philadelphia: Westminster, 1975), 108.

[66] See Jms 2:19; *LW* 30:12, 152.

[67] Friedrich Mildenberger, *Theology of the Lutheran Confessions*, trans. Erwin L. Lueker, ed. Robert C. Schultz (Philadelphia: Fortress Press, 1986), 89.

[68] McGrath, *Iustitia Dei*, 2:14.

[69] Council of Trent, Sixth Session, Decree on Justification, Canon 12.

[70] Braaten, *Justification*, 40.

[71] Timothy J. Wengert, *Law and Gospel: Philip Melanchthon's Debate with John Agricola of Eisleben over Poenitentia* (Grand Rapids: Baker, 1997), 126.

[72] Ibid., 118.

[73] Ibid., 127, 29.

[74] Ibid., 30-31.

[75] Ibid., 36.

[76] Ibid., 73, 92.

[77] Ibid., 92.

[78] Philip Melanchthon, quoted in Wengert, *Law and Gospel*, 78.

[79] Ibid., 98.

[80] Ibid., 135.

[81] Ibid., 160, 166.

[82] Ibid., 175.

[83] On this point, see also Forde, "Forensic Justification," 299.

[84] *LW* 31:51. Cf. Wengert, *Law and Gospel*, 67.

[85] Melanchthon, in *Melanchthon and Bucer*, 71.

[86] Luther especially stresses the idea of God's promises in relation to the sacraments in the *Babylonian Captivity of the Church*; see, for example, *LW* 36:37-49, 58-67, 82-85, 92.

[87] See *LW* 36:63, 66.

[88] On Luther's understanding of the real presence, see especially George Hunsinger, "Aquinas, Luther, and Calvin: Toward a Chalcedonian Resolution of the Eucharistic Controversy," in Niels Henrik Gregersen *et al.*, eds., *The Gift of Grace: The Future of Lutheran Theology* (Minneapolis: Fortress Press, 2005), 185-88.

[89] On what follows in this section and the next, see my *Paul on the Cross: Reconstructing the Apostle's Story of Redemption* (Minneapolis: Fortress Press, 2006), 34-45, 77-102. On the continuity between Jesus and Paul with regard to their acceptance of "sinners," see especially Alexander J. M. Wedderburn, "Paul and Jesus: Similarity and Continuity," in Wedderburn, ed., *Paul and Jesus: Collected Essays*, JSNTS 37 (Sheffield: Sheffield Academic Press, 1989), 130-36.

[90] On what follows, see my *Paul on the Cross*, 166-89.

[91] As Christian Wolff notes, although Paul does not speak explicitly of "following" Jesus, he does communicate the same basic idea ("Humility and Self-Denial in Jesus' Life and Message and in the Apostolic Existence of Paul," in Wedderburn, ed., *Paul and Jesus*, 160).

[92] Kent L. Yinger, *Paul, Judaism, and Judgment according to Deeds*, SNTSMS 105 (Cambridge: Cambridge University Press, 1999), 290.

Chapter Five: Christian Life in the World

[1] American edition of *Luther's Works* (hereafter *LW*), ed. Jaroslav J. Pelikan and Helmut T. Lehmann (Philadelphia: Fortress Press and St. Louis: Concordia, 1955-1986), 31:366.

[2] *LW* 45:97.

[3] *LW* 28:127.

[4] Alister E. McGrath, *Iustitia Dei: A History of the Christian Doctrine of Justification* (Cambridge: Cambridge University Press, 1986), 2:13.

[5] *LW* 45:89.

[6] Paul Althaus, *The Theology of Martin Luther*, trans. Robert C. Schultz (Philadelphia: Fortress Press, 1966), 237-41. See *LW* 25:245, 260; 27:20-21, 64; 32:28, 229; 34:152, 167.

[7] *LW* 27:64-65.

[8] Small Catechism IV, 4; Large Catechism IV, 65.

[9] See Timothy J. Wengert, *Law and Gospel: Philip Melanchthon's Debate with John Agricola of Eisleben over Poenitentia* (Grand Rapids: Baker, 1997), 191-200.

[10] For a general introduction to Luther's thought on this subject, see Paul Althaus, *The Ethics of Martin Luther*, trans. Robert C. Schultz (Philadelphia: Fortress Press, 1972), 43-82.

[11] See Frank Thielmann, *From Plight to Solution: A Jewish Framework for Understanding Paul's View of the Law in Galatians and Romans*, NovTSup 61 (Leiden: Brill, 1989), 34-45. For this idea in the Hebrew Scriptures, see especially Jer 31:33-34, 32:39-40, and Ez 36:26-27.

[12] On the variety of Jewish beliefs on this point, see N. T. Wright, *The Resurrection of the Son of God*, Christian Origins and the Question of God 3 (Minneapolis: Fortress Press, 2003), 129-206.

[13] On these and other characteristics of Jewish apocalyptic thought, see especially David C. Sim, *Apocalyptic Eschatology in the Gospel of Matthew*, SNTSMS 88 (Cambridge: Cambridge University Press, 1996), 31-53; Walter Schmithals, *The Apocalyptic Movement: Introduction and Interpretation*, trans. John E. Steely (Nashville: Abingdon, 1975), 20-28, 40-45.

[14] This idea is found even in Luther; see Althaus, *Ethics*, 18; Althaus, *Theology*, 246n3, 247n106-7; cf. John Calvin, *Institutes of the Christian Religion* 3.14.18; Formula of Concord 1, IV, 15.

[15] Herbert Boyd McGonigle, *Sufficient Saving Grace: John Wesley's Evangelical Arminianism* (Carlisle: Paternoster, 2001), 150-51.

[16] Ibid., 249-51, 261.

[17] Ibid., 248.

[18] Althaus, *Theology*, 243. See also Gerhard O. Forde, "Forensic Justification and Law in Lutheran Theology," in H. George Anderson, T. Austin Murphy, and Joseph A. Burgess, eds., *Justification by Faith*, LCD 7 (Minneapolis: Augsburg, 1985), 282-83.

[19] See Forde, "Forensic Justification," 282-87; Gerhard O. Forde, *Justification by Faith: A Matter of Death and Life* (Philadelphia: Fortress Press, 1982), 50-51.

[20] *LW* 25:327, 333.

[21] *LW* 25:336.

[22] *LW* 15:21; 22:177, 260, 359; 27:84.

[23] *LW* 19:27.

[24] See *LW* 42:11; 51:373.

[25] *LW* 31:299. To explain Luther's thought in this regard, Oswald Bayer makes a helpful distinction between "metaphysical" and "ethical" progress (*Living by Faith: Justification and Sanctification* [Grand Rapids: Eerdmans, 2003], 64-67).

[26] Formula of Concord 1, II, 18.

[27] See *LW* 34:165; cf. McGrath, *Iustitia Dei*, 2:16.

[28] Avery Dulles, "Justification in Contemporary Catholic Theology," in Anderson *et al.*, eds. *Justification by Faith*, 269.

[29] See Dulles, "Justification," 266.

[30] Christopher J. Malloy, *Engrafted into Christ: A Critique of the Joint Declaration*, AUS VII, T&R 233 (New York: Peter Lang, 2005), 275-80.

[31] See Dulles, "Justification," 269.

[32] See Malloy, *Engrafted*, 47.

[33] See Gerhard Ebeling, *Luther: An Introduction to His Thought*, trans. R. A. Wilson (Philadelphia: Fortress Press, 1970), 168; William H. Lazareth, *Luther on the Christian Home* (Philadelphia: Muhlenberg, 1960), 85.

[34] Formula of Concord 1, VI, 1.

[35] Formula of Concord 1, VI, 4.

[36] Formula of Concord 2, VI, 5.

[37] Formula of Concord 1, VI, 3; 2, VI, 16.

[38] Calvin, *Institutes* 2.7.12.

[39] Calvin, *Institutes* 2.7.14.

[40] Calvin, *Institutes* 2.7.12.

[41] For a summary of these criticisms, see Ken Schurb, *Philip Melanchthon, the Formula of Concord, and the Third Use of the Law*, Ph.D. Thesis, The Ohio State University (Ann Arbor, Mich: UMI, 2001), 22-85.

[42] Formula of Concord 2, VI, 9, 21.

[43] Formula of Concord 2, VI, 20.

[44] See Scott R. Murray, *Law, Life, and the Living God: The Third Use of Law in Modern American Lutheranism* (St. Louis: Concordia, 2002), 60.

[45] Formula of Concord 2, VI, 3.

[46] Formula of Concord 2, VI, 10.

[47] Formula of Concord 1, VI, 2, 6; 2, VI, 3, 12, 17, 21.

[48] See Ex 31:12-17; Lev 25:1-55; 27:16-24; Deut 5:12-15.

[49] In this regard, Walter R. Bouman argued that the parenesis of the New Testament constitutes the Torah for Christians ("The Concept of the 'Law' in the Lutheran Tradition," *W&W* 3, no. 4 [1983]: 422).

[50] See, for example, James A. Nestigen, "Changing Definitions: The Law in Formula IV," *CTQ* 69, no. 3/4 (2005): 267-68.

[51] Formula of Concord 2, VI, 21.

[52] Werner Elert, *Law and Gospel*, trans. Edward H. Schroeder (Philadelphia: Fortress Press, 1967), 47-48.

[53] See Scott Ickert, "The Uses of the Law," *LF* 25, no. 1 (1991): 20.

[54] See, for example, Mark C. Mattes, "Beyond the Impasse: Re-Examining the Third Use of the Law," in *CTQ* 69, no. 3/4 (2005): 277; Theodore L. Jungkuntz, "The 'Third Use of the Law': Looking for Light on the Heat," *LF* 12, no. 4 (1978): 10.

[55] Elsa Tamez, *The Amnesty of Grace: Justification by Faith from a Latin American Perspective*, trans. Sharon Ringe (Nashville: Abingdon, 1993), 21.

[56] Ronald Baesler, "Justification: Another Side to the Story," *CurTM* 27, no. 1 (2000): 32.

[57] *LW* 45:91.

[58] *LW* 35:368.

[59] *LW* 29:122.

[60] *LW* 35:370-71; cf. *LW* 30:204; 44:108-9.

61 Luther scholars have debated whether Luther's thought on this subject is best represented by speaking of two "kingdoms," "realms," "governments," or "rules." However, as David M. Whitford notes, Luther spoke only in terms of two realms (*Reiche*) and two governments (*Regimente*) contained in these realms ("*Cura Religionis* or Two Kingdoms: The Late Luther on Religion and the State in the Lectures on Genesis," *CH* 73, no. 1 (2004): 44. For a general background to Luther's teaching in this regard, see William H. Lazareth, *Christians in Society: Luther, the Bible, and Social Ethics* (Minneapolis: Fortress Press, 2001), 110-16.

62 *LW* 45:88.

63 *LW* 45:90-91.

64 *LW* 45:89.

65 *LW* 45:94.

66 Robert Benne, "Lutheran Ethics: Perennial Themes and Contemporary Challenges," in Karen L. Bloomquist and John R. Stumme, eds., *The Promise of Lutheran Ethics* (Minneapolis: Fortress Press, 1998), 22.

67 Ibid., 22.

68 Brent W. Sockness, "Luther's Two Kingdoms Revisited: A Response to Reinhold Niebuhr's Criticism of Luther," *JRE* 20, no. 1 (1992): 98.

69 Craig L. Nessan, "Liberation Theology's Critique of Luther's Two Kingdoms Doctrine," *CurTM* 16, no. 4 (1989): 259. See also *LW* 45:104-6.

70 Walter Altmann, "Interpreting the Doctrine of the Two Kingdoms: God's Kingship in the Church and in Politics," *W&W* 7, no. 1 (1987): 47.

71 See especially *LW* 45:94.

72 For a summary of the ways in which Luther spoke to the social and political issues of his day, see Walter Altmann, *Luther and Liberation: A Latin American Perspective*, trans. Mary M. Solberg (Minneapolis: Fortress Press, 1992), 78, 85-129.

73 *LW* 44:127-32.

74 Craig L. Nessan, "Reappropriating Luther's Two Kingdoms," *LQ* 19, no. 3 (2005): 309.

75 See Bernhard Lohse, *Martin Luther's Theology: Its Historical and Systematic Development*, trans. Roy Harrisville (Minneapolis: Fortress Press, 1999), 332-35.

76 Reinhold Niebuhr, *The Nature and Destiny of Man: A Christian Interpretation* (New York: Charles Scribner's Sons, 1951), 187, 191-92, 204.

77 Gerhard O. Forde, *On Being a Theologian of the Cross: Reflections on Luther's Heidelberg Disputation* (Grand Rapids: Eerdmans, 1997), 95.

Chapter Six: Redeeming the Gospel

1 Formula of Concord 2, XI, 48.

2 On this point and what follows, see my book *The Letter and the Spirit: Discerning God's Will in a Complex World*, LV (Minneapolis: Augsburg Fortress Press, 2005), 12-57.

3 I owe this observation to Gordon Jensen, who commented that in Luther's day, the Roman Catholic theologian Jerome Emser was more upset about Luther's translation of *ekklēsia* as *Gemeinde* instead of *Kirche* than about his interpolation of the word "alone" in Rom. 3:28 so as

to affirm that justification was by faith alone; see Heinz Bluhm, "Emser's 'Emmendation' of Luther's New Testament: Galatians 1," *MLN* 81, no. 4 (1966): 377.

[4] Robert W. Jenson, "Triune Grace," in Niels Henrik Gregersen *et al.*, eds., *The Gift of Grace: The Future of Lutheran Theology* (Minneapolis: Fortress Press, 2005), 18-19.

[5] See, for example, *LW* 10:13-14; 24:252-53; 25:220, 356-59; 26:366; 27:219-21; 29:122-23; 31:160-61; 35:367-68.

[6] Augsburg Confession 2, VII, 1.

[7] Augsburg Confession 2, V, 2.

[8] See, for example, David G. Truemper, "The Lutheran Confessional Writings and the Future of Lutheran Theology," in Gregersen *et al*, ed., *The Gift of Grace*, 131-46; Erik T. R. Samuelson, "Roadmaps to Grace: Five Types of Lutheran Confessional Subscription," *Dialog* 45, no. 2 (2006): 157-69.

[9] On this understanding of the Lutheran Confessions, see Carl E. Braaten, *Principles of Lutheran Theology*, 2nd ed. (Minneapolis: Fortress Press, 2007), 40-42.

INDEX OF SUBJECTS AND NAMES

INDEX OF BIBLICAL CITATIONS